D0776851

Economic Policy Reform in Egypt

ECONOMIC POLICY REFORM IN EGYPT

Iliya Harik

University Press of Florida
Gainesville/Tallahassee/Tampa/Boca Raton
Pensacola/Orlando/Miami/Jacksonville

02 01 00 99 98 97 6 5 4 3 2 1

Library of Congress Cataloging-in-Publication Data

Harik, Iliya F.
Economic policy reform in Egypt / Iliya Harik.
    p. cm.
Includes bibliographical references and index.
ISBN 0-8130-1483-2 (alk. paper)
1. Egypt—Economic policy. 2. Egypt—Social policy. I. Title.
HC830.H37 1996
338.962—dc 20   96-38520

The University Press of Florida is the scholarly publishing agency for the State
University System of Florida, comprised of Florida A & M University, Florida
Atlantic University, Florida International University, Florida State University,
University of Central Florida, University of Florida, University of North Florida,
University of South Florida, and University of West Florida.

University Press of Florida
15 Northwest 15th Street
Gainesville, FL 32611

To Lenny Binder

Contents

TABLES

Acknowledgments

Research on this book started in the early eighties, and I have called on the goodwill of a large number of people in Egypt and elsewhere, most of whom gave freely of their time and knowledge. Though it would be impractical to mention everyone by name, I remain grateful to them all. In ways that are not easily manifest, this work has been enormously enriched by the wealth of Egyptian scholarship, both written and oral, constituting a debt I owe to colleagues and scholars in that country.

A number of colleagues and friends have read and made helpful comments on parts of this manuscript. Alfred Diamant, Jim Christoph, and Dana Chabot critiqued the first part of Chapter 1. Kathryn Firmim-Sellers and Dan Siskin read the whole chapter and gave useful feedback. Dr. Naim Sherbiny of the World Bank gave helpful advice regarding Chapter 4, on agriculture. Dr. Munir Bashshur of the American University of Beirut made a critical and insightful reading of a former version of Chapter 7. Dr. Kamaal Husni Bayyoumi of the National Center for Educational Research, Ministry of Education, Cairo, read parts of Chapter 7 and made useful suggestions. I remain thankful for Dr. Galila el Kadi for her critical reading of Chapter 8. I am especially indebted to Dean Ali Hilal and his colleagues at the College of Economics and Political Science at Cairo University for giving me the opportunity to be part of their research endeavors and symposia during the lengthy research period for this book. Patricia Withered and Eve Alexander have kindly and diligently helped me prepare this manuscript in ready form for the University Press of Florida. And with his computer skills, Steve Flinn of the Political Science Lab has rendered me a great and generous service.

Material support for research was provided in 1987–89 by the Social Science Research Council, Fulbright and Fulbright-Hays grants, and the American Research Center in Egypt. I am also grateful to Indiana University for making it possible for me to take time out over a number of years for field research.

It goes without saying that no one mentioned above, organizations or individuals, bears any responsibility for what has been maintained in this book by the author, who alone takes responsibility for the entire project.

Abbreviations

ASU	Arab Socialist Union
CAPMAS	Central Agency for Public Mobilization and Statistics
GDP	Gross domestic product
GIE	Government industrial enterprise
GNP	Gross national product
GOE	Government of Egypt
HPC	Higher Policy Committee
IMF	International Monetary Fund
ISI	Import-substitution industrialization
LDCs	Less-developed countries
£E	Egyptian pound
MKA	Mu'tamar al Khubz al 'Arabi (Arab Conference on Bread), Cairo, 16–19 July 1988
MOA	Ministry of Agriculture
MOI	Ministry of Industry
MOS	Ministry of Supplies
MQM	Magaalis al Qawmiya al Mutakhassisa (National and Specialized Councils)
NICs	Newly industrialized countries
NPI	National Planning Institute
STA	Sharikaat Tawdhif al Amwaal (Money Investment Funds)
USAID	United States Agency for International Development

Chapter 1

Introduction

The Integrative Development Model

This book is about a valiant national development project that went awry. It did not have to. The beginning was auspicious. Strong and decisive measures had been taken by its authors to correct past injustices, build new institutions, and seek social and economic growth. The new leaders were young and angry reformers; they were determined, honest, idealistic. Yet, something happened in the process to mock the ideals of men whose strange makeup of innocence and worldliness can be understood but not forgotten. The legacy they inherited and the challenges they faced were not ordinary and certainly had something to do with the protracted developmental crisis in which the national project landed. The lessons of their tortuous but also treacherous path are as many and varied as the number of different perspectives that are brought to bear on them. The following narrative is but one of those perspectives.

State and Government

Since the Revolution of July 1952, the idea of an active and dominant government in society has been the sine qua non doctrine of economic development. Today, "the question of whether the state should even try to be an active economic agent" is uppermost in the consideration of many development theorists.[1] The question must therefore be addressed here, too. In this study, the role of government in the Egyptian economy has been examined critically. Though the record of intervention has been empirically shown to be adverse to economic development and general welfare, an active role of government in society has been presented here as inevitable and essential. An explanation of the apparent contradiction between a critique of government intervention and a claim for its necessity thus becomes mandatory.

Since the Egyptian model of government-led development is generic and common in so many countries of the Third World, its assessment here would not be complete if it were to be confined to a mere empirical presentation of policy outcomes. Inquiring, however briefly, into the theoretical foundations of the model provides greater understanding of both the potential and the limitations of government intervention.

The State

I begin by drawing a distinction between the concepts of government, state, and society. The term *state* is used in the literature to refer either to government, as in the structure which is in charge of making binding decisions; or to a country in its aspect as a juridic entity, as in the statement "member states of the United Nations." Noting the increasing use of *state* in the sense of "government," Giovanni Sartori writes, the term "became less and less coextensive with *res publica* (the politically organized society as a whole) and more and more narrowly identified with the structures of command (authority, power, coercion) that impinge upon society."[2]

The term *state* in this book will be synonymous with the politically and legally organized society. The state is a juridic entity in which the status, rights, duties, and responsibilities pertaining to all individuals and groups within a specific space and time are defined. As a community politically organized under a constitution, the state includes government officials and ordinary citizens alike. In "modern Western political thought, the idea of the state is often linked to the notion of an impersonal and privileged legal or constitutional order."[3] It is not a separate structure standing in an external relationship to citizens; the very concept of citizenship is a legal one and would be meaningless unless predicated on an existing civic order. Where there are no formal laws, there are no citizens, and where public law exists the community that it binds is a civic order. The state, in other words, is the juridic order in which individuals are defined as citizens, officials as government, and objects as property.

The use of the term *state* in the literature confuses the issue by counterpoising society as a structure in an adversarial relationship to the state. In fact, citizens and officials are separated not by mutual externality but by the different functions assigned to each. The dualism tends to blur the universal character of the state as a system in which everyone is a member. The state concept is coextensive with society and territory. The universality of the institution outweighs the importance of its being an institution possessing the prerogative of the legitimate use of force.

Civil society is not possible to define without reference to a state order. The term *civil* is defined in the dictionary as "of or relating to citizens; of or relating to the state or its citizenry."[4] Should the state and civil society be considered separate and external to one another, then there would be no common basis for any joint enterprise between them—or indeed any intercourse.

Where private space is tight, public space will be extensive, and vice versa. A range can be perceived here defined in zero-sum terms, and in which there are as many combinations as there are degrees between zero and unity. In a state system identified as a democracy, it is not the absence of rules that makes free space but their presence. One practices religion freely by virtue of rules making practice permissible and protected. Hence, one speaks of the right to worship freely. The same may be said of private property.

The concept of private property makes sense only in the context of the state or some communal order with a structure of command. Individual and group rights are socially defined and acquire meaning and force only when acknowledged by others, such as organized communities or a state. If one claims a private space but no one else recognizes that claim, then it is neither private nor a right. What is private is so by virtue of being part of a civic order, of having been recognized as such by the public.

Defining the *state* in this study as the "civic order that binds society and defines political relations" calls into question the extreme view of private property as a realm outside state jurisdiction. Private owners cannot, for instance, use property in ways that conflict with the civil code. Property is a bundle of rights that can be aggregated and disaggregated, and rights are socially not individually or divinely defined.[5] In the privatization process, property rights are disaggregated; some remain accessible to the public, while others are transferred to private agents.

Privatization occurs when a government withdraws some of its prerogatives in society. Privatization laws invest property rights in private citizens instead of in the government. The property privatized remains, however, subject to state laws, which are enforced by the government. Nationalization or privatization, in effect, are attempts to redefine particular authority relations involving transfer of jurisdiction over property rights.

Changes in economic policies discussed in this book refer to modifications in the jurisdiction of government; this book does not contemplate withdrawal of the state from society. Under privatization or structural adjustment policies, rules governing economic activities change; thus, ipso facto, the character of the state changes.

To sum up, *state* stands for (1) a juridic entity: it is the body politic legally defined with respect to authority relationships within the whole social order; (2) universality: it includes all citizens and its jurisdiction covers everyone and everything within a specific territory; (3) normative rules: persons are defined by law as citizens, and objects are defined as property; and (4) supremacy: the laws of the body politic serve as the highest in the land and constitute the final authority for the resolution of conflict.

Government

The term *government* refers to the organized body of officers in charge of legislation and the command structure of the state system. They make and implement policy by virtue of state rules which determine their selection and the functions assigned to their offices. The state is a more encompassing concept than government and includes the inputs to public life and other activities of ordinary citizens.

The dichotomy often made in the literature on privatization between state and civil society should be expressed in terms of government and society to avoid conceptual confusion. It refers to the distinction between the organized body of officers in charge of maintaining and operating the civic order, on the one hand, and citizens who play other roles in the body politic, on the other. There is a constant tug of war between the two sides over redefining or interpreting the system to allow each side more space. The conflictual relation between government and citizen amounts in effect to efforts to redefine private and public spheres. The government oversteps its limits and usurps citizens' rights when it claims to be identical with the state. The great expansion of government functions under the July Revolution was of this genre, where the vast majority of citizens were reduced to some kind of government functionaries.

Theoretical Implications

We may now be in a position to answer the question regarding a government's role in the economy and society. Since rights acquire meaning only within a state order, then whatever is legally defined as a right is publicly endorsed. Hence, a citizen's rights must be guaranteed. If a right is acknowledged in the state order but is not accessible, a situation tantamount to rendering state rules null and void ensues. Thus, although some rights constitute a promise of accessibility and not a grant or a gift, adverse conditions that make their attainment unfeasible are equivalent to their denial.

Herein lies the basis for an activist state system in the area of social and human rights. The view of the state as a civic order endorses the idea of public responsibility, thus evoking the full political engagement of citizens in policymaking. Neo-orthodox views which underplay, if not overlook, the role of politics in economic development are based on an unrealistic perception of society as an aggregated set of atomized individuals. In contrast, the perspective outlined above underlines the point that individual prerogatives are socially defined and can therefore be socially denied. That is why international organizations such as the International Monetary Fund and the World Bank see in government a necessary instrument of economic reform, despite the neo-orthodox foundation of their approach. Hopefully, this perspective sheds some light on the orthodox paradox in the literature on structural adjustment.[6]

Two principles identified above explain why liberalization of the hegemonic patron state is necessary. First is the principle of rights as publicly endorsed claims, and second is public responsibility as an essential feature of a civic order. If a government is obliged to protect and fulfill the rights of its citizens, then failure to do so becomes a serious breach of the civic order. Hence, a government should not claim what it cannot honor, as the patron state system in Egypt did. By assuming all responsibility for the civic order, the Egyptian Revolutionary regime took away the responsibility of citizens and assumed more than it could fulfill, making a travesty of public commitments. Second, the perspective that defines the state as a civic order encompassing all those bound by its rules views citizens as bearers of basic civil prerogatives not charged to government. When a government takes away such prerogatives, it distorts the essential features of the civic order. In short, a government's responsibility to ensure rights, and its obligation not to usurp civil prerogatives, calls for government to play an active but circumscribed role in society.

Accordingly, the philosophical foundation for the patron state's involvement in welfare and the economy in Egypt are not in question. What is in question is the government's assumption of all responsibility in the state, the methods used to attain the civic rights for which it had claimed responsibility, and its failure to fulfill those rights. It is therefore possible to be critical of the Egyptian government's involvement in the economy without being against the principle of government activism. That activism will be defined further in the conclusion to this book, in the context of empirical findings.

The Patron State

The state system that was developed under Nasser and his successors is the subject of this study. That system will be referred to here as the patron state. The patron state is made up of a set of rules in which the provision of livelihood of citizens and the management of business enterprises fall in the public domain as a responsibility of government. The government in a patron state is a provider and an entrepreneurial manager whose tools of trade are central planning and control mechanisms. The authoritarian character of the July Revolution soon extended from the political arena to the marketplace. Justification for the regime's daring move was made in ideological terms: to put an end to political corruption and divisiveness, to introduce a beneficent order, and to establish a more efficacious path to development. Needless to say, many observers saw political motivation behind the patron state's project.

While most contemporary state systems carry out managerial and welfare functions, in the patron state those functions are quite extensive. Because of widespread poverty and low labor productivity in the less developed countries (LDCs), society places heavy demands on government, which drown it under unusual financial burdens. Needless to say, the task of uplifting a society from its low economic and social levels is daunting.

The greater the dependency of society, the greater the tendency for the government to assume extensive responsibilities. Societies in LDCs are often characterized by a high level of domestic dependency, where the ratio of dependents to wage earners is high. Another indication of dependency is a distribution of income in which a high ratio of the population falls below the poverty level.

Though poverty is not a new phenomenon in Egypt or other countries, in the contemporary era the poor have become characterized by mobility: demographic, geographic, and psychic. Such mobility means the politicization of poverty, where masses of poor people make claims on the government and are open for mobilization by political entrepreneurs. The politicization of poverty leads to the government assumption of welfare functions and to political conditions conducive to the rise of populist leaders with potential for extensive interference in the economy. Such is the environment in which the patron state emerges.

The public space in the patron state system is very extensive and overshadows private spaces. For example, though in a liberal democracy information falls under private space, in a hegemonic system such as the patron state, information is defined as part of the public domain and therefore controlled by the government. The Revolutionary regime's redefinition of public and private spaces has extended the government's role and responsibilities to an unprecedented extent. Its right to such a role was determined ideologically by the regime leaders—ex cathedra, one might say. The public was not consulted but directed and induced to go along with the wishes of the regime. The government's ability and competence to perform all the extensive functions assigned to it had to be acquired through experience, a major risk given only minor attention by the emerging leaders. This study will deal with how the patron state system performed in those respects.

The leaders of the Revolutionary regime of 1952 did not choose the label "patron state" to designate the system which they set up. Arab socialism was the term they chose. Their model was an eclectic one that drew inspiration from Marxism, Islam, and the experiences of socialist regimes of the nonaligned movement of the Third World.

THE STATE CAPITALISM THESIS

Not all observers agreed with the leaders of the Revolution in what they had claimed was a socialist program. Many saw it as state capitalism. After all there were serious questions for the regime to answer before it could claim to have built a socialist state system. How could a system that emerged from the ranks of the military, that had minimal support initially from industrial labor, that preserved private property in agriculture, and that monopolized power in the hands of the original junta be socialist? From a political economy point of view, the objection to the socialist claim was that the government held a quasi-monopoly over all vital, and some not so vital, enterprises, in addition to being the direct manager of and sole decision maker in certain firms.

Some scholars have, moreover, objected that the status of workers in this so-called socialism was not affected by the new order. The worker on the assembly line experienced "no difference in his effective relation to the means of production and to his employers."[7] Moreover, the surplus from public sector firms was transferred, according to Alan Richards and John Waterbury, to the private sector: "In this process of accumulation, the state transfers surpluses on its own operations, profits if any, and external rents to the private sector. . . . This has been the predominant process of accumulation in the Middle East."[8] That was the case "in Egypt since 1974,"[9] according to Waterbury.

It is difficult to find any empirical evidence in support of the view that the government in Egypt was in the service of private interests.[10] Rather than being the beneficiary, the private sector remained under some severe official restrictions until the early 1990s. For the thesis that the government is in the service of the private sector to be upheld, a number of questions would have first to be answered satisfactorily. If the government had shed its largesse on the private sector, then why did the private sector continue to grow ever so slowly more than ten years after the open-door policy? Why, indeed, has the organized private sector continued to be so small in all the Arab states, with the exception of Lebanon? If governments, as it is claimed, had surrendered "surpluses," "profits," and "external rents" to the private sector, then what explanation is there for the crippling restrictions and controls that continued to riddle the private sector until the early 1990s in Egypt? How this happened and why is especially important in view of the fact that the public sector still dominates the national economies of Egypt and most Arab states, not to mention others in the region. Note that in Egypt, industrial investment by the public sector was still as high as 78 percent of total industrial investment as recently as the late eighties.[11]

Mark Cooper and John Waterbury have been among the first to join the argument claiming Egypt to be a state capitalist regime.[12] Following the reasoning of Milovan Djilas, E. V. K. Fitzgerald, and ʿAdil Ghunaym, Waterbury maintains that "Egypt undeniably entered a state capitalist mode in 1957,"[13] and exited out of it in 1974.[14] There has since been a widespread acceptance of this thesis in the political economy literature of the Middle East.[15] The idea is based on observations that national capital is mostly accumulated by the government, that the role of the public sector is dominant, and that government officials run the economy.[16] Waterbury, though, seems to be alone in maintaining that by 1973, "Egypt returned to something resembling capitalist economic orthodoxy" and that "individual companies [were] urged to sink or swim on their own through the reintroduction of market mechanisms in determining levels of investment and profits."[17]

Class considerations—which remain nebulous, overdrawn and hardly relevant—cloud the debate. As shall be discussed, the economy continued to be heavily regulated in Egypt, and the public sector companies were still dominant, subsidized, protected, and directly managed by the government years after Waterbury committed his convictions to writing.

Aside from the fact that the Egyptian economy had not reached a semblance of capitalist orthodoxy before the 1990s, the state capitalism thesis remains as vague as Arab socialism. I argue here that Egypt never entered a stage that can be called "state capitalism" nor exited to capitalist orthodoxy. To characterize the cosmetic changes made in the seventies under the open-door (infitaah) policy as a transformation to a capitalist economy is quite an extraordinary statement.

A description of Nasser's model as state capitalism raises serious questions of theory and practice. To be able to refer to a government, individual, or other entity as capitalist, one must first ask these questions: Is the actor involved in a competitive relationship with other actors in a free market, and does the system operate on the principle of maximization of profits, and if so for whose benefit?[18] More modestly, one may ask if the actor has been driven by the profit motive at all, leaving maximization aside. Can one speak of capitalism without a free, or relatively free market? Finally, how can the thesis of state capitalism in Nasser's Egypt be reconciled with the regime's role as provider of basic needs and general welfare?

I question the claim that by establishing a near-monopoly on accumulation, the regime acted capitalistic. Mercantilism is one thing; capitalism is another. The very attribution of capitalism to a government is conceptually discordant, even self-contradictory, for monopoly is not the same thing as capitalism. Only where a public sector enterprise is truly autonomous, seeking profits and competing in a free market, can one speak of a government operating on a capitalistic basis. This definitely was not the case in Egypt. The question will, however, be addressed again in the empirical chapters of this volume.

THE EXTRACTIVE STATE THESIS

The argument outlined above is a variant on a common thesis in development literature claiming that policy in most developing regimes is extractive. Extraction implies the existence of a beneficiary, usually a small class such as "state bourgeoisie,"[19] or the private sector, either independently or through the instrument of government. The idea of extraction, in addition, suggests exploitation of some group.

I maintain in this volume that the exploitation thesis attributed to the patron state fails to explain the process of economic policies established after the July Revolution. This point is made clear in the following discussion of the integrative development model.

The Integrative Economic Development Approach

A main thesis of this study is that the July Revolution regime had a grand development design of its own which the leaders wished to implement by force or inducement. Once a commitment is made to a development plan, policy measures can be largely explained by the necessities of maintaining and coordinating the various components of that national design Specific policies and governmental decisions will be examined here under the perspective of the integrative approach to the economy laid down by the Nasser regime, whose main tenet was a balanced economy. The stamp Nasser imprinted on the economic system remained basically in place until the end of the 1980s, with some adjustments.

The integrative economic development approach represents a grand design centrally administered and encompassing the entire national economy, which ideally is self-contained with mutually reinforcing parts. It is based on an equilibrium model which, to achieve and maintain, requires the application of extensive managerial powers of a central omniscient agency. To maintain this model, capital and other resources are transferred directly and indirectly from one industry to another and one sector to another. The goal of the transfers is to maintain a balance among the parts of the national project and keep the whole enterprise in tune, rather than to achieve greater efficiency or productivity. The process involves artificial balances between costs and prices, wages and cost of living, needs and services and between sectors.

Capital transfers made in the patron state often give the appearance of being extractive measures. I shall argue, however, that they were the mechanism for integrating the economy on the basis of an equilibrium model and that they were universal rather than class-based. Integrating the economy required a high degree of control and artificial balance between production and distribution, as well as between one production unit and another. It is in the light of this economic integration approach that the class and domestic extraction theses fade in importance.[20]

Stated as an ideal type, the integrative model appears like a highly rational endeavor with a great deal of order, discipline, and uniformity. In reality, the structure developed ad hoc and was sometimes disjointed, cumbersome, and sluggish. Nevertheless, this rational ideal was the objective and principle that guided the leaders of the regime.

Authors of the integrative development model showed marginal interest in competition or profits, and their conception of growth was not tied to individual enterprises but had a global character—growth for the entire economy or entire sector. Hence, an individual enterprise may be losing money, but the loss remains immaterial in view of the contribution the firm is supposed to make to other enterprises or to society. An industry's importance is in its functionality rather than its profitability. An auto assembly plant of the public sector, for instance, was not created by the regime with profit (revenue for the government) as the main objective, for indeed little of that materialized, but rather to generate value added at home. The national economy was perceived to benefit from the auto plant by the jobs created, the stimulation of forward and backward linkages, the payment of taxes, and the reduced need for foreign exchange. Even productivity took a backseat in relation to accommodating unutilized labor surplus. From the integrative economic development perspective, the narrow concept of profit occupies a secondary role compared to the presumed services performed for the economy and society as a whole.

Under that same perspective, the auto plant was seen to provide additional benefits unrelated to profits. The products that public sector firms produce serve a social function—to provide affordable commodities for the public. In theory affordable because of efficient production, but in practice because of artificial pricing. The practice was referred to as the *social returns* of a firm, a euphemism for artificially depressed pricing.

Viewed analytically, depressed pricing is not consistent with capital accumulation or growth, whether for the government or any other producer. The Revolutionary regime imposed prices on major parts of public and private sectors alike, a practice that survived in limited doses until 1990. Whenever the public sector happened to generate a surplus, part of the surplus was channeled in a number of directions, including workers, the government's operating budget, or other firms suffering from losses. A losing firm was not liquidated or abandoned but subsidized, for even a losing firm had a function to perform for other firms, the economy, and society. Thus, its value is assessed relative to its functionality rather than its productivity or profitability. Hence, the government assumed a lax attitude toward interfirm or intersectorial settlement of debts. When a public sector firm operated at a loss because of unpaid bills by other firms, employment policies, or "social" responsibilities, it was subsidized by the Treasury. Public sector banks often acted as the instrument, extending loans to losing government-owned enterprises, with little hope of repayment. There is nothing capitalistic about this design in any shape or form, let alone state capitalism.

When considering the global development design one should not overlook the invisible or unstated political motives of the regime. Extension of public sector enterprises to some business areas may have been related to the regime's desire to prevent the private sector from stepping in by default. The nature of the patron state system, its conception of itself, and its role in society make the incidence of competition or a strong private sector an anathema, and unless the government steps in to fill the gap, the "undesirables" would. Years after the open-door policy was launched, the private sector continued to be discriminated against and excluded from certain areas of enterprise.[21]

Extensive expansion of the public sector served in part to contain the space available for private entrepreneurs. One may think of such unlikely undertakings of the public sector (nationalized or government-initiated) as movie theaters, restaurants, retail stores, and even textiles as economically rational because they fulfill for the model the function of limiting private space, not because they produce a profit.

That is why the infitaah, the open-door policy, was cosmetic, not a serious break with the established order.[22] Neither by background, temperament, nor ideology was Sadat prepared to break away with the integrative development design set in place by the Revolution. A departure would require an extensive plan plus revolutionary zeal and commitment. Moreover, Sadat was not about to undermine the system that brought him to power and maintained him there. It is not even certain that he knew how to undo the integrative model, had he possessed the will. Radical reform would require a change of regime, as has occurred in Turkey, Argentina, or Russia.

Expenditure on welfare was not why the economic development strategy failed; that commonly accepted thesis should be seriously reconsidered. The problem was rather in the structure of an economic strategy premised on artificial transfers of distorted nature and such accompanying deleterious effects as diversion of resources from productive to nonproductive units. Resources transferred to inefficient enterprises meant in effect poor investment choices that rewarded the inefficient and curtailed the efficient. As shall be seen in the empirical part of this book, what was spent on welfare was quite modest, and those subsidies usually considered a form of welfare were in fact a primitive and inadequate wage system.

The Global Nature of Import Substitution in Egypt

The managed and integrative approach toward the economy that emerged under Nasser and his successors was characterized by import-substitution industrialization, for reasons quite familiar in countries with a very low industrial base and a deficit in the balance of payments. Insofar as the Revolutionary regime opted for public ownership of the means of production, regulation of the residual private sector, and integrative management of economic development, it went far beyond the question of import substitution.

Import-substitution industrialization (ISI) since the Nasser period was global in character and thus differed both from the first phase of ISI under the monarchy and from those newly industrializing countries that pursued ISI. Protective measures under the former regime were introduced selectively and on a limited scale, as compared with the later period.

The crucial correlates of the ISI model of the Egyptian regime are globalism and etatism. The plan was to make Egypt self-sufficient in every respect and therefore produce everything it needed. As a result the development drive became massive, requiring excessive capital, raw materials, technology, and organization, most of which were in scarce supply. The other aspect of the global model was governmental assumption of almost total responsibility for the economy, in the sense of being directly responsible for investment, industry, agriculture, and services. Official attitude was definitely hostile toward private initiative. Discouraged businesspeople lay low, migrated, diverted capital out of the country, or resigned themselves to the limited and regulated role assigned to them.

Another aspect of the Nasserite ISI model was the exclusion of transnational corporations, except in rare activities such as oil exploration. Exclusion of foreign businesses, whatever benefits such exclusion may provide to Egyptians, meant additional strains on investment capital and technology. Egypt decided to go it alone, and continued to do so through the mid-seventies, though by then only with great reservation.

The global model of ISI remained in effect until 1990, when finally the Egyptian government resigned itself to serious cooperation with the International Monetary Fund (IMF) and other aid donors. Since that period the pace of reform has moved faster, though public sector enterprises remain in place and protection is applied selectively.

Unlike other countries such as South Korea, Taiwan, Brazil, and Mexico, the Egyptian record with the ISI model has not been successful. The difference may well be in the fact that none of the countries named had, like Egypt, pursued an ISI model in a global manner. In most of them, the government acted as a partner or supporter of the private sector, transnational corporations were very active, and self-sufficiency was not an objective, at least not for long. Moreover, unlike Egypt, the newly industrializing countries eventually shifted to export-oriented strategies. Egypt did not. Little attention was given by the leaders of the July Revolution to the fact that in an increasingly interdependent world extremism in economic nationalism tends to depress growth.

The integrative development model adopted by the July Revolution was to a large extent a response to the lack of confidence in the free market. Like in many LDCs, the market economy in Egypt at midcentury was characterized by serious distortions and imbalances: selective monopolies, considerable domination by foreign businesspeople, sectoral imbalances, limited access to capital, a small number of economies of scale, a small entrepreneurial class, and widespread poverty. The episode described in this book tells of the paradoxes involved in efforts by the Revolutionary regime to free the Egyptian economy and society from those distortions, not by corrective steps but by surgical measures replacing the free market by a managed economy.

THE STRATEGIC MINORITY AND THE COALITION REALIGNMENT

The Free Officers captured power by virtue of the strategic position they occupied in the power network of Egyptian society. As army officers with command over men carrying arms, they were in a better position than most to capture power should they desire or find it necessary to do so. The unrest of the early fifties and rapid changes in the social order cried out for someone to take over and reestablish order. The young officers did not have functional or binding links with the politically organized groups in society. They were neither rootless nor a social minority but a strategic one: a minority by virtue of their position rather than the color of their skin or their class.[23] They were the few who occupied sensitive positions from which they could leap to capture supreme authority. Not owing their political power to any particular group, they were in a position to be more creative than they would have been otherwise.

The Revolutionary regime started by trying to sever the link between class and power, be it economic or political. Delinking class from political power required the adoption of surgical procedures. The extremes of power and wealth on the one hand and those of deprivation and powerlessness on the other had to be removed. The top was undercut, the center was broadened into one bona fide and protected whole, and a safety net was provided for the deprived masses.

Political alignments contributed in a major way to the ability of the regime to hold on to power through very trying times and bold experiments, and that remains one of its uncelebrated achievements. From the very beginning, Nasser redrew the social map, pegging his political fortunes around a centrist position, which remained in effect into the nineties.

Having diminished to a negligible force the classes who combined economic and political power, the regime had no stop sign left in its course toward full hegemony over the country. By 1957 the Free Officers had defeated their political opponents: imperialists, royalists, national political parties, and the Muslim Brotherhood. Their way to full mastery of the land was henceforth open and free-wheeling. In effect, the strategic minority maintained their autonomy, built up a mass base of support, and implemented their national project.

There is some congruence between the managed equilibrium of the integrative economic development model and the political balance of regime alignments, for the elements of the national project of the July Revolution could hardly be identical with the interests of any single class or group. They made each class or group suffer in some way or another, including the main beneficiaries of the Revolution: peasants and industrial workers. The aristocracy was destroyed, wealthy businesspeople and large landowners were cut down to size and made to operate under restrictions not to their advantage, professionals and managers of the nationalized private sector were reduced to the status of poorly paid government employees, peasants were subjected to crop and price controls, industrial workers were deprived of their rights to strike and freely run their trade unions, and intellectuals were made to express the ideas and wishes of the regime rather than their own.

Though deliberately deprived in some respects, all the above-described groups—with the exception of the royal family, the aristocracy, and leaders of politically organized groups—received something in return. The landed class continued to enjoy relative wealth and some standing in the administration; the barons of industry and expert managers headed the new and the nationalized government enterprises; intellectuals and professionals continued to enjoy job security and prestige; industrial workers enjoyed job security, guaranteed employment, fringe benefits and limited participation in management; and peasants received the benefits of land reform and new government-provided facilities. In short, the redistribution of resources covered almost all classes brought together into the center, though nearly all paid a price they would not have paid without the regime.

Class struggle or links of solidarity among members of the coalition were officially prohibited. Since the interests and needs of each and every one of the five categories—peasants, workers, intellectuals, soldiers, and native capitalists—could be secured only through the regime leaders and not from one another, it was pointless for them to fight one another, though there was room for some competition within the narrow frame set by the regime.

It would be disingenuous to argue, as some have done, that business groups or the bourgeoisie have been the prime beneficiaries of the new order, simply because most of their business deals were of necessity with the government.[24] Worse still is the argument that the leaders of the three regimes under the Revolution were instruments and servants of the bourgeoisie. Being a business client of government, practically a hostage, can hardly be considered an advantageous position for a person in business. Controls were imposed on them with respect to size and kind of enterprise, marketing, finances, pricing, hiring, and firing. It is not realistic to call such an environment hospitable, let alone advantageous, for private entrepreneurs. The remnants of Egyptian entrepreneurs were given an opportunity to make a reasonable living but were allowed no real economic or political power.

The political genius of the regime, the reason it enjoyed relative stability throughout its years in power, lay in its relative success in building up a center-based coalition that delinked it from actual power and its practice of attending to the needs of the various segments of society on a one-to-one basis. Life was not without tension, but the stress remained at a tolerable level. Sadat's open-door approach of the early seventies did not change the basic contours of the coalition, though it shuffled names and weights. Moreover, Sadat did not recreate the private sector, he simply gave it more room.

THE NATURE OF TRANSITION

By the 1980s Egyptian leaders had realized that the integrative development model was not self-sustaining. But as was clear to observers, the regime had not fully abandoned the beliefs on which the model rested. Moreover, these leaders showed no commitment to a new or different vision of the future. Taking small measures and temporizing continued to be the order of the day. Though convinced of the need for some reform measures, Egyptian leaders of the seventies and eighties were still not sure that the free market litany preached to them by the international financial agencies would solve their problems. They feared its social and economic effects and were not convinced that it would solve the chronic crisis. Established in the habit of maintaining full control, the very idea of a loss of control generated mental disorientation and tremendous fear. The economic crisis and ensuing debate put them in the unenviable position of having to contemplate the dismantling of the edifice they had built and upon which their power rested. To the extent that they were convinced that some reform was necessary, what to do remained a dilemma. Though they could not stay in place, they were unsure of the steps ahead of them.

Faced with the inevitable, Egyptian leaders kept their sights on what was essential, separating it from what was negotiable. The unchangeable was the power coalition made up of the professional politicians of the ruling party, organized labor, business associations, and the military. It was seen therefore that changes in policy should not cut deeply into the interests of the alignment members.

To the extent the economy created by the integrative development approach was highly interdependent, the regime realized from the beginning that genuine reform that would end the drain, waste, and chronic depression would have to be radical and revolutionary. Such an approach would not be politically possible to sustain without seriously hurting major partners in the political coalition and leading to its demise. Hence, the economic and political transition was slow and gradual. The crisis was to be managed, not resolved.

Not fully convinced of a new vision, the regime sought to temporize and cut around the edges. It searched for soft spots where it could create new openings and moderate the crisis. Those spots were found in areas that could supplement, rather than restructure, existing institutions. For instance, encouraging the private sector could reduce the economic burden of the government without interfering with the regime's economic bedrock (the public sector) and benefit many members of the coalition, including businesspeople, some members of the bureaucracy, and the military. This was particularly engineered so as to preserve the benefits of another major partner of the coalition: organized labor. The private sector, it was stipulated, would have to function under rules similar to those of the public sector and was not allowed to compete with it. Other soft areas that provided the regime maneuvering room were found in policies that would take effect slowly, such as the phasing of official employment of new entrants into the job market over a number of years, a gradual reduction of subsidies, and a value-added tax.

Reform policy did not go so far as to integrate Egypt into the world economy. Selective imports, limited opportunities for international capital, and tourism do not constitute global integration. As shall be discussed, official rhetoric notwithstanding, exports remained firmly restricted, and their value did not show significant progress. The public sector continued to dominate the economy and to remain artificially protected from collapse and from the private sector.

Paradoxically, it was changes in the global economy that permitted Egypt to retain a considerable measure of autarkic tendencies. The rapid increase in rent revenue from foreign aid, remittances by expatriates, Suez canal fees, oil, and tourism allowed the economy to remain afloat, if not prosperous, providing ample room for officials to procrastinate and temporize. The political value of Egypt for Western countries often served to dilute the effect of pressure from the IMF and the World Bank. However, Egypt's need for international cooperation and the system's failure to deliver the economic goods remain the main incentives for policy change in the patron state.

THE DOMESTIC POLICY APPROACH

The object of this study is to explore economic development, which is considered here as a product of the exigencies of domestic politics, not only of the science of formal economics. The emphasis here on domestic policy is not borne out of neglect or underestimation of the importance of the international environment. Rather, the choice is made on the basis of two assumptions and one analytical consideration. First, domestic economic policy in Egypt was made with a considerable degree of national independence and therefore must be considered as the crucial factor in assessing the development record of the regime. National independence does not negate the international constraints, which were willingly accepted or suffered by the national decision makers in Egypt. Those constraints were addressed and encountered with all their consequences.

Second, those governments subject to the same kind of international constraints Egypt has experienced have shown marked variation in economic development performance; hence, the variation must be attributed to other than international pressures on the local economy. Moreover, in Egypt during the period under consideration, international constraints were accompanied by positive international support. Since the Nasser period Egypt has been a major economic beneficiary of the international system. During the turbulent period of the Nasser regime, support was provided by the bloc of communist nations, while under Sadat and Mubarak support came from the United States, Western Europe, and the oil-rich countries of the Middle East.[25] It is too easy in a world with a fresh memory of colonialism to overlook the positive contributions international actors have been making toward a healthier development environment.

Third, a line had to be drawn somewhere to make this extensive analytical inquiry feasible and meaningful. The field of domestic policymaking is sufficiently vast to require a full-length study by itself. I thus left assessment of the weight of international factors for other specialized studies. Moreover, it was necessary to limit the study to a small number of policies, six to be exact, to keep the inquiry from extending beyond a manageable size. Those policies are industrialization, agriculture, subsidies, foreign exchange, housing, and education. Four of the policies are at the core of every economic development strategy, and two are in the supportive area of services. While there are no other compelling reasons for choosing these particular policies, it is hoped that the six policies will provide sufficiently convincing evidence to support generalizations about the Egyptian development approach.

THE HISTORICAL PHASES OF POLICY CHANGE

This inquiry starts with the Nasser regime in 1952 and ends in 1990. Since it is organized thematically rather than chronologically, a historical synopsis may prove a useful introduction.

Economic policy in Egypt went through several phases, which will be identified here briefly. Under the constitutional monarchy, the economy operated under a limited form of ISI, enjoying surplus holdings in foreign-exchange reserves and depending on commodity export of raw material to Western markets, mainly cotton.[26] Industry accounted for 10 percent of GNP,[27] agriculture was the dominant sector, and the country enjoyed self-sufficiency in food and some consumer products. The private sector was responsible for most economic activities in industry, agriculture, finance, and services. Foreigners and foreign residents dominated industry, finance, and services sectors. The government role in the economy was by and large confined to moderate regulation, maintenance of irrigation, and the providing of some limited support to business.

The first phase in the economic policy the Free Officers established under the new order extends from 1952 to 1958.[28] During that period, the Nasser regime challenged the principle of private property, starting with agricultural land. Moderate land reform measures were introduced in three stages, starting in September 1952 and peaking in 1961. Large private estates were broken up and anything in excess of the newly set limit was distributed to landless tenants. Market institutions were replaced with an officially managed cooperative system encompassing the provision of inputs and the marketing of the produce. In manufacturing and industry, the new regime tried initially to support the private sector, while providing "guidance" as to amounts and types of investments. In the meantime it started to take measures to involve the government directly in the economy.

The second phase, from 1958 to 1973, starts with the institution of socialist measures in 1958, which peaked in 1963 with almost total government hegemony over the economy.[29] Egypt moved from partial and selective import-substitution policies under the monarchy to global policies whose objective was almost total self-sufficiency (iktifaa' dhaati). This phase also coincides with the first Five Year Plan (1959/60–1964/65), in the middle of which the regime changed course from partial reliance on the private sector to almost total takeover by the government. Acts of nationalization, which started in 1956 and were initially limited to the subjects of the culprit states in the Suez invasion, spread to national businesspeople and enterprises. Most private enterprises in industry, manufacturing, trade, insurance, finance, and other services were taken over by the government.

It was Nasser's view that transforming the means of production to public ownership was not limited to nationalization but included government control of private enterprises through regulation.[30] Control, in his view, was the key question. What was not nationalized was regulated. During this phase, the public sector became responsible for about 75 percent of industrial output and 90 percent of all new investment in industry.[31]

The first Five Year Plan was supposed to rely on domestic sources of finance, but in fact the government resorted to borrowing heavily from foreign sources at unfavorable rates after it had used up the country's foreign-exchange reserves.[32] Economic growth was at 5.5 percent on the average during the years of the Plan, a respectable but not very impressive rate when considered relative to the amount invested or when compared to other countries of the region during the same period. By 1965, though, the financial resources of the government were almost depleted and the government was not able to undertake a second national five year plan.[33]

In sectoral terms, industrial growth reached 8.5 percent annually during the Plan years, then dropped to 3 percent between 1965 and 1970. In agriculture a growth of 3.3 percent fell short of the Plan's target of 5 percent, and by 1975 it had dropped to 2 percent. The financial crisis that hit Egypt starting in the last years of the Plan was further aggravated by the 1967 war and a subsequent period of economic stagnation, which lasted until 1975. Low growth, shortages of investment capital, consumer goods, and spare parts and growing dependency on foreign imports for food marked the period immediately before the open-door policy was initiated in 1974.

For a brief period, exports grew during this phase and started to become more diverse. The proportion of manufactured goods in Egyptian exports rose to 30 percent, compared to 8 percent in the period before the Revolution. Countertrade with the communist countries, though, constituted a large component of this rise in manufactured exports. That ratio, however, declined to 12 percent in the seventies.[34] Self-sufficient in food production, Egypt changed during this period to dependency on imports. As a result of the self-sufficiency approach, Egypt, which has the third-largest population among some twenty Middle Eastern countries, ranked tenth in total volume of exports in 1990.

The public sector experienced in a fitful way its fastest expansion by the end of this phase.[35] According to Nasser, the public sector in 1963 comprised 80 percent of the means of production, 80 percent of export trade, 100 percent of insurance companies and banks, 100 percent of import trade, 100 percent of transport and communications, 50 percent of contracting companies, and a little over 25 percent of domestic trade.[36] Those enterprises left alone involved mainly small- to medium-sized firms, most employing ten persons or less.

The third phase starts with the open-door policy (infitaah), in 1974 and lasts more or less until 1990, the effective date of the agreement with the IMF. It was launched by President Sadat in 1973/74 as he prepared to shift Egypt's foreign policy to a pro-Western stance. It may be considered as much an effort to build a favorable image in Western capitals as a step to reduce the government's huge economic burdens.

The open-door policy consisted of modest measures intended to relax official constraints imposed on management of the public sector and the small private sector, particularly in construction, tourism, and finance.[37] An open invitation to foreign capital to invest in Egypt was made and sweetened with tax holidays.

None of the major features of the integrative economic development model changed significantly, though, before 1988. Subsidies to individuals and public sector companies expanded, privatization was avoided, price and crop controls persisted, foreign trade continued to be mostly in government hands, foreign-exchange controls stayed stringent, and administration of the economy remained highly centralized despite formal changes. Growth in industry and agriculture remained very slow, though the private sector's share of GDP was growing.

Commenting on the persistent national government's obsession with self-sufficiency in the eighties, Heba Handoussa, the observer with the most intimate knowledge of Egypt's economy and industry, wrote: "One of the most distinctive characteristics of industrial policy in Egypt since *al infitaah* is the clear contradiction between the government's stated objective of encouraging investment capital and production for export and the actual policies followed . . . which make for invigorating investments and production for import-substitution."[38]

The infitaah did not bring back either the free market or capitalism; instead it slowly prepared the country for such an eventuality. Rather than withdraw, the government continued to weigh heavily on the economy and the productive process in general. The private sector remained barred from large areas of industrial activities. Not until 1993, for instance, were private entrepreneurs allowed to enter the import market of fine wheat, and even then they were not permitted to deal in other kinds of wheat. Restrictions on exports were not lifted until 1992.[39]

Egypt's external revenues during this period, especially the years 1975–84, rose sharply largely because of the region's oil boom and the improvement of Egypt's international position. Under the infitaah, government expanded rather than reduced its size. Public revenue as a percentage of GDP rose rather than declined.[40] Government expenditure went up sharply, and public employment increased at 3.7 percent annually.[41] By 1979, five years after the infitaah, the public sector's share of GDP increased from 45.1 percent to 53.6 percent.[42] The expansion, however, started to slow down by the early eighties. Recession hit by 1983/84 as a result of the decline in international oil prices and other external revenues. The balance of payments and budget deficits peaked in 1986, while debt service almost tripled.[43]

Despite the easing of the restrictions on the private sector under the infitaah, statistically the picture differed little in 1990 from that of 1963. The public sector remained responsible for 70 percent of investment, 80 percent of foreign trade, 90 percent of banking, 95 percent of insurance, and about 65 percent of value added.[44] The government continued to have a near monopoly on infrastructure projects (water, electricity, transport, telephones), employing 50 percent of workers in the formal sector, and its shares of credit came to 60 percent, making it the largest receiver. This may have constituted the beginning of a mixed economy, but just barely.

By the end of the seventies a few foreign banks had opened offshore branches in Egypt, and foreign investors responded slowly and in a limited way.[45] Restricted from fruitful areas of investment by official policies, Egyptian entrepreneurs exploited to the hilt the small opportunities opened to them in imports of consumer goods. Because of continued government restrictions on private sector engagement, however, private sector imports by 1979 had not exceed 25 percent of total imports.[46] In the first phase of infitaah, as should be expected, businesses moved to meet the shortages in consumered goods by means of imports or production, to the extent allowed. Afloat with cash from external sources, the consumer goods market flourished and conspicuous consumption gave a bad name to infitaah.

The second major feature of the open-door policy period is the Egyptian economy's rapid movement toward a rentier system.[47] Starting with the first few years of the open-door policy, the major part of national income came from services and external sources such as expatriate remittances, foreign aid, fees from the Suez canal, oil royalties, and tourism.

The eighties under President Husni Mubarak witnessed extensive investments in infrastructure made possible through loans, treasury bonds, and foreign aid. Electric power was multiplied, the telephone network was repaired and extended, roads and bridges were built, and extensive work was done on the sewer system. In contrast, spending on health and education lagged behind. The indifferent performance of industry was reflected by its low contribution to the GNP: 15 percent in 1988, a drop from 20 percent in 1960, despite marked growth in the oil industry. The period also witnessed the reassertion of the self-sufficiency principle openly advocated and championed by President Mubarak.

Despite difficulties, the private sector has grown faster than the public sector during the Mubarak years. The observation that the growth has been in trade and services is no longer true. A shift started to take place from trade to industry by the early eighties. By 1985, the private sector was contributing about 40 percent of industrial production[48] and more than half the GNP. In terms of industrial investment, the private sector's contribution in 1965 was a meager 2.5 percent. By the late eighties it rose to 23 percent, still low but markedly higher than in the 1965 figure. Generally, private investment rose from £E40 million in 1973, less than 9 percent of total investment, to £E2.6 billion, or 35 percent of total investment in 1986/87.[49] In contrast, the public sector has continued to suffer from liquidity, debt, low productivity, and losses, despite the greater attention given it under President Mubarak.

The Mubarak regime continued to resist pressure from international sources represented by the IMF until 1990. Even when the regime gave in and signed an agreement in 1987, it did not honor it because of the serious budgetary crisis. The tilt in the tug of war between the IMF and the Egyptian government started to move in the direction of the latter by 1990/91. The government then took serious measures to reduce the deficit, liberalize foreign exchange, and reduce tariffs, subsidies, and price controls. It also took steps toward privatization, selling or renting some government-owned hotels and local government enterprises in the provinces, and inviting consulting agencies to examine the best ways to proceed with privatizing large government industrial enterprises (GIEs). Egyptian officials claim that the government's target is to sell 85 of the country's nearly 300 public sector companies by 1997. Though the government has made impressive progress in the direction of structural adjustment since 1990, the pace of reform remains slow, in line with the gradualist Mubarak approach.

Chapter Two

Industrial Policy and Decision Making

PERCEPTION AND PERFORMANCE

Since the early years of the Revolution, industry took a center stage in the development perspective of the new leaders. As in most developing countries, industry was viewed as the way of the future and a ticket to the modern era. Put in official language, industry is "the only path to economic progress and continued development."[1] Private entrepreneurs were encouraged, indeed pressured, to invest in industry, and the government itself joined in with private capital in some large industries, such as iron, steel, and railway equipment. The fifties thus showed growth in industrial investment and production. However, as of 1958 the Revolutionary regime started to turn socialist in orientation and, in the process, nationalized most existing industrial firms, banks, utilities, insurance companies, international trading, and other businesses. Other means of control were imposed on the remaining, small private sector.

Though industry became the favored sector in investment allocations and the driving force of the new development strategy, it did not in fact become a dominating sector overshadowing all others. The following allocation figures, which compare investment ratios of agriculture and industry, will bear this out. During the fifties and sixties, investment in industry hovered around 25 percent of total investments (table 2.1). During the first Five Year Plan (1960–65), at the height of the socialist drive, agriculture received almost as much as industry. According to Hansen, "annual agricultural investment increased by 2.0 percent of GDP between 1952 . . . and 1967, [while] annual industrial investment increased by only 1.1 percent of GDP." It was after 1974, during the infitaah period, that industrial investment (6.9 percent of GDP) outpaced that of agriculture (2.2 percent of GDP). Investment in infrastructure was the largest. Nevertheless, the increment in industrial investment in the first four years of the eighties was at a slower rate than that of agriculture.[2] The figures that show an increase in industrial investments beginning in 1969/70 (see table 2.1) reflect heavy investment in petroleum, which could be seen as a tilt in favor of industry. This relatively small discrepancy in sectoral allocations puts Egypt outside the circle of countries, developing and communist alike, who

Table 2.1. Sectoral allocation of investments

	Agriculture (%)	Industry (%)
1952/53–1956/57	11.4	23.8
1957/58–1959/60	14.9	25.7
1960/61–1964/65	23.4	26.6
1965/66–1967/77	21.8	27.4
1969/70–1973	14.6	33.9

Source: Drawn from Mabro and Radwan, The Industrialization of Egypt, 47.

plundered or at least neglected agriculture in the interest of industry. The indifferent results of Egyptian development must therefore be due to factors other than lopsided allocation policy.

Upon assuming power, the leaders of the Revolution perceived the government as a reform agency and an *animateur*, mainly of private business. However, their readiness to intervene in the national economy and expand the role of the government was in evidence from the very start, even before they adopted socialism as an official ideology. As the regime turned socialist by the late fifties, its perception of government's role in the economy took a more aggressive bent. The government became increasingly perceived as the major agent of change and as a business entrepreneur in its own right. This emphasis on industry by the new regime was viewed by at least one Western economist as justified, given the parameters of the Egyptian economy at that time.[3]

By the end of the sixties, however, it was clear that the industrialization drive was not producing the expected results. A sharp decline in industrial output started in 1964/65, the last year of the first Five Year Plan, and for the years 1966/67–1967/68 it showed a negative growth.[4] Efforts to remedy the situation in the following two decades produced indifferent results.[5] This is even more surprising in view of the fact that Egypt was in a favorable position during the fifties for an industrial takeoff, yet it failed to make the leap forward.

Though one sometimes gains the impression from the literature that Nasser's development troubles started with his emphasis on heavy industry, there is no real evidence to support that claim. Heavy industry remained limited in scope (table 2.2), while emphasis was placed on consumer goods in the industrial sector. When the investment ratios in the various industries during the first Five Year Plan are tallied, it becomes clear that heavy industry was not the target of the industrialization drive under either Nasser or those who followed him. The investment share of consumer goods industries reached 30 percent of total industrial investments under the Plan, while heavy industries received only 11 percent, and 48 percent went to intermediate goods industries.[6] Much of this expenditure on intermediate goods, however, went to petroleum.

The Limits of Autonomy

In the absence of effective, organized interest groups and of political parties, national decision making regarding domestic affairs becomes by and large the function of the personal judgment of the ruling elite and an expression of their internal agreements and disagreements.[7] To maintain the stability of its autonomy, the regime first subdued its opponents and then built a supportive coalition of organized labor, small private manufacturers, the peasantry, the army, and the intellectuals. We are concerned here with the first two groups.

Industrial workers were dealt with harshly at the start of the Revolution, then co-opted into the coalition as a favorite social group and patronized by the regime. In return for favors received by labor, trade unions lost their independence and decision-making ability to the government. In contrast, manufacturers were first wooed and favored by the regime only to be discredited and their enterprises mostly nationalized by the 1961/63 period.[8] As large manufacturers were removed from the scene, small ones were drawn into the coalition. Both organized labor and small manufacturers and business associations remained part of the official coalition until 1990. In effect, the regime enjoyed a high degree of freedom in setting its industrial policy objectives.

Though autonomous, Egyptian leaders were not complacent. They tended to tune in to the public mood in order to gauge the limits of their powers and the potential for greater mobilization of the masses. When, through oversight or misreading of a situation, they stepped on areas sensitive to the masses, the public let them know in no uncertain terms. Sadat was caught unaware in January 1977 by a violent eruption of public anger expressed through indiscriminate looting and burning; Mubarak had his turn in 1986 when a special group, the central security guards (al amn al markazi), expressed themselves in the same manner. He was also caught unawares later by wildcat strikes.

Table 2.2. Ratio of value added in the industrial sector according to type of industry, 1950–1971

	1950	1952	1960	1970/71
Consumer goods industries	73.0	69.8	68.4	63.0
Intermediate	23.8	25.2	27.1	29.6
Capital goods industries	2.2	3.8	3.5	6.3
Other industries	1.2	1.2	1.0	1.2
Total	100	100	100	100

Source: Muhieddin, "taqyim istraatijiyat al tasniyʿ," 188.

Because of relative democratization during the Mubarak period, social and professional groups have become more involved in voicing their views publicly and engaging in dialogue with government officials. While the regime has become more open, it still enjoys undiminished powers for making economic policy.

Since Mubarak is basically a stabilizer rather than an innovative leader or an expert in economic matters, his policy has been to maintain the economic legacy in its totality, with all its problems and promises. Indeed, he went one step further by reaffirming the policy of self-sufficiency, already underplayed in the Sadat lexicon.

Some policymakers in Egypt claim that official decision making regarding the economy is the product of rational considerations free from interference by interested parties. This is not, however, a view to be taken at face value. At least during the Mubarak period, interested parties have been given more attention by the government, though their impact on shaping policy is hard to assess. Private business groups acting through the ruling party, the National Democrats, have had direct access to the higher authorities. These business groups have been able to solicit the authorities and negotiate individual and group issues with the government. Trade unions have continued their alliance with the regime. International actors, however, together with the worsening economic crisis, had the most visible impact in steering the Mubarak regime toward privatization and liberalization at the end of the eighties.

As for the rationality said to be enjoyed by an autonomous decision-making body, the issue is less than clear-cut. From the little we know, it seems clear that a rational planning model based on the principle of maximization of profit for the government as an entrepreneur has not been the main consideration. There is no evidence that efficiency was a major policy objective nor that policy was intended to stimulate economic growth. On the other hand, global equilibrium and political considerations have been of primary importance in the making of economic policy. Central planning does not have an unquestionable claim to rationality.

THE DECISION-MAKING SYSTEM

The highly centralized and autonomous decision-making power of policymakers and the institutional fragmentation at the implementation level contributed in no uncertain terms to the indifferent results of industry and the economy in general. The integrative economic development strategy in turn accounts for the chronic economic crisis produced by the serious distortions in economic policies. In this section I discuss the decision-making system, especially as it applies to industry, and other instruments of the integrative policy approach.

An analysis of the decision-making structure in the public sector will show that some problems of Egyptian industry are institutional, reflecting the integrative strategy. The general development policy has always been made at the highest level of government in a highly centralized fashion. Reform efforts made in the seventies and later in the eighties with the stated objective of achieving decentralization were more formal than real, and decision-making power remained authoritarian and centralized.[9] The interdependence of all the parts of the economic and welfare systems makes it practically impossible to give the public sector autonomy, as will be discussed.

The guiding principles of economic policymaking since the 1952 Revolution have changed very little. Decisions reflect the perceptions, values, and political purposes of the top leadership as they are embodied in the integrative global approach to development. It represents a central intelligence guiding and controlling the process.

At the top stands the president, who is both heir to the edifice and its central pillar. As head of state with indefinitely renewable tenure, the president is very sensitive to the impact of economic decision making on the regime. The regime is his project, and he is keen on making sure that the project does not collapse. It is important for him to take into account the opinion of the experts on what makes the national economy deliver within the framework already in place, but preserve the right to act on his own. At the same time, he is fully aware of the populist nature of his regime with all its implications for economic policymaking.

The Egyptian president rules over a nation in which a majority of citizens live on the borderline of economic insecurity and a majority of the population are below the politically volatile age of twenty. The cities that are densely populated are potentially explosive. The president is fully aware that the majority of people are concerned about the basic needs of housing, food, health, and educational services. He will do everything within his ability not to pose a threat to the continued flow of those services to the public, especially the urban population. And this urban population, it is important to bear in mind, has constituted the majority of Egyptians for the past twenty years or more. The fact is that most of the Delta and good part of the densely populated province of Giza are suburbs of Cairo, Alexandria, and a few other cities. Statistics on urban-rural divisions thus do not reflect the real sociological aspects of demographic conditions in Egypt.

Economic difficulties, however, require government leaders to perform a fine balancing act between withholding and granting basic public demands. Ministers and experts are expected to understand the president's position, if they are to survive. They usually leave the broad lines of policy for him to draw, and those policies they propose must be foolproof on this vital issue of the president's position regarding the survival needs of a populist regime.[10] Those parameters still leave considerable room for the president's experts to maneuver and differ with one another.

Sadat and Mubarak inherited an economic system not of their own making. Nasser laid down the foundations of the patron state and left massive government responsibilities and burdens to his successors. Those who followed could not, even if they had wished, reverse the existing order without risking their political survival. In effect, they honored the legacy they had inherited and maintained the basic economic approach. However, on economic matters, both Sadat and Mubarak had almost the same cast of mind as Nasser and showed commitment to the global equilibrium approach in which the government played an integrative role. The current gradual shift toward a market economy and privatization has been too recent to allow for much speculation about the future role of the government in the economy. The shift is in line, though, with the gradual adjustment process started by Sadat in 1973 and resumed by Mubarak in the late eighties.

The temperament of each president also left its mark on how the economy was run. President Sadat occasionally and arbitrarily intervened in minute details of policy, such as setting the price of eggs or other commodities, regardless of legal or economic considerations. President Mubarak has been less impetuous or conspicuous in that respect, leaving details to his cabinet ministers, so long as they abide by the principle of price support and the self-sufficiency policies. He has shown greater attention to economic matters than his predecessor and has repeatedly given backing to the public sector, self-sufficiency, and price controls. He has also paid serious attention to rebuilding Egypt's infrastructure.

There is nothing capitalistic about Mubarak's perception of business as run by the government, neither in terms of competition nor pricing. Pricing of public sector products are based on the principle of so-called social returns, an official euphemism for administered low prices. This is naturally the antithesis of the principle of maximization of profit or promotion of growth. Like his predecessors, Mubarak has been firmly wed to the idea of selling public sector products at a price determined by the purchasing ability of low-income consumers. As late as 1989 he remained proud that the public sector supplied low-priced consumer goods. For instance, faced with a steady rise in the price of chicken meat during that year, he advocated the expansion of the public sector in poultry, an industry thus far dominated by the private sector, in order to supply the market with poultry products at low prices. The public sector farms' prices are lower, not because they are more efficient—far from it—but because their prices are officially determined.

Specific economic policy decisions are made by the council of ministers under the guidance of the president. Specific cabinet ministers and other high-ranking officials, such as the governor of the Central Bank, function under organizational constraints dictated by the offices they occupy. All have their own ideological biases and political interests to protect. Their differences may not always be resolved, especially if the president is undecided on a course of action or is not attentive enough to settle the point.[11] In other cases, the problems may have become so intricate and intractable that policymakers resign themselves to the status quo with all its faults and risks. Only a determined president with clear economic vision could face such a situation frontally and make a policy change.

Trade unions and business associations, studies have shown, are actively involved in the making of economic decisions, but their influence and success is at best spotty.[12] Perhaps the most important foreign agent influencing the making of economic policy in the late eighties has been the International Monetary Fund, and behind it the advanced industrial countries, creditors of Egypt and guarantors of its place in the world economy.

THE HIGHER POLICY COMMITTEE

Under President Mubarak, the pricing policies, especially of vital products, have been determined by the Higher Policy Committee (*Al Lajnat al 'uliya lil-Siyasaat*), a coordinating body made up of high officials, mainly cabinet ministers and the governor of the Central Bank.[13] It is headed by the prime minister, and in 1988 it included the following ministers: Defense, Foreign Affairs, Planning, Agriculture, Interior, Supplies, Industry, National Economy, Finance, International Cooperation, Petroleum, Education, Information, the minister in charge of cabinet affairs, and the minister in charge of Peoples' Assembly affairs. The membership of the Minister of Defense in this committee is due to the fact that the Ministry of Defense has extensive industrial enterprises straddling military as well as civilian products. Since those activities are shrouded in secrecy and reliable information is not available, they will be overlooked in this study.

The Higher Policy Committee (HPC) sits as a commissar of last resort over most operations of the public sector, dictating what to charge for products and services, what to produce, how, and by what means. Expansion, imports, and loans all have to be approved by the HPC. Usually, it reserves for itself the critical issues, leaving other matters to line ministries. Also, when there is a difference between ministers, the HPC acts as arbiter.

The directors of the general organizations, the five large umbrella agencies running the public sector industries,[14] had responsibility for day-to-day management of their industrial firms. On paper, some autonomy was introduced to public sector firms during the infitaah period;[15] however, most remained subject to both the minister and the minister's staff.[16] Under Mubarak, the HPC gained more power at the expense of the directors of public sector firms and individual ministers. Often ministers and high officials had to find ways to circumvent the HPC.

Decisions are reached in the HPC by general agreement or by following the sense of the meeting. Usually, this is preceded by much deliberation, bargaining, and sorting out of differences among individual ministers before the formal cabinet meeting. The collective nature of policymaking here can frustrate cabinet ministers, who, though in charge of their own ministry, are unable to affect the vital issues of the department they govern. One such official, and an influential one at that, was Yusuf Waali, the Minister of Agriculture. When his frustrations reached the limit, he resorted to public criticism of the cabinet of which he was a member. In January 1983 an article he had written severely criticizing the government for its policy regarding agriculture, pricing, and other issues was published in Egypt's leading economic journal.[17] He did not lose his job for the indiscretion, nor did he resign. On the contrary, he turned more political, towed the line, and subsequently advanced up the power ladder.

On the implementation level, the HPC leaves many differences unsettled among the various ministries. The compromises the HPC reaches do not always relieve a minister from the economic bind in question. The following example, which shows how one minister tried to get around the HPC's strictures, reveals unresolved problems and overlapping ministerial jurisdiction. It concerns the pricing of industrial commodities in which the imported component is significant. To protect themselves, some government industrial enterprises (GIEs) priced their products in dollars as well as Egyptian pounds. The practice developed to shield companies whose products include large components of imported parts for which payments were made in hard currency. Since there is more than one price tier of foreign exchange, industrial firms stand to lose money if they sell at the artificially priced foreign exchange in the domestic market. To illustrate, in 1987 a twelve-foot refrigerator was priced at £E400 and at $280. In May of that year, the government raised the dollar value from £E1.35 (the incentive rate) to £E2.16. The depreciation of the Egyptian pound raised the cost of foreign exchange for the company, yet the price of its refrigerator remained unchanged at $280. Consequently, customers found it advantageous to pay for the company's products in Egyptian pounds. That in effect cut the true dollar price of the refrigerator to $183, a major loss to the company.

The Minister of Industry could not unilaterally raise the price charged for the industrial commodity subsequent to the depreciation measure, and obviously could not afford to sell below the production cost of $270. Searching for a way to circumvent the decisions of the HPC in order to cut losses, he made it mandatory for customers to pay in dollars, thus prohibiting payments for refrigerators in Egyptian pounds, a practice well-known in the country.[18] However, this course led to conflict with the Minister of the National Economy, who was eager to reduce the local demand for foreign exchange.

Here the interests of the Ministry of National Economy conflict with those of the Ministry of Industry (MOI). The MOI has to maintain the flow of hard currency needed for regular operations of industrial firms under its control, even when the Central Bank is unable to supply it with foreign exchange in adequate amounts. To make up for a shortfall in hard currency and to avoid selling at lower-than-cost prices, the MOI must demand payments in dollars from its customers. In contrast, the Ministry of National Economy wants to reduce the demand for hard currency in the black market, which is stimulated in part by the sale of domestically produced goods in dollars.

The argument of the MOI is that Egyptian industry needs in excess of $1 billion annually for imports of production components, and only about $500 million is secured through returns from exports. The balance has to be provided by banks, which could furnish at best $300 million. Thus, rather than resort to the black market itself, the MOI prefers to sell locally and in foreign currency those of its products whose imported components exceed 60 percent. Even then, company executives find themselves needing even more hard currency.

Faced with shortages in foreign exchange, government officials often advise firm executives to raise hard currency on their own, a clear invitation for them to deal with the black market, itself an illegal activity. For instance, in 1986, the Ministry of Supplies (MOS) asked the chief executive of the Egyptian Bottling Company to obtain hard currency for production purposes on his own, in effect from the black market, as there was no other source. Yet, he was required to sell his products at the same prices as before.[19] As is seen here, often the huge government bureaucracy fails to respond in time to changing conditions—such as exchange rates—and its practices rapidly become obsolete and harmful.

The open-door policy did not free the public sector from complex bureaucratic interference by the various ministries. Formal changes made in the administration of the state economic enterprises in 1971 and 1975 did not in effect lead to freeing GIEs from direct intervention by ministers. GIEs remained directly under the control of the line ministries, with nearly unlimited power of intervention by the respective minister.[20] As a World Bank study concluded, "in practice very little was achieved and the Government has retained effective control over all three kinds of key decisions": price formation, wage payment, and employment.[21]

Consider the 1975 reform law number 11, which was introduced to make up for the failure of the previous law of 1971 and to give more autonomy to the public sector enterprises. A higher council was created for the five separate sectors, but it remained quite distant and ineffective.[22] The more operative structure was the general assembly (jam 'iyah 'umumiyah), to which the law transferred some functions of the former general organizations, such as passing a budget, handling accounts, and supervising the enterprise's various projects.[23] However, the general assembly continues to be run directly by the line minister, while two other members represent the ministries of Finance and Planning and five other members are appointed by the Council of Ministers. Since the Minister of Industry is quite busy, it has been the practice that a large number, about ten general assemblies, are held and their business concluded in one day. The ineffectiveness of the general assemblies has resulted in the line ministry usually stepping in to fill the void and, in effect, run the enterprise. Moreover, the financial system followed by public sector enterprises was never affected by any of the reform bills.

In this fragmented system, a state economic enterprise is subject to various kinds of intervention from more than one ministry—Industry, Economy, Finance, Planning, Supplies, and others—plus separate supervisory agencies. Executives thus find themselves responsible to more than one authority, a situation that discourages them from taking the initiative and instead prompts them to avoid responsibility by declining to make decisions. Considerable conflict has been noted in the regulating forces—laws, decrees, and established practices—causing severe problems to public enterprises.[24]

The structural order of decision making just outlined may have its justifications, but it has also delayed and blocked reform efforts of the economy in general and the pricing system in particular. A cabinet minister burdened with heavy administrative duties cannot supply vision or guidance, and the firm's executive is too busy obeying orders to provide initiative.

OFFICIAL PRICE SETTING

The second major explanation of slow economic and industrial growth is the broad development strategy of economic integration, of which official pricing was one instrument. Based on that broad strategy, official pricing is a means for balancing resources to maintain an extensive import-substitution system and to provide services to meet welfare needs. It tends therefore to cut prices below market rates and sometimes below cost. Viewed piecemeal, such a pricing system may seem to be extractive. But, as shall be discussed in this book, it is a balancing mechanism of a general nature and an instrument of national policy closely associated with subsidies. Pricing of industrial commodities will be discussed here and subsidies in a later chapter.

From the time the government started to set prices on a wide scale in the early sixties, the ax fell heavily on the producer, whether the public sector or private entrepreneurs. Considering that the industrial private sector had shrunk to a small segment of the economy by the early sixties, the public sector bore the brunt of official pricing policies. There is a general agreement, even within government circles, that price controls have led to financial deterioration of public sector enterprises and to low profits.[25]

Until the infitaah period, the government set the prices for most industrial products. In 1959 the structural mechanism for implementing price fixing was set in place, and the Minister of Industry was empowered to fix the prices of industrial goods. In 1960 the government started to fix prices of medicine and pharmaceuticals. With the completion by 1963 of the socialist measures, most industrial products of the public sector were priced by the government. The price for petroleum products started to be managed in 1967, when the General Egyptian Organization for Petroleum established a pricing committee. Other price fixing of that period included public transportation, water, electricity, telephones, housing, and health services. The pricing structure of industrial output was based on the cost-plus basis, which removes incentives for cost reduction in the management of GIEs.

When President Sadat launched his infitaah strategy in 1974, price setting was only mildly affected by the new approach, despite the financial crunch faced by the government. Distortions in the scale of prices persisted, and in certain cases spread. In 1977, for instance, the government's poultry farms were made to sell at below production cost, and their losses in three years were estimated at £E18 million.[26] In contrast, private farms, whether individually owned or joint ventures, were allowed to sell at a small margin of profit, not to exceed official specifications. Official pricing was a basic instrument of the national economic strategy and could not be scrapped without changing the whole economy, too radical a step even for Sadat to contemplate.

Instead of a wholesale transformation, the infitaah approach aimed at scaling down the range of price controls for partial relief of the official financial burden on the government and on public sector firms. In 1975 price controls on industrial products amounted to 50 percent of output, and this figure was supposed to be reduced to 35 percent in 1978. However, the reduction was for the most part not implemented, according to then Minister of National Economy, Dr. Haamed el-Saayeh.[27] In a statement to the international Consultative Group meeting in Paris in December 1979, Dr. el-Saayeh stated there were "ministerial directives not to implement some of these price changes."[28] Rather than progressively reduce price controls in line with the infitaah orientation, the government reversed itself by 1980 and reasserted price controls for most firms in the public sector in an effort to control inflation.[29]

Even when efforts were made to reduce price controls, the actual change remained negligible. Prices set for the GIEs' products rose at the rate of 1.6 percent annually between 1973 and 1975, compared to 19.7 percent annually for private sector products.[30] Public sector prices later rose more markedly, by 10.1 percent in 1977, and continued to rise in 1980 and after.[31] The price escalation of public sector commodities, however, remained far below the general inflation rate for those years, estimated at between 20 and 30 percent per year. It also failed to take into account changes in the cost of foreign exchange.

Using price controls as a device to keep the cost of living low has been referred to by Hansen and Nashashibi as "depressed inflation."[32] In effect, "depressed inflation" means a policy that keeps prices and wages artificially down by administrative measures, rather than by improving productivity and cutting down production cost. Indeed, the policy of depressed inflation progressively hurt productivity, as the government had to divert resources from investment to price support to keep consumption levels from dropping. The transfer of surplus, however, was not limited to supporting consumers but also was used to maintain equilibrium within the productive system through providing raw materials and intermediate goods at rates affordable to inefficient firms.

The transfer in 1987 to the MOI of responsibility for obtaining raw materials for the production of basic goods distributed by the MOS added to the confusion. Until then the MOS provided raw materials at subsidized rates for commodities produced by the MOI for the former's benefit. The government instructed the MOI to use its own meager resources from exports to finance imports of raw material for basic goods in short supply. This added another strain to industrial firms, which generally are not allowed more than 5 percent profit at best, and of which many are suffering losses. The MOI had to raise the prices of that portion of basic commodities that was in excess of an individual's coupon share. Since most families need more than is allowed them by coupon, pressures on distribution centers became excessive in the first few months of 1988. This situation was further aggravated by chronic distribution problems.

Commodities sold below cost at the beginning of the industrial drive included automobiles and television sets. When the Nasr automobile was first produced in the early sixties, the government set its price at below production cost, as it did in the case of color televisions. The Nasr Auto Company, as can be expected, incurred financial losses, which were covered by the public sector banks. Then when the company failed to pay off its loans to the banks, the latter closed the company's credit line. Production shortages ensued, and many clients who had put money down for their desired automobile had to wait years before delivery was made.[33] Production was slowed not only by official pricing policies but also the emergence of a black market in automobiles. People who had bought cars from the company at below production cost could make a tremendous profit by selling the product on the black market, where prices shot up astronomically.

The practice of buying public sector goods cheap and selling them on the black or "undeclared" market continues to this day, though to a lesser extent. Those involved may be government officials, merchants, middlemen, or consumers entitled to the inexpensive product. In basic goods, a cadre of low-income women known as *dallaalaat* have emerged as black market peddlers of basic commodities bought at official prices from the government consumer societies (*al gam'iyaat al istihlaakiyah*).

Automobiles and television sets have since been considered luxuries and properly priced more or less, but not before damages had occurred. Their production (assembly), however, lacks the advantage of economies of scale; thus it would be less costly to import than to assemble locally. Since a high ratio of inputs is imported, these companies receive indirect subsidies through low-priced exchange rates and low-interest loans. The domestic market for assembly-type refrigerators and washing machines, in contrast, is quite adequate, and that industry was profitable until recently.[34] Moreover, the low profit margin the government allows firms producing refrigerators and washing machines prevents them from expanding or diversifying their production. Those who resort to loans lose money because interest rates are higher than the profit margins allow.

When financial transfers in the form of pricing ceased to suffice, the government allowed public sector companies to borrow from banks, a step which soon led to overdraft. State industrial firms, as we shall see, borrowed from banks above the allowed limit (*sahb 'ala al makshuf*), in the amount of £E2 billion in 1986/87, an increase in overdraft of more than £E500 million above the previous year.[35] According to the same source, annual imports by the sector constitute $1,300 million, while its exports amount to $671 million, 48 percent of which are textiles.[36]

Official prices for services follow the same pattern as that of industry. In 1986/87 Egyptian railways lost £E234 million, as reported by the Central Accounting Agency. Part of this loss was due to official price control, which sets ticket prices among the lowest in the world. Other reasons for the losses are high operating costs and expensive foreign loans.

Conclusion

The main bent of public discourse in Egypt conveys the strong impression that the bureaucracy is the main cause for the chronic economic problems and for the failure of Egypt to fulfill its development objectives. The official press plays a major role in propagating this view, which has crept into some scholarly works. It should be remembered, however, that the bureaucracy did not make national policy nor the rules under which it operates. Those were and still are being made by the top political leadership of the country: the president and his cabinet. The decision to create an enormous and overstaffed bureaucracy was a political one, and the restrictive and excessive regulations that followed were made by the same political leaders. The bureaucracy that administers these regulations is the most apparent source of irritation and an easy scapegoat. Explaining development failure as a bureaucratic problem is misleading. Putting the blame on the bureaucracy shifts the focus away from the main source of the development difficulties Egypt has experienced. Policy, not the instruments of its implementation, has been the source of these problems.

Leaders in a patron state make specific economic decisions under strong influence by their own grand economic design and by political considerations. The rationality manifested in the behavior of leaders has to remain in line with the integrative development approach on which the edifice of the Nasserite state rests. Then specific political risks have to be weighed carefully. The regime's commitment to the social returns policy of government industrial firms, for instance, does not serve to promote economic growth or maximize profits but rather to maintain the grand economic plan and, subsequently, the political survival interests of the regime. If by rational economic behavior one means maximization of profits and growth of an enterprise, the social returns policy and redundant labor and employment policies of government enterprises do not contribute to that objective. Cheap energy for the consumer, under Mubarak and his predecessors, is not a rational economic course of action, viewed from an economic textbook perspective; but from the patron state vantage point, Mubarak and his aides live comfortably with the idea and the practice. In contrast, investing in the improvement of infrastructure and energy sources, as the Mubarak regime has done, is a rational economic activity understandable from both perspectives.

Administered prices are a major instrument in the integrative development strategy to maintain the equilibrium desired by the planner. They constitute a transfer of capital from areas with surplus to areas with deficits, as was seen in the shifting of burdens between the Ministry of Industry and that of Supply. The transfers kept the total business machinery of the government in operation, albeit at a slow pace. The policy, in fact, is a major contributor to low growth levels, for it deprives those who produce a surplus from the means of renovation, research, and expansion. It also constitutes a deleterious tax on producers, who are in effect charged a social tax in order to keep a low-income population in the market for consumer goods.

In reality a tax, administered prices are called *social prices* to convey the idea that the objective of industry is to perform a special service for the public, that is, the provision of affordable goods. In fact no special favor was done by those cut prices, since they were made necessary by the official measures that kept wages low. Unfortunately, they also contribute to low industrial productivity and, ipso facto, fewer goods available to the public, hence, greater incidence of widespread shortages and a black market.

The inadequate decision-making institutions that developed in the industrial sector did not come into existence by chance or by oversight. They were part of a centralized structure deliberately created to give the government total control over production and distribution and to maintain the global balance dictated by the objectives of its developmental strategy. The same obsession with control may have been the reason for the fragmentation of decision-making institutions at the implementation level. By avoiding the creation of a strong and cohesive agency to take charge of industry, the regime may have been guarding its power from institutional competitors. That may also be why institutional reform of the management structure of the industrial sector never produced autonomy for individual enterprises. In terms of the integrative development strategy, individual enterprises were not important by themselves but by virtue of their functionality to the entire sector, the total economy, and society.

Chapter Three

Industry
The Performance Record of Integrative Development

During the Nasser period, industry witnessed vast expansion under the watchful eye of the government, which extended its range of activities in the public sector to include the manufacturing of such diverse products as chewing gum and automobiles. However, the production of capital goods remained a small sector throughout this same period. Acting as the central brain in a vast field of operations, government coordinated the various activities and made vital decisions regarding investment allocation, employment policy, pricing, and quantities of output. The provision of inputs and distribution of outputs was managed in such a way as to guarantee the continued operation of all firms regardless of performance. The survival of a public sector firm was never in question, since the driving principle, the reason for its existence, was to play a functional role in the rest of the economy and to supply domestic market needs, rather than earn profits. With guaranteed security and absence of competition, quality products and efficiency were not a policy priority. Above all, the system had to operate in unison, assuring mutual support to all parts of the whole.

For the integrative approach to work, transfer of resources and distribution of burdens is necessary. The first part of this chapter discusses how equilibrium was maintained in the manufacturing sector through the manipulation of various kinds of transfers; the second part will be devoted to a discussion of the actual performance of GIEs and the mounting need for change and reform in the late eighties.

SECTORAL TRANSFERS

It was imperative under the integrative development model to introduce mechanisms that would keep the entire economy marching at a relatively comparable pace. Transfer mechanisms thus became the rule of the day. Such mechanisms included price controls, subsidizations, mandatory distribution of output, taxation, and special assistance (*i'aanah*). As the market was officially controlled and managed, the outputs of various government-owned firms were distributed to other public sector firms and agencies. Given the different paying capacities of various firms, intra- and intersectoral accounts became complicated. Debts between various ministries or public agencies were allowed to linger, thus permitting the weaker industries to draw on the resources of stronger ones. By creating equilibrium artificially, the government contributed to severe economic distortions and eventually to poor performance of GIEs. An extensive topic in and of itself, subsidization will be covered in Chapter 5. Here I focus on the other transfer mechanisms.

Transfers are made indirectly through the Treasury, which collects from all and redistributes the returns. Writing about the late seventies, Handoussa maintained that the "state appropriates more than 80 percent of profits available for distribution on shareholders and workers, and companies have an unreasonably low claim over their own profits for the purpose of reinvestment."[1] She shows that GIEs contributed the largest share to the Treasury in 1978—£E332 million—compared to the next largest, trade, whose share came to £E140. Industry's share amounted to 42.7 percent of the total share of all public sector contributions.[2] In return, industry received £E120 in subsidies,[3] which increased considerably later on. The Treasury's high collection rate is confirmed by the World Bank in the early eighties. An International Bank of Reconstruction and Development report maintained that "public sector companies were required to transfer 65% of the surplus available for distribution to the Treasury."[4]

Sectoral transfers tended to support traditional industries. Industries such as metals, engineering, petroleum, and energy indirectly subsidized textile, chemical, and food industries. For example, direct governmental assistance to the textile industries in 1985/86 came to £E101,452,000, which exceeded "profits" made by textile firms by £E17,019,000. Similarly, aid to chemical industries came to £E120,889,000, which exceeded returns by £E24,157,000. In contrast, engineering industries received only £E21 million, though the sum was raised in 1986/87 to £E72 million, exceeding profits by £E14,817,000. Metals industries, petroleum, and energy received no cash assistance at any time during the three years (1984/85–1986/87) under consideration.

In the early eighties, traditional industries such as textiles showed positive economic returns, whereas metals industries were in the red.[5] The transfers made here by the government were obviously an economic distortion, which illustrates one of the serious problems of central management. Unequal transfers from GIEs are reflected also in tax rates. Based on the available data from the Ministry of Finance, food industries of the public sector pay the lowest tax rate, 10.87 percent of the surplus (al faa'id) in 1985/86 and 14.42 percent in 1986/87. This compares with 42.89 and 52.09 percent for pharmaceuticals during the same respective years. The Petroleum Authority paid the government 40 percent on its operating profits.[6] The taxes GIEs paid, including those of petroleum and energy in 1985/86, came to £E216,051,000. The industries hit hardest by taxes are, in descending order, pharmaceuticals, energy, petroleum, metals, and engineering. These industries bear a major share of the responsibility of transfers to the rest of the sector, even though among them only petroleum was operating profitably.

In addition to taxes, GIEs had to pay a variety of annual charges to various government departments. For instance, the Treasury claimed £E89,916,000 as its share (hisat al khizaanat) from GIEs in 1985/86. Other official exactions (for supervision, Bank Nasser, and other miscellaneous fees)[7] came to £E25,857,200. And there were other payments, such as profit distribution (15 percent) to workers and distributions to stockholders (mainly government) in varying amounts. When all official claims for the year 1985/86 are added up, they come to £E331,824,000, or 41.5 percent of returns. When distributions to workers and the government are included, the figure rises to about 46 percent.

GIEs that suffered losses as a result of government policies cut down on production, resorted to loans, or sought subsidies from the Treasury.[8] As a result, most GIEs operated at below capacity and therefore at high production cost,[9] a state of affairs still persistent in 1988.

The plight of GIEs was of course compounded by the imposition of "social prices," low prices affordable to low-income people, and to other governmental agencies and companies. In order to soften the harshness of price controls on producers, especially in public enterprises, the government resorted to transfers in the form of subsidized inputs, such as raw materials and energy. Public enterprises also benefited from low-interest loans and foreign exchange, when available, both at lower rates than those paid by the government for acquiring them. Cutting the interest rate, as a practice, goes back to the seventies and persisted throughout the eighties. As for foreign exchange, the free-market rate instituted in May 1987 reduced the GIEs' benefits from that source.[10]

Critics of the government assert that subsidized foreign-exchange rates result in costly and unnecessary support across the board for all kinds of goods, from automobiles and color televisions to playing cards. However, the fees of government banks on foreign exchange were sufficient to balance the artificial rates with cost, sometimes adding a margin of profit. In addition, government holdings in foreign exchange were so limited that executives were encouraged by the government itself to resort to the black market to secure the needed hard currency. In 1983, for instance, the "own-exchange" policy in financing imports was extended to the public sector.[11]

Some of the surplus taken from the industrial sector was redistributed in other ways, such as an outright cash payment (i'aanah) to weak firms. In 1985/

86, the government contributed £E293,757,000 to GIEs, which left it with a meager surplus from the manufacturing sector of £E38 million. Direct government support for industry started to rise sharply in value in the seventies from less than £E1 million in 1971 to £E102.4 million in 1978.[12]

Financial support for GIEs, however, was neither in sufficient amounts nor always available. For instance, in 1979, the investment needs of the food industries amounted to £E129 million, while the Treasury allocated only £E39 million (including self-financing). Under those conditions, the Minister of Industry resorted to bank overdraft loans, which reached £E41 million that year[13] and exceeded £E2 billion by 1984/85.

Other transfers take the form of unsettled accounts among the various ministries and public agencies. Interagency debts are monumental. Of particular interest is the debt—and resulting chain of dependency—of the Ministry of Supplies to the Ministry of Industry, and the Ministry of Industry to the Ministry of Petroleum and Energy.

Under the official perspective, industrial firms were not just economic enterprises but service organizations producing to fulfill a social purpose. They not only had to shoulder the responsibility of keeping one another afloat but they also had to provide social benefits to the public in the form of employment and low prices. In a discussion of ailing firms, the Minister of Industry exclaimed, as if addressing his colleagues in the cabinet, that if government could not provide the sum of money necessary to tidy up the ailing companies, then "leave me the profits of industry for two years only and I take it upon myself to turn over (bi tasliim) [to the government] all the public sector industrial companies with full operating capacity and with their profits doubled."[14] Curiously enough, this item of news was prefaced by a statement attributed to the same minister announcing that as of April 1989, there will be a gradual reduction in the prices of locally produced television sets! He stated that 250,000 units would be produced by 1989, and the price change would start with a minimum 20 percent reduction, which he hoped would eventually reach 40 percent.

Planned reductions in prices were not limited to television sets but were to include refrigerators and washing machines. Although indicators showed a rise in the prices of refrigerators and washing machines internationally, the Minister disclosed that studies were underway to keep prices constant. The steps being taken to maintain prices, he added, should be considered in actual fact a price reduction, because elsewhere prices are rising. The directors of these companies, according to the Minister, should consider saving on cost of production. Those last two recommendations were made by the Minister on the same occasion without an explanation of how GIEs could perform such feats when cost of production was going up.[15] His credibility has not been improved by the fact that the HPC has deprived managers from the enabling legislation to reduce production cost.

It is hard to reconcile these announcements about planned price reductions of GIE products with complaints made by the same official that price controls have caused losses in government-owned industrial firms. One possible interpretation is that the Minister of Industry was not in charge of pricing industrial goods but subject to the dictates of the HPC. Keeping prices low is in line with the regime's philosophy, which states that public sector products should be a source of inexpensive goods for the masses. Similarly, the losses of a company are not a sufficient reason to raise its prices or to liquidate it. The official view is that industry should contribute to other sectors of the economy and to social services and welfare.

Official demands on industry in Egypt are not of the same genre encountered in advanced industrial societies. Industry in the latter case is supposed to produce competitively, contribute to national economic growth, and pay its social dues in taxes. Under the patron state, industries were to meet national needs of goods in amounts sufficient to replace imports, and at a price affordable to the public. When the affordable price happens to be lower than cost, the concerns of the producers are ignored. Being a government agency, however, the producer can afford to relax, knowing full well that some losses can be reclaimed from the Treasury or through cutting back the quantity and quality of goods. The adverse effects of that approach on the economy cannot be sufficiently emphasized.

PERFORMANCE OF GOVERNMENT INDUSTRIAL FIRMS

In 1990, there were still 388 public sector companies, 116 of which were GIEs under the Ministry of Industry. The rest of the government-owned industries were under other ministries, such as Electricity, Health, and Defense. Except for a few firms that shifted to joint ventures with international corporations, no significant change had affected the public sector since the early seventies. Most of the growth in manufacturing occurred in the private sector, primarily since the eighties. Despite its growth, private investments in industry continued to be relatively small due to continued official restrictions and to reluctance of the government to privatize the economy.

Operating in the Red

Though differences among officials and observers exist regarding the performance of GIEs, all agree that net returns have not been commensurate with the volume of investments.[16] The total sum and the rate of profits in the late eighties do not reflect much change from the early seventies, when profits from the public sector industries were reported at 2.4 percent, or about £E102 million,[17] on a "total fixed investment" of £E4.245 billion.[18] According to Dr. al-Qaysuni, three times Minister of Finance and twice that of the National Economy, the public sector in 1977 did not meet more than one-third of investment capital needed from its own revenue.[19] Though the public sector contributed 40 percent of all production that year, the net return to the Treasury was less than £E150 million.[20] Many of the public sector companies that do not generate losses turn out small profits not consistent with the total subsidies they receive, their large investments, and their significant positions in the economy. Qaysuni argues that after discounting various expenses from listed profits, what remains as net profit is negligible.[21]

It would be instructive here to compare the reported net profits of the public sector with the returns the government makes on trading in agricultural goods. As mentioned earlier, farmers were compelled to sell some of their products at low prices to the government. Net gains made by the government on agricultural commodities came to £E179 million in 1974/75. In comparison, the reported net profits of GIEs for the previous year came to £E102 million, less than what the government earns in profits from the monopoly sale of one agricultural commodity, cotton.[22] Anyone considering this situation with a rational economic behavior model in mind would have to raise serious questions regarding the adequacy of Egypt's agricultural as well as industrial policies.

The number of government industrial firms making net losses, according to official accounts, rose from four in 1974 to sixty in 1978.[23] The losses suffered by companies producing basic consumer goods only was estimated by the Ministry of Industry at £E110 million in 1980. A former Minister of the Economy, Dr. Sultan Abu-ʿAli, disclosed in a statement made at the Annual Convention of the Society of Egyptian Economists on 28 November 1988 that out of 116 public sector industrial firms, 78 companies suffered losses in 1986 and again in 1987. The total profits of the successful companies came to £E355 million in 1987, while losses of those who were unsuccessful reached £E581.2 million during the same year.

The Public Economic Authorities (al Hayʾaat al Iqtisaadiyah al ʿAammah), which perform public services like communications and transport, some of which are directly related to production activities, showed a deficit of £E489 million in their budget for fiscal year 1988/89.[24] The ratio of returns to general current revenue (ijmaali al iraad al jaari) was less than 6 percent in sixteen out of twenty-two Public Economic Authorities, as reported by Abu-ʿAli.[25] The Treasury finances the capital deficits of the public economic authorities,[26] and the amount of financial support (al daʿm) given them in the fiscal budget of 1988/89 came to £E979 million.[27] The figure represents the difference between the expenditures made by these authorities (£E1,258 million) and revenues (equivalent to £E279 million). Benefiting from this support are sixty-seven service organizations (*hay'aat khadamiyah*) in various sectors offering general services at cost or less.[28] As for new investments in these organizations, the Treasury allocated £E1,126 million for that fiscal year and £E896 for the previous year, to enable these public organizations to increase their services.[29]

Deficits of GIEs in the Eighties

The financial crisis of government industrial firms has persisted under three successive presidents. Currently, GIEs are beset by liquidity problems and a heavy debt burden. The balance sheet of GIEs shows serious financial problems and low returns.[30] The surpluses shown in three consecutive years— 1984/85, 1985/86, and 1986/87—from the entire government industrial sector, including petroleum and energy, were £E586, £E583, and £E577 million, respectively. When petroleum and energy are excluded, the returns drop to £E292, £E416, and £E429 million for the respective periods.

Reported profits give way to severe losses when the value of subsidized inputs, low interest rates on loans, low-priced foreign exchange extended by the government, plus debt service are all taken into account. Careful examination of the GIEs' balance sheets shows actual losses rather than profits. After-tax figures for 1985/86 show very low returns, excluding petroleum and energy. Total returns that year amounted to £E389,665,000 after taxes, but before interest on debt and various other governmental charges were paid (table 3.1).[31] In 1987/88, this figure dropped to £E371 million.[32] When interest on

Table 3.1. Comparison between returns of government industrial firms and interest paid on debts, 1985/86 (in thousands of Egyptian pounds)

Type of industry	Returns after taxes	Interest paid on debt	Ratio of interest to returns
Textiles	63,112	133,068	210.8
Chemicals	70,055	60,963	87.0
Food	110,396	93,356	84.5
Metals	60,510	24,810	41.0
Engineering	57,693	73,066	126.6
Mining	5,553	11,665	210.0
Pharmaceuticals	22,346	20,893	93.5
Total	389,665	417,821	107.2

Source: GOE, Ministry of Finance, *Al Hisaabaat al Khitaamiyah.*

the GIEs' debt is taken into account, the balance shows them in the red. The sum paid by the GIEs for debt service in 1985/86 came to £E417,821,000, which when subtracted from returns shows a deficit of £E28,156,000. Years of low returns from government industrial firms have resulted in a chronic liquidity problem, and by 1980 industry was borrowing heavily from banks.

As the table 3.1 shows, interest paid on the GIEs' debt surpassed the returns from their operations. The same is true for the other two years for which data is available, 1984/85 and 1986/87. In effect, GIEs had been making net losses for the three years under consideration, not gains as official reporting to the public indicated. The enormous debt they incurred remained a tightly controlled secret until 1991, when officials started disclosing in their statements that the debt of the GIEs was huge, amounting in one report by the Minister of Industry to £E45 billion.[33]

The liquidity problems of the GIEs continued to be quite severe in 1984/85 and in the following fiscal year, when they borrowed heavily in overdraft (al sahb 'ala al makshuf) an amount of £E2.2 billion. Textile, chemical, food, and engineering industries were by far the largest borrowers. Engineering led the pack in 1985/86 and borrowed in overdraft £E659,615,000. Among the 116 under the Ministry of Industry, 65 companies accumulated debts surpassing 50 percent of their capital assets ('usul).[34] When borrowing by the petroleum sector is added, the total overdraft by GIEs comes to £E2.4 billion.[35] To judge from a public statement made by the Minister of Industry, overdraft continued at that high level during 1986/87.

Official statements regarding the performance of the GIEs, made for public consumption, are rosier than the revelation made above. For instance, the Minister of Industry reported in 1988 that the number of firms making losses fell to twenty-eight,[36] and out of these, only seven, he reiterated, were in serious trouble, meaning their annual losses amounted to more than half their capital assets. Some of these companies are manufacturing textiles with obsolete machinery; some are engineering firms, which suffer from badly conceived projects, poor management, and price controls. The alleged losses of the GIEs in 1987/88 came to £E196 million.[37] To judge from the record of the previous three years, the figure seems low. The rising cost of foreign exchange without an equivalent rise in prices—a condition likely similar to that faced by other industrial firms—is cited by the Minister as contributing to these losses.[38]

Disparate reports of ailing companies, though, suggest that the number of losing companies is still higher than the Minister admitted, especially if one takes into account the joint venture companies, which operate under the terms of law 43. The cabinet discussed the problem of ailing companies on many occasions that year but could not come to a conclusion regarding their fate. In June 1988 the cabinet ruled out privatization or liquidation of the twenty-seven ailing companies, a decision announced by the Minister of Industry.[39] The Minister disclosed that the accumulated losses of most of these firms amounted to 50 percent of their capital and that seven firms were in a very critical financial position. A solution, he added, would require massive intervention in the form of injecting up to £E250 million to make them solvent again.

Losing GIEs include, in basic and intermediate goods, vegetable oils, soap, dairy products, poultry, fertilizers, animal feed, pesticides, cement, many basic chemicals, and medicines. Soft drinks had been losing money since 1978—the loss in one of them, Coca-Cola, reached £E4 million in 1981—yet the HPC did not move until 1983 to raise the prices of its products.[40] Subsequently, government-owned soft-drink companies started to turn in a profit.

The absence of losses on the balance sheets of some GIEs producing basic food products may be deceptive. The record shows no losses partly because the Ministry of Supplies provides the Ministry of Industry with an input subsidy and partly because their market is guaranteed and their stocks are sold in their entirety. In 1987 the MOS withdrew that subsidy, though it continued to insist on receiving the same products at the old rates. That proved costly to the MOI, which all the same continued to produce for the MOS while postponing the settlement of accounts until the respective ministers could reach an agreement.[41] The problem of settling accounts of intraministerial debts is still far from being solved.

The seriousness of what has been revealed about the performance of GIEs becomes clearer when it's known that they have been and still are the recipients of a larger share of national investment than any other sector.[42] In the first Five Year Plan under Mubarak (1982/83–1986/87), total public sector investments came to £E27.1 billion, or £E5.4 billion annually, equal to 25 percent of the GDP.[43] This does not include the phenomenal amounts invested in electricity generation during Mubarak's first and second Five Year Plans, 9.7 percent and 17.1 percent of total investments, respectively. The contributing share of manufacturing and industry combined, private and public, in the GNP remained at 33 percent.[44] For the nearly £E5 billion invested in GIEs annually, the returns do not seem commensurate with the effort.

The cumulative effects of years of low productivity and low returns by public sector firms have constituted a chronic drain, taking their toll on the national economy with its continuing deficits and huge foreign debts. It should be noted, though, that the sharp rise in foreign debt in the eighties could be directly related to the vast amounts spent on imported wheat and on infrastructure. One may grasp the magnitude of the issue when one considers that during the first Five Year Plan, £E3 billion were allocated for the sewer facilities of greater Cairo alone. In a speech in November 1988, President Mubarak stated that the government had spent £E22 billion since 1982 on infrastructure projects: drinking water, electric generators, telephones, sewers, and railways.[45] The data show that publicly owned industries have not been able to raise enough capital in profits to sustain their own operations and have proven to be a drain on the public Treasury, forcing those making profits to surrender the surplus in the interest of other firms.

Low returns in GIEs are often caused by government policies and managerial structure, not necessarily by low qualifications of the executives in public enterprises. The plight of GIEs is clearly the product of policies that place a sectoral burden on individual firms, forcing them to make sectoral contributions and forgo their own self-interest and advancement. Not being able to use a surplus for renovation and reinvestment, they end up with diminishing returns.

Official restriction, moreover, contributes to subterfuge. When excessively constrained by official pricing, public sector executives resort to trickery to evade bad financial effects. They produce less of the items whose price is set low by the government and a disproportionate amount of others. Thus a customer might not find the object wanted with the appropriate specifications but an abundance of other kinds.

To the plight of Egyptian industry, one must add the cultural tradition of no punishment for failure and no reward for good performance. Rewards are usually set across the board. The moneymaker and the loser are both rewarded alike with a 10 percent margin for managers and employees.[46] Moreover, the law organizing the public sector requires standard salary scale for all companies of the public sector, irrespective of the particular situation of each.

Attempts at Reform

The preceding should not give the impression that the government has remained unaware of or has ignored the problems. The dilemma, however, lay largely in the fact that the integrative development strategy calls for one thing and balancing the books of GIEs calls for another. The Sadat and Mubarak regimes, it should be repeated here, continued their commitment to the integrative development approach and therefore did not change their perception of government industries as service institutions. Under that perspective, GIEs were not allowed to operate as business enterprises. The critical factor is not oversight as much as unwillingness to change perceptions and bite the bullet. The government was also discouraged by the magnitude of the problem.

Successive governments, especially in the eighties, have tried to face up to the issue by taking piecemeal measures aimed at adjusting prices, devaluating currency, renovating factories, and the like, but they have failed to take the bull by the horns and introduce fundamental policy changes. An effort made by the Minister of Industry beginning in the mid-eighties to improve the performance of industrial firms was the product of a concerted effort by the highest authority in the state, the president, who wished to see an improvement in performance and some relief from the financial pressure on the Treasury. Yet, the same president insisted on the continuation of the social rather than the economic pricing system.

In effect, the drive for change amounted to a search for soft spots in the system, such as in policy implementation and details, and the creation of more room for the private sector. The modest results of such efforts are documented across the chapters of this book. While production was moderately improved and cost moderately reduced, the overall record of GIEs remained basically insupportable. The private sector, however, did make progress and continued to grow under a tolerable but not very hospitable official environment. Perhaps the main value of reform efforts has been the reduction of government intervention vis-à-vis the private sector, a development that could prepare the way for transition to a market-driven economy. Autonomy of GIEs as a solution has proved to be a chimera and, in a patron state, a contradiction in terms.

Problems of Government Industrial Enterprises

Some of the economic problems discussed above, which resulted from government hegemony over the type and amount of industrial investments, distribution of returns, employment practices, price controls, and production subsidies, will be briefly illustrated here by the examination of specific cases of business firms.

The Fertilizer Industry

Chemical fertilizer and aluminum plants are entirely public sector industries and among the largest in the economy. They reflect the typical problems already witnessed elsewhere in the economy. Obsolete equipment, overstaffing, price controls, and the wrong source of energy have contributed in a major way to making both industries very costly and uncompetitive.

A net transfer of resources is made from the energy industry to the fertilizer industry. The World Bank has found that the fertilizer industry receives heavily subsidized raw materials and energy. The price the fertilizer industry paid for natural gas was "8 percent of its economic opportunity cost (i.e., energy equivalent price of fuel oil); the fuel oil price [was] about 18 percent of the international price (FOB export price . . .); power price [was] about 14 percent of its opportunity cost."[47] It should be noted that these price assessments reflect the increase in the general energy prices introduced by the government on 1 May 1987. On that date, the government doubled the price of natural gas, increased the price of fuel oil four-fold, and raised the power rates to industrial users by 40 percent. Still, energy prices remained at the low rates indicated above, which ranged from 8 to 18 percent of their economic prices.[48] As for electricity, the industrial sector paid only 25 percent of its actual generation cost.[49]

Despite resource transfers and other subsidies, the fertilizer industry has remained inefficient. The cost of producing ammonia at the Kima Fertilizer Complex is seven times what it costs elsewhere,[50] while in the nine fertilizer complexes taken together, the higher cost is estimated at three to four times.[51] One reason for inefficiency is the social function the industry is called on to perform. In accordance with standard practice, production inputs are subsidized on one end of the scale and the price of the product is officially set low at the other end. These transfers are not necessarily balanced, for commodity price reductions often outweigh the value of subsidies. The Agricultural Production and Stabilization Fund, a government agency, sets the factory prices of fertilizers low in conformity with the general guidelines set by the HPC of the cabinet. The price is determined on the basis of the production costs provided by different companies, with a profit margin added to those costs. Since their production cost is covered as a matter of fact by the Treasury, firms have little incentive to cut costs.

The local farmgate prices for fertilizers are lower than international prices (of comparable imported products delivered to farmers). Based on data given by the World Bank, local prices averaged 34 percent of international prices.[52] The returns on equity of fertilizer plants in 1985/86 show that only the Abu Qir company had a reasonable return of 10.6 percent, with al Nasr Coke next at 2.9 percent, two others at 0.3 percent, and a fifth at 0.02 percent.[53] Thus, four companies showed a low profit and one showed virtually no profit at all. Three firms, SEMADCO, Abu Zaabal, and Kima faced liquidity problems due to price distortions.[54] In 1980, losses suffered by four companies were estimated at £E40 million,[55] though the Minister of Industry claimed that the fertilizer companies suffered losses for the first time in 1988. He attributed the losses to the higher exchange rate introduced in May 1987, which was not accompanied by an increase in the prices of the fertilizer products.[56]

According to the same confidential World Bank report, among the nine fertilizer complexes, only two—Abu Qir and Talkha II—are competitive, while four others could become so in the long run should new investments, rehabilitation, and rationalization measures be fulfilled. Three other companies are hopelessly uneconomical, the worst of which is the Kima plant.

The Kima Fertilizer Complex, started in 1960, has been producing ammonia, nitric acid, and ammonium nitrates. Its equipment is now obsolete, and it operates below capacity. The production of ammonia is not competitive, according to experts. "It costs about US$622/ton of ammonia (on the basis of economic prices of inputs) compared to the current landed price of ammonia (at Alexandria port) of about US$115/ton."[57] The ammonia plant at Kima is based on the most energy intensive process, and it "consumes 4–5 times more energy per ton of ammonia than modern, natural-gas based ammonia plants."[58] The artificially low prices of energy gave the industry the wrong signal, and its executives naturally did not have to be concerned about cost. Energy in the late eighties was provided at the nominal cost of 1.2 piastres (100 piastres equal £E1) per kilowatt-hour, or 10 percent of its economic price. The World Bank report concludes that its production cost has been "much higher than landed import prices" by 440 percent for ammonia and 247 percent for ammonium nitrate.[59]

Al Nasr Coke and Chemicals Company, like Kima, produces ammonia based on one of the least efficient feedstocks: coke oven gas. However, in this case its administered prices have been set high, and it has no incentive to cut down on its production cost.[60] Both companies, Kima of Aswan and al Nasr of Suways, have failed to renovate their obsolete equipment, a fact which contributed to low productivity and high production cost. Plans discussed in early 1988 with the World Bank to import ammonia for the Kima plant may make its operation more economical.

Subsidization of productive enterprises is generally supposed to stimulate growth and competitiveness. In the case of fertilizers, subsidization does not have this effect, due largely to price controls. The production subsidy for the fertilizer industry does not contribute to profit making or to saving and reinvestment. Financial statements by the companies showing profits are based on financial rather than economic bases and are thus distorted and difficult to assess. For instance, the World Bank report found that the farmgate prices of urea, ammonium nitrate, calcium nitrate, single superphosphate, and triple superphosphate were between 22 and 60 percent of international prices.

With production not up to sufficiency levels and imports restricted, a distribution quota was established. Thus farmers often did not receive sufficient amounts of fertilizers and resorted to black-market practices. Frequently, poor farmers would sell their shares to wealthy ones. Approximately 40 percent of fertilizers supplied to farmers found their way to the black market.[61]

The central agency that sets prices for fertilizers is the HPC, and the process directly involves the ministries of Agriculture, Industry, Commerce, and Supply. There are at present six fertilizer companies operating twelve fertilizer plants. The companies are supervised by the Chemical Industries Organization, a chemical industry holding company under the Ministry of Industry. Production cost and distribution is determined by several different agencies, which makes for a very cumbersome process. The World Bank report determined that the agencies concerned lacked skilled managerial personnel to carry out reviews and that these agencies leave very little flexibility to company managers.[62]

The vicious circle of the artificial equilibrium approach can be clearly seen in operation here. In effect, the government, believing in its planning ability and its omniscience, tries to create a balance by determining the cost of inputs and those of outputs, often through the mechanism of artificial pricing. The fertilizer producer receives subsidized inputs and is then subjected to product price controls. The farmer then receives fertilizers at low prices and sells to the consumer at rates that reflect the low-priced inputs subsidy. However, salaried consumers whose wages as employees of the government are kept low could not be considered the beneficiaries of the official balancing act. In short, the fertilizer industry has been shackled by central government interference of all kinds and involving value transfers in the prices of inputs and outputs.

Aluminum and Electricity

Unlike fertilizers, which are produced solely for local use, aluminum is for both local use and export. As an industry that consumes much energy, it was once believed to be an answer to the surplus electric power expected from the completion of the High Aswan Dam. One aluminum-producing complex, Nag Hammadi, and the Kima Fertilizer Complex together consume two-thirds of the total capacity produced by the High Aswan Dam.[63] Contrary to expectations, the surplus energy produced by the High Aswan Dam vanished before the Nag Hammadi industrial complex started operating in 1975. Egypt has since been relying on fossil fuel as a source of energy. In the early seventies, hydraulic power accounted for 70 percent of Egypt's electricity, but the level dropped later to 38 percent and again to 20 percent in 1987. Electric power generated by means of petrol and natural gas made up the difference. Petrol-generated electricity became the major source of electric power in 1980.[64]

The present regime has invested and continues to invest heavily in the generation of electricity. In 1981, Egypt's electric power reached nearly 18 billion kilowatt-hours; six years later it jumped to 45 billion kilowatt-hours, 80 percent of which was based on petrol and natural gas. The country's needs, however, have not been fully met, and the government is currently building several new plants, for which it is borrowing funds from international sources, including a $270 million loan from the African Development Bank granted in 1988.

The use of electric power in Egypt has been much criticized, and conservation efforts, if they exist, are not very effective. Consumption for domestic uses is one of the highest in the world, 45 percent of the total capacity, whereas industry's share amounts to only 55 percent. In contrast, the share of domestic consumption in both India and China is only 10 percent, while in Sweden it is 25 percent.[65] Still, expansion rather than conservation seems to be the future course in official plans.

Consumption of electricity is growing at over 10 percent annually, which requires the addition of 600,000 kilowatt-hours every year.[66] Nevertheless, no serious efforts are being made to stem consumption, and no price increases were envisaged in 1988 according to the Minister of Electricity.[67]

The prices of electricity in Egypt for both domestic and industrial consumers (excluding firms operating under law number 43) are some of the lowest in the world.[68] In 1982, the price of electricity was raised from 0.3 piastre per kilowatt-hour to 1 piastre (0.45 US cents), and it stayed at that fixed rate until 1987. In 1988, one kilowatt-hour cost the consumer for domestic use 4 piastres on average. For some industries, such as aluminum, and the Kima fertilizers firm, the price paid was 1 piastre per kilowatt-hour in that same year.[69] In 1985 a USAID report estimated that Nag Hammadi Aluminum was paying only 7 percent of the long-run marginal cost of electricity.[70] The Electric Authority of Egypt (*Hay'at Kahrabaa' Misr*) disclosed that in 1975 the price charged the aluminum company constituted 58 percent of production cost. In 1985/86, the price per kilowatt-hour constituted 38 percent of cost, causing the authority £E27 million in losses, according to the prime minister's office.[71]

As has already been mentioned, aluminum is an energy-intensive industry. The Nag Hammadi Aluminum plant is by far the largest single consumer of electricity in Egypt, and it utilized 11.6 percent of the 26,175 million kilowatt-hours nationally available in 1984/85.[72]

The World Bank maintains that the electricity cost alone required to produce a ton of aluminum in Egypt is greater than the price for a ton of finished aluminum on the world market—US$1,260 compared to a world price of US$1,100, a loss of US$160 per ton.[73] The USAID report goes on to state that Egypt's electricity cost of producing a ton of aluminum rose to $1,560 in 1986, while the world price of aluminum rose to only $1,200 per ton. Electricity is generally considered as a very expensive source of energy for the production of aluminum and fertilizers. Recommendations by the World Bank to close the aluminum plant in the interest of Egypt's national economy have so far been ignored.

Egypt has been heavily subsidizing foreign consumers of its aluminum products, according to the World Bank. Egyptian officials, on the other hand, claim that profits have been made on aluminum exports.[74] The data provided by the Electricity Authority of Egypt show that export of aluminum generates profits while domestic sales incur losses. It is claimed that aluminum sells locally at a loss of £E250 per ton and a gain of £E1,250 per ton from export.[75] However, due to various distortions in costs and prices, industry profit figures given by Egyptian officials remain unclear.

Multitier pricing of aluminum products have had a deleterious effect on the industry and the national economy. There are three rates: one low for companies of the public sector, one higher for companies operating under law number 159, and one high (thus comparable to international rates) for companies operating under law number 43 of 1974. As a result of the various rates, some companies that pay the lower rates choose sometimes to sell their share of aluminum at the higher rate rather than engage in the productive process themselves.[76] In effect, the price policy has contributed to the expansion of the black market to industrial corporations.

The Pharmaceutical Industry

Medicines have a definite social welfare value and it is to be expected that prices will be controlled. Indeed, the price of medicine in Egypt is among the lowest in the world.[77] For instance, cough medicine costs around 30 piastres (about 13 cents). Not surprisingly, the medicine subsidy is high. The exact amount may never be known, as officials juggle the figures depending on what they wish to emphasize, an act made possible by the multiple exchange rates. In 1988, the subsidy was said to be £E170 million, as reported by the Minister of Health.[78] The figure £E788 million is attributed to the President's speech to Egyptians in London in September 1988. It seems certain that the latter figure was computed on the basis of the free-market exchange rate.

The pharmaceutical industry is an example of Egypt's drive to attain self-sufficiency. It may be worth noting here that Egypt produces locally almost all (87 percent) of medicine needed domestically for human use. The percentage was planned to reach 92 percent by the end of 1990. This is extremely high for a country whose pharmaceutical exports do not exceed a few million dollars. Most pharmaceutical patents, though, are of foreign origin, and imports of inputs are still very high. Indeed, most foreign pharmaceutical firms in joint ventures with the public sector acquiesce in the official price controls of medicine because they are able to make up losses by the profits the home firms gain selling ingredients to the Egyptian subsidiaries.

Some small profits shown in official figures in the early seventies seem to have dissipated in the eighties. The pharmaceutical industry of the public sector, for instance, showed £E16.7 million in profits in 1975. Of that sum only

£E2 million remained as net profit, and this profit was appropriated by the government.[79] In 1988 it was reported that the public sector pharmaceutical companies lost £E67 million, an amount equal to that incurred by the small private sector companies.[80]

The industry has not in recent years been able to fulfill its promise to satisfy the domestic market needs, a problem compounded by the outright prohibition of imports of certain medicines.[81] Egypt imports a very small amount of finished medicine, worth around £E100 million, only 20 percent of which is imported by the private sector. The government has opted since 1986 to prohibit the import of a specific number of medicines outright. Before 1987 imports were subject to approval by rationing committees (lijaan al tarshiid), which caused a great deal of confusion and dissatisfaction in the business community. Price controls and limited funding has led some public sector enterprises to cut back on research and resort to patented products instead.

Officials admit that most government-owned firms in pharmaceuticals are suffering from financial liquidity problems. In 1985/86 pharmaceutical firms of the public sector earned (after taxes were paid) £E22,346,000, while the interest on their debt amounted to £E20,892,000. The ratio of their debt service to earnings that year was 93.5 percent,[82] a figure that later went much higher. They badly needed renovation yet lacked resources, "due to the large gap between production cost of medicine and sale prices."[83]

Official pricing policies, which created severe financing problems for state industrial enterprises, have also caused serious problems for private companies. Though some private pharmaceutical industries began operating in the seventies under investment law number 43 and later under law number 159, most were begun in the eighties. Pricing policies have seriously hampered the growth of this burgeoning private industry, whose share is still 12 percent of the local market. Investment laws number 43 and 159 guarantee a free pricing hand for private companies, yet the Ministry of Health has practiced a supervisory role over them; in the eighties the ministry imposed official compulsory pricing on both foreign and Egyptian investment companies.

Private sector sources maintain that some firms closed as a result. One American firm had cut back to nearly 50 percent of its normal operating capacity by 1988. While it had not dismissed workers, it ceased to accept new ones. The company relied almost entirely on imported ingredients and therefore was susceptible to changes in international prices and exchange rates. In 1987 two joint venture companies laid off 50 percent of their employees subsequent to a conflict with the Minister over compulsory price setting.

Another company, ABI, functioning under law number 159 by Egyptians, found itself in serious trouble in 1988 due to restrictions imposed by the Minister of Health. ABI produced a large array of medications,[84] primarily some fourteen drugs usually in short supply locally. Unable to sell at the officially set prices, the company's inventory rose dangerously high and it suffered from lack of liquidity. Another private company in Alexandria resorted to the courts to force the minister to lift the official price controls to which it attributed its large losses.[85]

Private pharmaceutical companies claim that the law exempts them from price controls (decree number 1141 of the Investment Authority [*Hay'at al Istithmaar*], 1983), since they do not receive any subsidized inputs, imported or otherwise. Apparently, in 1988 the Minister of Health overruled the pricing committee and determined the prices himself, which provoked complaints from the industry as well as from the Chamber of Chemical Industries. The minister agreed in September 1988 to allow the companies to raise the prices of some products that are not for critical illnesses by 15 to 30 percent. The price change took effect in 1990. Since the base price is quite low, the permitted increases did not in most cases add more than a few piastres per medicine.

The problems of the pharmaceutical industries are of the same genre as other industries: pricing, foreign exchange, liquidity, import substitution, high dependency on imported ingredients, and shortages in supplies. Most of these problems are related to the government's ambitious objective of self-sufficiency, control policies, and restrictions imposed on the private-sector industries.

The Textile Industry

Textiles are the oldest industry in the modern manufacturing history of Egypt, and the most extensive. One would have expected the textile industry after nationalization in the sixties to be relegated to a secondary role, to decline in size, or just to hold their own in view of the regime's express wish to move into heavier and more modern industries. Instead, the industry expanded and became the recipient of substantial investment capital. Moreover, textiles have continued to benefit from the policy of low-cost raw material, especially cotton. The advantage they gain in cheap inputs is a direct loss to the peasant cultivator, who is compelled to plant cotton yet receives very low prices for it. The emphasis placed on traditional industries led one Egyptian economist to take the Nasser regime to task for not pursuing a heavy industry policy and for the limited growth of industries producing intermediate goods.[86]

In the seventies, many government-owned textile firms started to show losses. They were overstaffed, poorly managed, and suffered from liquidity problems. Attractive opportunities in the private sector and abroad, moreover, siphoned off many of their skilled personnel and workers. The government-owned textile firms continued to be a poor performer in the eighties and to receive financial support from the state budget. Severe liquidity problems in the industry led textile firms to borrow heavily from banks. For instance, in 1985/86 the textile industry borrowed in overdraft £E518,698,000, while their return before taxes was only £E84,433,000.[87] The textile industry is thus the most indebted of all Egyptian industries, and its debt service is 210.8 percent of its return.[88] Unsold inventory in the industry as a whole that year came to £E140 million. In 1986/87 three large textile firms of the public sector lost £E60 million and were declared to be insolvent by the Minister of Industry.[89]

Being insolvent, however, does not mean that the firm is liquidated. No publicly owned industrial firm has been. For instance, in 1988 the Misr-Halwan Textile Company was declared by the Minister of Industry as one of the companies to which the rules of insolvency apply. Yet, the minister added that he would recommend to the council of ministers that the firm remain in operation.[90] Whether he had in mind the fate of sixteen thousand workers or something else entirely remains unclear, but it should be mentioned again that the regime has opposed liquidating any government industrial firm.

The price system had at one point contributed to expanding the black market. Industrial companies operating under law number 43 of 1974 paid prices for yarn that were 28 percent higher than prices paid by other companies. Consequently, many companies found it in their interest to sell the yarn rather than to use it for production of textiles.[91] This state of affairs came to an end when the government recently decided to charge one price for yarn.

CONCLUSION

Examination of industrialization policy has shown how artificial equilibrium dominates the economy in the patron state. Transfers of resources from one firm or sector to another created economic distortions, though they were not extractive or malicious. Rather, they represented discrepancies between the scarcity of available revenue and expenditure, official business costs and returns, production and consumption.

In countries pursuing an industrialization-first strategy, excessive taxation policies are sometimes limited to agriculture and reflect an urban bias.[92] In Egypt, however, exactions were made from most productive sectors, including those owned by the government itself. Redistribution of resources by the government thus represented a national scheme to centrally collect returns from productive enterprises and make transfers according to a logic dictated by a national design.

Though industry was emphasized in the development plan, it was not markedly favored over agriculture. True, cotton producers suffered disproportionately from official policies, but they were not singled out as victims of excessive taxation. To the extent that cotton was the largest earner of hard currency up to the mid-seventies, the diversion of its returns to the government and to the textile industry could be viewed as a large transfer of resources away from agriculture. At any rate, cotton dropped in the seventies to sixth place as an earner of foreign exchange, and agriculture ceased to be the backbone of the economy.

On balance, the terms of trade slightly favored the urban areas, especially in matters of consumer subsidies.[93] However, considering the strongly established urban bias prevalent before the Revolution, the near-parity practiced since the sixties constitutes a great step forward. Currently, we witness some characteristic urban problems in rural areas, especially in housing and bread making.

It is in the nature of the patron state to tax accessible sources of wealth regardless of whether the parties victimized are politically favored or not. In addition to planned transfer of resources, government's unrestrained and often wasteful expenditure policies put a premium on securing additional revenue for the Treasury regardless of method.[94] Since economic policies in Egypt led to little generation of surplus for reinvestment or use for other expenditures, the government sought to transfer revenue away from those productive groups who were actually the makers and holders of material values. The most accessible resource, of course, was public sector firms, which were made to pay for one another and for welfare in the form of underpriced products and redundant employment. Other revenue generators, such as exporters, contractors, and professionals, fall in the same category and will be discussed elsewhere.[95]

Official subsidies lowered the production cost of GIEs, which was offset, however, by price controls and other impositions. The quid pro quo in this case is a very poor alternative to welfare or a proper wage scale, since it impoverishes the producer and the national economy and hardly satisfies the consumer.

As previously discussed, the number of government enterprises suffering from losses because of officially set prices and other causes was very high by the seventies and early eighties and continues to this day, despite concerted efforts by the government to remedy the situation. Government public enterprises suffer from chronic and severe liquidity problems, which limit their ability to invest or to operate at full capacity.

Under the integrative model, government economic firms are viewed as institutions with a primarily social purpose. The priority for a government industrial firm in Egypt is not necessarily to grow, to maximize profits, or to generate additional investment capital but rather to maintain a national development design based on interdependence.

At the outset of the Sadat presidency, the regime was already entrapped by two decades of its own policies and no longer in a position to quit its earlier commitments nor able to move forward. Sadat thus opted for a very slow adjustment process, which dragged on from 1973 forward and continued, under his successor, into the early 1990s. No shock treatment was tried by the patron state in Egypt.

Why does government not liquidate an enterprise with endemic losses that has been officially declared insolvent? A private operator would have no choice but to close a business that is losing money year in and year out. In the public sector, however, a firm is viewed from a different perspective. There is a tendency for the government to extend the definition of a service industry, such as railways, to almost every public sector enterprise. Railways may lose money, but governments will subsidize them because transport is considered a public responsibility, essential for the economy, and one that meets the needs of low-income groups. But in the patron state, the idea that a firm is a service industry is extended to all other government enterprises, including textiles, dairy farms, or aluminum firms. Thus, a textile company ruled insolvent by the Minister of Industry is recommended for continued operation by the same official. The company's employment of sixteen thousand workers and its relevance to suppliers and other businesses are considered as important services to the economy. Hence, textiles and dairy products assume a new function—service to the national economy—and therefore are protected and supported regardless of their financial returns. They cannot be judged as separate firms that have to stand on their own. Social functionality of a firm takes precedence over economic growth.

The record of public sector industries shows that in the patron state economic growth per se loses some of its saliency in favor of the service that enterprises perform maintaining equilibrium for the polity and society. One has to conclude that the patron state's commitment to growth is questionable and at best compromised.

Of the many possible principles of distribution, the doctrine of social returns of industrial firms is the least productive for welfare and growth. Since the policy undercuts the major source of funding, not only for economic growth but also for welfare itself, it is obviously self-defeating. Without growth, there will be no revenue with which to support distribution. It is not the policy of attending to basic needs that is in question here but rather the instruments used to finance them.

The patron state, which starts out with the idea of achieving greater control over the economy, ends up losing effective control over its course, though it maintains control over its management. The slide away from a position of power, one that could steer GIEs in a new and corrective direction, has had a deleterious effect, not only on industry but on the economic and political behavior of the public. It has already been noted that government officials have driven, indeed encouraged, corporate executives into the black market. Cynicism, resignation, lack of desire to try, and disrespect for the law have been visible attitudes manifested in Egypt since the end of the sixties. The Egyptian experience with government economic hegemony shows that the more control is sought, the greater the slippage. Eventually, the government became trapped by its own policies, which made change progressively more difficult.

The tendency among Egyptian intellectuals to blame bureaucracy for the poor performance of industrial firms may be no more than a form of self-delusion. Few would doubt that there have been poor managers who brought failure to their companies, but that happens in the private sector as well.[96] Though managers of GIEs undoubtedly share part of the blame, it should be remembered that responsibility falls squarely on policy and policymakers. The bureaucrats most responsible were those appointed by policymakers on patronage rather than merit bases. Under Nasser and Sadat, individuals considered loyal (ahl al thiqah) were promoted to executive positions regardless of merit. But the question goes beyond recruitment shortcomings to the elite perception of the regime's survival needs as coterminous with strict control over all economic activities. Excessive controls tie the hands of managers, take away their initiative, and generate fear of responsibility.

Two observations are appropriate here. First, it is government policies, not those of managers, which are responsible for whatever adversities are encountered by public enterprises. Bureaucracy has long served as a whipping boy for critics who do not want to admit political realities or are not aware of them. Second, the propositions sometimes made that government economic enterprises, like private ones, behave in a capitalistic manner, seeking to maximize profits, is not supported by the facts in the Egyptian case. The few executives who do behave that way are a rare specimen. Most have to follow an approach dictated by higher political authority and inspired by social and political considerations.

Political leaders continued in the eighties most of the practices that had encumbered government industrial enterprises for nearly thirty years. Executives remained deprived of the full rights to draw up policy; hire and fire; determine investment and prices of products; and decide what, how much, and for whom to produce. Firm managers are, moreover, not allowed to dispose of returns in the best interest of the enterprise. Had it not been for the influx of rent income—such as large injections of foreign aid—since the mid-seventies, the economy would have collapsed long ago.

Despite the rent income, Egypt was in a very difficult financial situation during 1987 and 1988. The government was compelled to negotiate the rescheduling of its enormous debt of over US$40 billion. Unable to reduce its annual deficit of nearly £E10 billion, Egypt had difficulty in 1988 convincing the IMF of its ability to carry out reforms. A special campaign conducted by the president was launched to rally European supporters to side with Egypt in its bid to reschedule $3–4 billion dollars in interest payments. President Mubarak had to harp, unfortunately, on the often-used theme that Egypt is too vital politically for the West to let it go under. Luck, as it were, struck again: the Gulf crisis of 1990 raised the political value of Egypt internationally, and relief arrived at a critical time.

The debt-ridden industrial sector corresponds to the national economy with the exception that the GIEs are indebted to Egyptian, mainly government, banks, while the national debt is owed to foreign banks and governments. The financial drain on the national economy caused by costly public sector industries is usually viewed from a fiscal point of view as harmful, which indeed it is, especially when accumulated over many years. However, when debt is kept within the bounds of a sound ratio of loans to capital, it should not be an intimidating factor in policymaking. In the wake of the debt phobia resulting from the LDCs' hopeless debt situation, this becomes a point that should be particularly remembered. In Egypt, the ratio of equity to debt in the public as well as the private sector has been very high.

Despite commendable efforts recently to renovate and rehabilitate GIEs, the sector remains sluggish, operating inefficiently and below capacity. The regime continued into the early nineties its reluctance to liquidate any government-owned firm, no matter how uneconomical its performance. Sales of GIEs to private parties remained limited to tourism and small provincial projects. Some fifty major enterprises, including industrial ones, were being studied for privatization, but little progress had been made by the early nineties.

Chapter Four

Agricultural Policy
Private Ownership and Public Control

Immediately after taking over, the Nasser regime introduced land reform measures that established a ceiling on the size of private estates and distributed seized farmland to landless tenant farmers. In a few years during the fifties, a sophisticated developmental strategy in agriculture emerged with little or no external advice. During this early phase of the Revolution the idea of growth had not yet been submerged by the global integrative development strategy.

The early reform strategy seemed to meet the most agreed-on recommendations by students of development from different schools of thought. Its elements included (1) growth through public investment, land reclamation, land consolidation, and expansion of perennial irrigation; (2) land reform through the redistribution of resources and institutional change; (3) the provision of material incentives in the form of private ownership and profits; (4) support and encouragement of small owner cultivators through the establishment of cooperatives; (5) acquisition of hard currency by continued emphasis on cash crops; and (6) the provision of basic needs to the rural population, such as health services and education.[1]

In one sense, the approach can be seen as a cultural statement defining the identity of the new leaders, not only as to the questions of modernization and social justice but also vis-à-vis the peasantry, who in Egyptian national consciousness represent the authentic and oppressed Egypt itself. Liberation of the peasant stood as a symbol for the liberation of the primordial Egyptian, not just as part of an economic plan.

Though the reforms of the fifties remained intact throughout the period under consideration, the sixties showed the mark of the integrative development model imprinted on them. Farmland, except for a small number of publicly owned farms in reclaimed areas, remained privately owned, but its use fell increasingly under government controls. In effect, agriculture became subject to management by the central government and to the customary transfers made to maintain a national economic equilibrium. Policies that seemed extractive were actually part of that grand design, as opposed to discriminatory measures against agriculture. No discrimination against agriculture is in evidence here.

The Urban Bias and Extraction Theses

Agriculture in Egypt was not neglected, as has been the case in so many African and Middle Eastern countries; it received a fair share of public investments. National investment in agriculture amounted to about 11 percent of total gross fixed investment in the mid-fifties and reached nearly 25 percent during the first Five Year Plan.[2] This indicates considerable commitment to agriculture regardless of whether that investment went to irrigation, land reclamation, or the old lands. The agricultural growth rate of 3.3 percent during the first Five Year Plan was reasonable, though it fell short of the projected 5.1 percent.

Despite all its excesses, the Nasser regime did not extract or impoverish the rural sector in order to finance industrialization. Though policy instruments in agriculture were similar to those in most African countries, agrarian reform and welfare policies balanced the picture.[3] The regime's reputation and mystique were tied up with the cause of peasant liberation, agriculture was the major contributor to the budget, and industrialization relied heavily on agricultural raw material. Hence, agricultural growth had an immediate relevance to the regime, morally and materially. It should also be pointed out that draining resources from agriculture to build up industry has become less of an imperative due to the availability of external finance. Loans and foreign aid had already started to affect policy under Nasser and grew in leaps and bounds later on.

The question of agriculture should be viewed in terms of total transfers between what comes out of and what goes into the countryside. When the terms of trade are taken into account, it will be seen that the Nasser regime achieved a relative balance in allocating resources to the countryside. Economists who gauged the terms of trade have shown that the net transfers of financial surplus out of agriculture amounted to about 5 to 7 percent of the total agricultural income during the period from 1952 to 1970.[4] When nonagricultural services extended by the government to the countryside—such as health and education—are added to the picture, the net financial transfer could well melt away.[5] If by "taxing the countryside" one means targeting it alone as an object for victimization or extraction, then the July Revolution could be considered free from that charge. For there is no doubt that the Revolution was positively inclined toward the peasantry and contributed more to it than had any other regime during the entire history of Egypt.[6]

In the eighties, however, the gap between inflow of resources and outflow from agriculture widened, though the gap described in table 4.1 does not show the inflow to rural societies from services such as education, health, and housing. The private sector was encouraged to reclaim desert lands and cultivate them. There was also a change toward partial relaxation of crop pricing policies, as we shall see.

Overall, the record shows that it is not enough to favor small farmers and have a sound development strategy. The affected group needed to have a say in the adoption of policy instruments that translate the overall strategy to practice and affect them most directly. Egyptian peasants suffered mainly from the political structures that deprived them of political influence at the national level.

Political hegemony at the center and the comprehensive national planning of the economy precluded a democratic option for peasants. Had peasants been able to make their voice heard in decision-making councils, the story of Egyptian agriculture could well have been a success. Though farmers remained

Table 4.1. Transfers out of agriculture due to price distortions, 1980 (in million £E)

Resource Transfers out of agriculture due to price differentials	
Rice	-202
Wheat	-93
Cotton	-617
Sugarcane	-240
Maize	-59
Meat and dairy products	224
Total	-987

Inflow of resources to agriculture via inputs and subsidies	
Chemical fertilizers	96
Pest treatment	46
Animal feed	103
Sugarcane irrigation	1
Various subsidies	3
Irrigation maintenance	106
Energy	22
Machinery	30
Total	407
Net transfer out of agriculture	-580

Source: Nassaar and Mansur, "al siyasaat al si'riyah," 39.

private operators, the government linked them to the rest of the economy and determined the size of their contribution to the grand development design, just as was the case in industry.

The single political party, the Arab Socialist Union, served as a communications channel between the local community and the provincial administration, but did not include the national government. The linkage between the party's provincial cadres under Nasser and the national leadership was structurally nominal and personally nonexistent.[7] While peasants enjoyed a measure of local autonomy and exercised their rights of political participation under a tutelary form of local democracy, they lacked mediating agents influential with the central power.[8]

The chasm between national and local levels deprived peasants from the full benefit of local organizations created by the Nasser regime. Agricultural cooperatives and village councils remained vulnerable to the whims of the provincial and national governments, almost without a shield to fend for themselves.[9] Though active political participation at the local level prevailed and peasant leadership was encouraged, local cadres had very little opportunity to voice their interests in the councils of the national government. Just as is the case with most single party systems, messages flowed downward from the center to the periphery. The regime that introduced land distribution and cooperatives is the same that introduced an official policy of crop controls, administered prices, and forced requisitions.

Peasants, further from the center of power than the urban population, and realizing fully that there is a price for everything, were eager not to jeopardize their gains. As for urban producers, by the sixties most had become public sector firms, pliant instruments of the political elite, while those private entrepreneurs who remained in business were on the defensive.

It was under the liberalization policy era of Sadat (1970–81), however, that agriculture suffered in a more pronounced way. Beginning in 1973, agriculture went through a period of benign neglect. Public investment in agriculture was drastically cut back, and a decline in growth rates followed. Official investment was, on the average, 5.3 percent between 1976 and 1982, then it picked up moderately under the Mubarak regime.[10] Private investment in agriculture did not improve until the mid-eighties, with the relaxation of price controls and the introduction of incentives in land reclamation.

The policy of infitaah affected agriculture in very minor ways. Some of the land reform farms that had stayed under the control of the Ministry of Agriculture and Agrarian Reform were sold during the Sadat period to farmers, while land sequestered for political reasons was returned to their original owners. There also were some changes in the law protecting tenant farmers, though most recent tenancy changes were caused by economic forces. As we shall see, limited shifts in cropping patterns occurred, despite official controls, in favor of fruits, vegetables, and animal husbandry.

After the mid-seventies, a market-induced shift in favor of tenant farmers occurred at the expense of landowners. This was due to the profits made mainly from growing fodder for animal feed, demand for which had increased markedly by the mid-seventies subsequent to official policy support for animal husbandry and dairy farming. Owners felt they were entitled to an increase in rent commensurate with higher land revenues. At the time land reform was introduced, rent was fixed at seven times the value of land tax. Plans to correct what owners considered to be a new distortion in the rent system have been a regular item for discussion in the Ministry of Agriculture, the cabinet, and the Peoples' Assembly. However, no basic change was introduced by 1992.

The Government's Control over Agriculture

Though agricultural land remained in the private hands of small farmers, agriculture does not qualify as a private business sector. Like the rest of the economy, agriculture was brought under control of the central government and tied to the grand development design in line with the integrative development model of the regime.

While land title remained in private hands during and after the Nasser regime,[11] other rights pertaining to the freedom of usage were curtailed by government policies. If one is to define property as a bundle of rights, then very few property rights were retained by farmers. The government controlled most property rights: cropping patterns, trade in inputs and outputs, prices, and export. In addition, requisitions for some grain products were imposed. Ceilings on land possession and the tenancy laws, though reformist and in the interest of small farmers, nevertheless constituted limits on property rights. Though relaxed in the eighties with respect to reclaimed desert lands, most of these limitations were still in place in 1990. The limited relaxation of economic controls that did occur in the eighties could have been due to the electoral leverage farmers enjoyed then.

The managed approach, however, did not always make for change. Interdependence between the various departments of government generated internal forces against change in agricultural control policies. For instance, the Ministry of Industry depended on agricultural outputs to keep its firms running, and thus deprived the Ministry of Agriculture from making policy in the best interest of farmers. Any changes in cotton or sugarcane acreage or prices could have a vast impact on the industrial and trade sectors. Similarly, the Ministry of Supplies, which is in charge of providing food products at affordable prices to consumers, had a great stake in what is planted and at what price it was to be sold. It exercised pressures on the Ministry of Agriculture to keep farm products low in price. Like the Ministry of Industry, the Ministry of Supplies played a major role in determining agricultural policies. The same could be said of the government export agencies and the Ministry of National Economy, which determined the official rates of foreign exchange. The interests of the peasants were lost in this interlocking array of various and sometimes conflicting government concerns, often couched in terms of national interest and the interests of citizens.

Again, as in other entrepreneurial activities of public sector agencies, maximization of rates of production and of profits were given a secondary role in favor of governmental interests that were inimical to growth and detrimental to producers. Moreover, the capacity of the government bureaucracy to coordinate and implement excessive controls proved to be wanting, and the government found itself gradually losing control over the behavior of peasants. Even though such loss of control was less evident in agriculture than in other spheres of activity, black markets and evasion of the laws became permanent features of the countryside.

The Producer and Policy Controls

Most of the control policies in agriculture since the Revolution have had counterproductive effects on development in the economic sense of the term, and an anti-civic effect on the conduct of ordinary citizens in cultural terms. The policies in question here include crop and price controls, compulsory requisitions, and collective marketing of inputs and outputs. Though some controls predate the Revolution, it was during the latter period that national planning became comprehensive and government intervention extensive.

Crop Controls

Crop controls constitute a discriminatory act against the interests of farmers and may be considered even more serious than price controls. The Ministry of Agriculture designates the kind of field crops farmers must plant each season, according to a rotation and a consolidation plan. The guiding principle of a government cropping plan is the perceived needs of the economy and public order. Such objectives prove to be a heavy burden for producers whose main interest is to make a living and receive positive rewards for their investments. Since some field crops fetch less than other crops and cost more to produce, the opportunity loss to farmers is sufficiently serious to lead many of them to evade the law, plant something else, and pay the fine if caught (usually around £E20 per feddan). This is particularly true in the case of cotton, which is expensive to grow—it takes longer to mature and is vulnerable to pests—and fetches a low price. The World Bank has estimated that the number of farmers evading the cropping law reached 180,000 in 1974. Sugar producers diverted some 40 percent of their produce away from the lower-priced official markets.[12] Thus, the area actually planted with cotton in 1974 was 9 percent less than that designated by the government, while that for sugarcane, rice, and onions was less by 14, 31, and 35 percent, respectively.[13]

Low prices paid by the government to farmers, among other things, served as a disincentive against growing the officially designated crop. Farmers continued to evade the law that forced them to plant crops subject to administered prices. In contrast, crops that go for animal feed, such as clover (*bersim*) and maize, gained acreage over the same period.[14] Bersim was particularly lucrative because of the high demand and lack of official control over its market. Moreover, the area planted with vegetables and fruit, which enjoyed a relatively free market, rose markedly for the same period, at about an average of 12,000 feddans annually for fruits and about 5,500 feddans for vegetables.[15] Though some changes in cropping patterns had occurred, mainly through law evasion, on balance Egyptian cropping maintained the basic character it held since the fifties. Agriculture failed to respond effectively to its comparative advantage due to official restrictions.

Official cropping patterns discriminated against small farmers. First, farmers in the neighborhoods of cities and towns were allowed to depart from the rotation and plant fruit and vegetables to supply the urban population. This raised the burden on other farmers, mostly small, to provide strategic crops—such as cotton, rice, wheat, and sugarcane—subject to compulsory deliveries. Second, requisition quotas were set per feddan of land, regardless of the farm size. The burden on small farmers was felt more strongly because requisition cut deeply into their supplies.

It is tempting, for a political economy student, to consider the advantages possessed by fruit and vegetable farmers as a political measure to garner support among special interest groups.[16] Such an interpretation would be highly impressionistic. Growers of fruits and vegetables are on the whole larger and wealthier, but they too have suffered from the same strictures of the government's policies, in particular price controls and export regulations. Moreover, many of them were in disfavor politically between 1961 and 1970. Most large landowners suffered economically from the tenancy laws, which remained unchanged. The advantage from converting to fruits and vegetables was relatively small, especially in the absence of adequate export facilities.

The compulsory cropping pattern has not only deprived farmers from an adequate reward and discouraged growth but also deprived the country from taking advantage of high-yield crops particularly suited for export. Egypt's weather, perennial irrigation, and proximity to Europe and to Arab oil producers made it a prime candidate for producing high-price export crops, particularly fruits and vegetables. But central planning, with its inflexibility and compulsory nature, prevented this possibility from materializing. The private interest of the producer is not totally denied nor despised but considered to be a function of the national plan. Farmers, hence, are compelled to grow cotton while they could do better with other crops.

With the increase of evasion by farmers in the eighties, the government vacillated between severity and leniency, at times pardoning violators, at other times threatening them with dire consequences. In May 1987 the Minister of Agriculture threatened to raise the fine for evading the cropping pattern from £E20 to £E200 per feddan in order to enforce conformity to the official production plan,[17] though no such action was reported to have actually taken place.

Price Controls and Requisitions

The exchange cycle of the agricultural economy seems at first sight quite paradoxical. Everyone was paying reduced rates: farmers were paying reduced rates for inputs (through subsidies) and low rents to landowners, landowners were paying low tax rates, the government was paying low prices for agricultural produce, traders were buying agricultural produce from government marketing agencies at modest prices, and consumers were paying low rates for agricultural goods in the marketplace. It seemed like the best of all possible worlds, yet there was something wrong with this cycle, for it concealed the identity of the parties who paid the real cost of agricultural products: the farmers and the government.

Since the national government assumed responsibility in the late fifties and early sixties for pricing most commodities and services, in public and private sectors alike, it showed a distinct tendency to determine prices on the following bases: (1) the purchasing capacity of low-income families; (2) the need to provide low-cost agricultural raw material for industries; (3) revenue making for the national budget; (4) price stability; and (5) limited market considerations. The interests and needs of the individual enterprises were obviously not uppermost in official consideration.

The practice of underpricing commodities is officially referred to as the social basis of pricing, in contrast to the economic basis, another of the many euphemisms Egyptian officialdom resorts to in order to tone down the harsh-sounding effects of direct statement.

Administering prices in agriculture is a policy set in motion with the establishment of agrarian reform cooperatives in the fifties, which was then extended to the remaining crop farms in the early sixties as part of the expansion of the cooperative system and the nationalization of trade.[18] Land ownership, cultivation, and returns from sales, however, remained firmly the private domain of farmers.

While the mechanism for fixing prices has changed from time to time, most price controls in agriculture remained intact into the late eighties. Pricing decisions were centralized in the Higher Policy Committee of the cabinet, which can overrule pricing decisions made by the relevant minister.[19] This is necessary since more than one ministry is affected by the pricing decisions of a particular minister. In agriculture, the ministries of Supplies and Industry are most affected by the pricing of agricultural commodities; these ministries are also the most influential, after the Ministry of Agriculture.

Price and crop controls were most stringent with respect to export commodities, such as cotton and rice, which earned hard currency revenue for the government. Since the mid-fifties, farmers who were beneficiaries of land reform were required to deliver all or part of their crops to government purchasing agencies at low prices. Collective marketing was expanded in the early sixties to cover all farmers. Through its agent, the Cooperative Credit Bank (Bank al Taslif al Taʿawuni), the government imposed compulsory deliveries (tawrid) for export crops such as cotton, rice, sugarcane, onions, and garlic; and for products destined to meet the food needs of the consumer, such as wheat, maize, fava beans (ful), lentils, and a few others. Requisitions are compulsory deliveries of a share of the yield per feddan at a low price set by the government. In the case of cotton and sugarcane, the entire yield had to be turned in to the government purchasing agencies to supply the textile and sugar industries or to meet the export quota. As will be discussed further, the margin of profit made by the government out of these crops was much larger than that made by producing farmers.

Inability or unwillingness of the government to adjust to changes in the world prices on which it was dependent is clearly manifested in the case of fertilizer price fixing. Before the spectacular rise in oil prices in 1973, farmers paid the government 87 percent more for their fertilizers than world market rates. However, between 1973 and 1976, world prices for fertilizers escalated, and farmers paid only half the world price.[20] In the first period the government overcharged, and in the second it oversubsidized. This is a clear instance of equilibration, where the major interest of the government lies in keeping the system balanced and functioning, thus it takes away from producers when possible and subsidizes them when production cost is excessive.

There is a cultural component to the circuitous way of managing resources. To the extent producers are usually associated with the bourgeois class, they enjoy little esteem and much abuse in the culture and ideology of modern Egypt. In the memory of contemporary Egyptians, producers are associated with large landlords, who are not always of the same native stock. Though land reform reduced this class to the point of marginality, voices in the press were quite loud accusing beneficiaries of land reform of becoming bourgeois.[21] The ideological sensitivity, in effect, was directed toward small farm producers and urban producers alike.

Resources Transfers

Benefits that accrued to the government from requisitioned goods were passed on to consumers, individuals, and industrial firms. In 1975, for instance, subsidies to consumers for basic agricultural goods were as high as US$1,054 million, whereas producer subsidies reached only US$261 million.[22] On balance, the government retained nominal returns only; this can be seen from table 4.2, which shows the adverse economic effects on farmers of agricultural price-setting policies during one year.

It is clear from table 4.2 that the government acts almost as an intermediate agent, transferring the value generated by the producer to sustain the government's inefficient enterprises and to satisfy the domestic consumer.[23] The transfers made during the years 1973 to 1976 applied to export crops (in effect an indirect tax on peasant producers) and reached 60 percent for cotton, 80 percent for rice, 70 percent for sugar, and 60 percent for onions. Then the situation started to improve for producers, as international prices declined, taking with them an incentive for export, a government monopoly. In addition, the government started after 1973 to slightly raise the farmgate prices for some agricultural products, though very timorously.[24] At the same time government policy started to favor meat and dairy producers, to reduce the burden of imports. Other crops remained unaffected. For instance, farmgate prices for rice rose only 3 percent during the period from 1968 to 1974, whereas world prices climbed from $147 per ton in 1972 to $542 per ton in 1974, a 268 percent increase.[25]

Table 4.2. Consumer and producer transfers on major crops, 1974/75 (in million £E at parallel exchange rates [1 £E = $1.50])

Crop	Transfer from producers	Transfer to consumers	Transfer to treasury
Rice	-562	518	044
Wheat	-078	334	-256
Cotton	-254	122	132
Sugar	-400	040	360
Maize	-120	249	-129
Meat	214	-242	028
Total	-1,200	1,021	179

Source: World Bank, *Agricultural Price Management*, ix.

Government policies in agriculture, as in other areas, kept prices down, on the one hand, and subsidized production, on the other. Thus, price distortions existed on both ends of the scale, inputs and outputs. Subsidized agricultural inputs, however, did not make up for farmers' losses from selling at low, administered prices.

The production inputs subsidy constituted a fraction of the surplus acquired by the government. The "value of input subsidies does not compensate for the value of product taxes," estimated by the World Bank to be, for the whole sector, 30 percent of value added.[26] The "transfers to Treasury from profits by the Cotton Organization summed to £E348 million, whereas the direct producer subsidies paid by the Agricultural Prices Stabilization Fund on all crops for all purposes amounted to only £E187 million over the period extending from 1973 to 1976."[27] If one "adds in the exchange rate gains, the transfers out on cotton alone more than pay for all the direct producer subsidies, all public sector investment in agriculture and all the current expenditures of both the Ministries of Agriculture and of Irrigation."[28]

The gap between revenue to farmers from the sale of crops and that of the government continued through the eighties. In 1980 the transfer outside agriculture from rice, wheat, cotton, sugarcane, maize, meat, and dairy products amounted to £E987 million. In contrast, subsidies from the Treasury to agriculture (for chemical fertilizers, concentrated animal feed, irrigation allowance for sugarcane, combating the boll weevil, maintenance, and others) came to £E355 million.[29] Similarly, comparing subsidies to producers with those to consumers shows clearly the direction of the bias.

The distribution policy of subsidized inputs did not take into account farm size, thus subsidies to agriculture benefited larger farmers disproportionately. Shares of inputs distributed by the government were the same for each feddan, causing those who had larger estates to receive more support. Moreover, the farmers, mostly large ones, who evaded the law regarding the cropping pattern still received subsidized inputs. Those farmers who continued to abide by the cropping plan and plant cotton or rice were the small farmers who lacked the influence required to successfully evade the law or the capital to convert their acreage to other, more profitable crops.[30] Here again we find that those who are socially and economically disadvantaged receive less, even under a system seeking global equilibrium. Those who are better endowed, in terms of material resources, status, and skills, enjoy a greater share than their poorer counterparts.

It is curious that the national regime that did the most for small farmers should turn around and tax them heavily. But on the other hand, it is in the nature of the ambitious patron state to reach out to accessible sources of revenue, regardless of their particular character, in order to obtain funds for welfare, unprofitable public enterprises, the finances of an expensive government machinery, and other extensive expenditures. Thus, it would be a mistake to consider the adverse policy as directed against peasants per se; it affected all revenue generators, including government industrial firms.

The government also made resource transfers in the marketing of agricultural commodities, a policy that persisted through the eighties. In 1982/83 the returns to farmers from each feddan constituted a fraction of that gained by the government. Comparisons between the farmers' and the state's returns for a number of crops are shown in table 4.3.[31] It is therefore no surprise to see that the area planted with these crops shrank, despite the compulsory nature of the cropping pattern (see table 4.4).[32]

The decline in acreage for some major crops was not halted until 1986, when the government made price changes in response to severe shortages in the domestic market. Though the government has often complained about unreasonable growth in the consumption of sugar and warned against its ill effects on health, its concerns for meeting consumers demands caused it to ignore its own advice.

Table 4.3. Distribution of returns from some agricultural commodities to farmers and to the government, 1982–83

Crop	Farmer's returns (£E/feddan)	State's returns (£E/feddan)	Ratio
Wheat	120.6	184.2	0.66
Rice	019.8	346.2	0.06
Maize (shaamie)	023.8	032.4	0.73
Sugarcane	135.2	875.6	0.15
Garlic	255.0	959.2	0.21

Source: Nassar and Mansur, "al Siyasaat al Si' iyah," 33.

Table 4.4. Changes in areas planted with certain crops (in thousands of feddans)

Crop	Base year (1970)	End year (1984)	Difference
Wheat	1,305	1,178	127
Rice	1,142	985	157
Cotton	1,627	984	643
Sugarcane	251 (1981)	249	2
Garlic	9 (1952)	9 (1986)	0

Source: Nassar and Mansur, "al siyasaat al si'riyah," 29; CAPMAS, Statistical Yearbook, 1952–1986, 35.

In the mid-eighties, the government started to improve prices for farmers. But most progress in freeing prices has occurred since 1985/86, with gradual lifting of price controls on vegetables and fruits, though controls remained on some produce.[33] By 1988 compulsory requisition had also been reduced and limited to three crops: cotton, sugarcane, and half the rice product per feddan. Voluntary procurement remained in effect for many field crops, including wheat, and was made feasible by improved official prices.

Providing incentives, as a policy change in the eighties toward sugarcane shows, produced positive results. Sugarcane farmers were officially supported, beginning in 1986/87, with better prices, grants, and loans for mechanization and irrigation. The area planted with sugarcane thus increased in 1987 to 263,000 feddans. Moreover, strong efforts were made to encourage the planting of sugar beets. Expansion of the area for sugarcane continued in 1988, and the cabinet decided in September of that year to add 21,000 feddans.[34] International prices of sugar rose dramatically in 1988, and Egypt was then importing 32 percent of its sugar consumption, about 1.5 million tons annually. Sugarcane yield per unit in Egypt ranks as second-highest in the world. On the other hand, per capita consumption of sugar is one of the highest in the world, and with the very high subsidization policy, the consumer has no incentive to cut back on sugar intake.

This case shows that incentives to individual farmers will stimulate growth, market conditions permitting. In contrast, data show that price controls lead to decline in acreage planted and volume of produce. The answer to shortages in agricultural goods cannot, in a country with limited cultivated area, be conversion of larger acreage to the crops in short supply, because that would come at the expense of another commodity and lead to shortages elsewhere.

IMPACT OF POLICY ON PRODUCTION

Both growth and investment in agriculture suffered since the late sixties. Deprived of incentives, farmers were less inclined to invest in land. Those who could diverted their investments toward livestock and fruits, a tendency that continued throughout the seventies and eighties.

The contribution of agriculture to the GNP ranged in the mid-eighties to about 21 percent and absorbed about 45 percent of the labor force, yet official investment in agriculture had fallen to around 8 percent. Moreover, most of that investment went to irrigation and drainage. When private investment is added, the total comes to 10.8 percent.[35] The second Mubarak Five Year Plan (1988–92) envisaged no changes in this pattern; investment in agriculture was designated at around 8 percent (3.1 for agriculture and 5.1 for irrigation and drainage) once again. In addition, production was adversely affected because farmers were not willing to invest when official policy made it difficult to obtain decent returns. In the case of cotton, farmers continue to this day to call it *mahsul al hukuma* (the government's crop), almost writing it off from consideration as a source of revenue.

Growth in agricultural production remained low throughout the seventies and early eighties, falling well below 2 percent. Until 1980 the long-run growth rate in aggregate agricultural production amounted to 1.3 percent per year, while for "the developing countries as a whole it has been 2.6% and of the developed countries 1.8%."[36] Some improvement occurred after the mid-eighties, and growth is officially estimated at about 2.8 percent, whereas Egypt needs a growth of at least 5 percent to keep up with its rapid population growth.

Improvement in growth rate has been associated with increasing liberalization of policy. Moderate growth in productivity in 1988 has been reported for wheat, maize, and sugarcane, among others. Increased production of wheat has been reported officially since the late eighties in response to improved prices and new technologies. By 1990 prices compared very favorably with international rates, whereas in the past farmers drew profit not from wheat grain but from the hay made of wheat stalks.

Officials often cite comparative figures to show that Egypt's productivity per unit of land in certain crops is one of the best in the world. They overlook the fact, though, that Egyptian agriculture is under perennial irrigation, and when comparisons are made with other agricultures under irrigation, it would appear that Egypt's performance could still improve.[37] Productivity per feddan has declined in Egypt as of the mid-sixties.[38] Adams attributes much of the decline to Egypt's very limited participation in newly developed technological innovations in world agriculture.[39] But since most agriculture is private, adopting new technology could not be separated from the availability of incentives for farmers. As long as farmers have little incentive to increase production, technology adoption will not be among their priorities.

The negative effect of price controls on production was well recognized by government officials. The Minister of Supplies stated in 1977 that official price fixing for rice, cotton, wheat, and beans led to a drop in production.[40] The same has been admitted by a Minister of Agriculture, Yusuf Waali.[41] In the following sections I discuss the adverse effects on production and the producer from governmental pricing of several agricultural products. The examples are from the eighties, at least ten years after the open-door policy was introduced.

Wheat

Prices of wheat on the world market went up dramatically during the seventies, adding a new strain on the large food import bill, despite concessionary arrangements with the United States. Imports of wheat rose from 2,207,000 metric tons in 1970 to 4,344,000 in 1980, almost a 100 percent increase in ten years. By 1986/87, wheat imports had risen to 5,240,000 tons. Imports of high-quality flour during the same period reached 550,000 tons in 1970 and 1,384,000 in 1980, again in excess of a 100 percent increase in ten years. Flour imports peaked at 1,799,000 metric tons in 1983/84.[42]

Imports surpassed growth in wheat production. Local production increased from 1,499,000 metric tons in 1960 to 2,033,000 in 1975, fell below that level for the following eleven years, and equalled 1,916,000 metric tons in 1986/87.[43] In 1987/88 local production responded to price incentives and rose to 2,722,000 metric tons.[44] In addition, new technologies contributed to the improvement in productivity.

Sharp increases in the international prices of wheat and wheat flour did not discourage the government from completely shielding the consumer by absorbing the increment through higher subsidies. Imported grain distributed at low prices during the seventies and eighties also caused local production to decline and per capita consumption of wheat and wheat flour to increase. The value of the wheat subsidy as a result skyrocketed.

The wheat and wheat flour subsidy cost the Egyptian government £E897 million in 1980/81. Ten years earlier, in 1970, the cost was as little as £E4.9 million. The following year it rose sharply to £E21 million and then to a whopping £E252 million in 1975, reflecting higher international prices subsequent to the revolution in oil prices. With the resumption of United States aid to Egypt in 1975, the wheat import bill dropped in 1976 to £E163 million. However, a sharp increase in demand and the continued escalation in international prices, which peaked in 1980/81, raised the bill again.[45] In per capita terms, the government subsidy for wheat rose forty-three-fold between 1970/71 and 1981/82.[46]

This heavy burden was aggravated by the tendency in the seventies to expand subsidies. For instance, in 1973 the government started to subsidize the high-quality wheat flour that goes into the making of pastries and French bread consumed by the upper levels of society. The import bill for high-quality flour that year was £E8,167,000; in 1980/81 it reached £E231 million, 26 percent of the total wheat and flour subsidy for that year.

In effect, consumption of wheat and wheat flour increased more rapidly than population. In 1960, when the population was 25.8 million, Egypt consumed 2,370,000 metric tons of wheat and wheat flour, making the per capita consumption 92 kilograms per annum.[47] In 1975 the volume consumed reached 5,361,000 metric tons, a per capita consumption of 145 kilograms. In 1983/84, consumption reached a new record of 8,796,000 metric tons, or 196 kilograms per capita.[48] In the span of thirty years (1950–80), the population increased

102 percent while imports of wheat increased 612 percent and local production 71 percent.[49] Egypt has one of the highest, if not the highest, per capita
consumptions of wheat in the world.

Egyptian consumers were not, as it may appear, eating twice as much bread
in the eighties as they did in the sixties; rather, they were sharing their bread-
basket with chickens and other domestic animals. Subsidized wheat and its
products had become far less expensive than animal feed, and thus found their
way into the troth. The price for one kilogram of wheat flour in 1986 was half
the price of a kilogram of animal feed. In 1988 a ton of flour cost £E110, while
a ton of animal feed cost £E160 officially and nearly £E300 on the black market. Not until 1987, after successive increases, did the wheat price surpass the
price of hay.

In addition to the use of wheat as chicken and livestock feed, part of the
sharp increase in wheat consumption could be accounted for by waste at various stages. Total waste from storage, transportation, and rejects at the dining
table was estimated in 1988 by some experts at 50 kilograms annually per
capita, that is about 29 percent of the per capita share of wheat consumption.
Ten percent of total waste occurs in storage and transportation, while 70 percent (equal to 20 percent of the per capita consumption) is diverted to nonhuman usage.[50]

Price distortions inevitably lead to irregular trading patterns and stimulate
the black market. And in fact, the wheat subsidy contributed to the emergence
of a flourishing black market in wheat and wheat flour.[51] Bakery owners have
openly admitted smuggling wheat flour,[52] and in 1986 anyone who wished
could watch the police intercept trucks of smuggled flour at the three main
exit bridges of Cairo: Imbaba, Shubra, and Mastarad. The price for flour is
generally higher in the countryside, where the demand for animal feed is the
greatest.

Shortages in the supply of wheat and distortions in its price were related to
administered prices at the farmgate. In 1985 the official price paid to farmers
for a kilogram of wheat was 12 piastres, whereas a kilogram of hay, a non-
controlled by-product, brought 16 piastres. It is no surprise that the area planted
for wheat that year dropped to an all-time low of 1.18 million feddans, with
production under 2 million tons,[53] whereas total consumption was 9 million
tons. Moreover, the amount obtained by the government through compulsory requisition was quite negligible.[54] For a few years prior to 1983, farmers
were freed from compulsory deliveries and the amount actually delivered
reached its peak of 447,000 tons. Subsequently, after the restoration of mandatory requisitions in 1984 and 1985, the volume dropped again to 209,000
and 148,000 tons respectively, an average of about 10 percent of production.[55]

In 1986 the government increased the price paid farmers for the procurement of wheat to £E40 per ton,[56] and by the end of the season removed the

mandatory nature of delivery. The effect was immediate. In June 1987 the Minister of Agriculture proudly announced during the budget debates in the Peoples Assembly that in response to improved wheat prices "the price of hay had fallen below the price of wheat" for the first time.[57] This, he explained, followed the freeing of wheat from compulsory deliveries. Raising the price paid to farmers has also increased the volume delivered to government warehouses, from 1.5 million tons to 2.5 million tons.[58] Though exaggerated in official figures, improvements had occurred. In 1988 both area in production and yield increased: the area expanded to 1.422 million feddans, a 3.55 percent increase over the previous year, and the yield rose to 18 million and 928 irdab (about 2.86 million tons), an increase of 4.32 percent.[59]

The distortions underlined in the analysis of policy regarding wheat were part of the larger scheme of creating balance in the economy as a whole. In this case, the intention was to balance the low purchasing capacity of the ordinary consumers with the prices of farm products that otherwise were beyond their means. This artificial equilibrium, as it turned out, compounded rather than solved the problem.

It is clear that excessive central control leads to a slide away from effective management and generates uncivic behavior. Subsidies to luxuries such as quality flour for making pastries and other sweets cannot be explained in terms of realizing an integrative approach to development. They were, rather, a deviation from the spirit of the national design by officials in alliance with beneficiaries. The behavior of the bureaucracy in charge of implementing the national design makes an excellent study of how government itself often fails to execute its own projects according to plan. In the end, policy changes in the late eighties demonstrated that incentives have positive effects on production, and the government started to break away from the integrative development model, though ever so slightly.

Fruits and Vegetables

The year 1988 registered a marked departure from the integrative development approach, for the government became more or less willing to consider each enterprise as an individual case and attend to its needs. Market forces were allowed a larger role in determining production and equitable pricing by government marketing boards. Thus, in that year, as part of the reform drive, twelve crops were freed from mandatory requisitioning and compulsory pricing. Only cotton, sugarcane, beets, and half the rice harvest remained unaffected. Prices offered by the government marketing boards, moreover, were raised. The process of gradual change had started earlier, and modest price improvements were already underway by 1984. By 1987 the government raised purchase prices for a number of agricultural commodities by 234 percent (table 4.5).

Table 4.5. Changes in official prices for certain crops (£E/ton)

Crop	Base year price (1984)	Updated price (1987)	Percent
Rice	110	200	182
Soya	285	375	132
Wheat	10 (irdab, 1982)	030	300
Sugarcane	20	030	150
Lentils	93 (irdab)	140	151
Ful	32 (irdab)	75	234

Source: Minister of Agriculture, *Ahraam,* 25 July 1987.

In response, production increased in most of these commodities, especially wheat and sugarcane.[60] In January 1988 the Higher Policy Committee decided to raise the farmgate price of cotton by £E30 for the new cotton season, an improvement but not a redress.[61]

Official controls on cultivation and trade in vegetables and fruits were less onerous. No mandatory deliveries were required as in other crops. However, there were mandatory price controls for both wholesale and retail. Some of the effects of official policy were similar to those in other crops, namely, shortages and an active black market. Parallel marketplaces for wholesale products developed outside officially designated areas and thus operated outside the official price range. There was no decrease in land cultivation area, though, for the returns from vegetables and fruits were still better than those of field crops, even with price controls in place. Moreover, official prices were difficult to implement, considering varieties and product quality differentials. However, the production of crops not subject to collective marketing, such as potatoes, more than doubled between 1972 and 1985, a production growth rate faster than any of the other major vegetables.[62]

Following the seventies, collective marketing of fruits and vegetables declined. Close to cities, farmers sold directly to customers and also at weekly markets. However, they were all supposed to abide by official prices.

Marketing of vegetables worked in the following way. In the seventies, wholesale traders would buy from farmers, then meet with officials of the Ministry of Supplies to determine the price. The Ministry of Agriculture was supposed to be a party in the decision making, but differences between the two ministries point to a subordinate role by the MOA. The MOA claimed it was not consulted by the MOS regarding production costs and pricing. The pricing estimate sent by the MOA was often ignored by the MOS, according to MOA officials.

Claims and counterclaims between the two ministries are hard to verify, but it is clear the issue of jurisdiction was never settled. Official underpricing was also a problem. Not fully appreciated were the costs of transport, packaging, waste, labor, and other intermediate functions.[63] At any rate, whereas previously official prices were set by committees from both ministries acting jointly, the MOA lost ground to the MOS, which took over the setting of prices. That development may reflect the prominence of consumer over producer interests. As was observed in the case of industry, responsibility for policy was not always fixed in definitive terms.

Later, price fixing of fruits and vegetables was transferred to the provincial level, to be carried out by local officials and merchants, a practice that lasted until price fixing was abolished in 1985. However, official price directives are still issued daily and distributed to retail merchants.[64]

In 1985, when the government lifted price controls over fruits and vegetables, free-market forces were allowed to take their course, and consent prices (*tas'irah wuddiyah*) replaced the compulsory price system.[65] A consent price is reached by agreement between the wholesale traders and the MOS, without interference from the ministry's police (*mabaahith al tamwiin*). In cases of violation, persuasive efforts were made by officials to keep things in line. Hence, the pricing of fruits and vegetables was one of the rare occasions on which the bureaucracy sought persuasion through dialogue—rather than decrees, police inspections, and other arm-twisting tactics—to solve a problem.

Control of the export market by inefficient public sector companies and complicated bureaucratic restrictions dampened business interest in exports of fruits and vegetables. Egypt's comparative advantage in this kind of agriculture was thus dissipated by the bureaucratic hurdles originally inspired by the self-sufficiency objective. As a result, the export sector remained anemic into the late eighties.

Poultry

An examination of the poultry industry will illustrate the problems attendant with transition in the patron state. The tension associated with the emergence of free enterprise in the midst of a centrally managed economy is quite instructive on the issue of change.

Consistent with the infitaah policy to encourage food industries in the private sector since the mid-seventies, poultry farms received generous treatment. In the early seventies, the industry was given a growth impetus in the form of low-interest loans, low tax rates, and direct subsidies for animal feed and medicine. Official support for production gave quick results, helping Egypt become almost self-sufficient in eggs and covering a high proportion of the demand for white meat.

Though mostly private, the industry's potential for export of eggs and chicken meat was not very promising due to the inefficiencies in production, as will be discussed later. Without a potential for export, the industry could not generate external income to balance the heavy import costs. In effect, the chicken industry remained oriented toward the satisfaction of the domestic market in conformity with the established strategy of import substitution. Critics charge that the chicken industry in Egypt is in the nature of an assembly plant operation rather than a viable enterprise. Though the observation is by and large true, it may still be a little harsh. For although dependency on imported ingredients used in veterinary products and chicken feed is high, the industry made progress in all other operations, including local production of hatchery eggs and baby chickens. Backward linkages nevertheless remained limited, and very little progress was made in the production of chicken feed and medicine domestically, though the potential was there. The competitiveness of the industry was affected more by lack of managerial skills and experience among its new entrepreneurs than by official measures.

One harmful official measure was removal of the corn subsidy in 1987 in line with government efforts to reduce the budgetary deficit. The speed with which the subsidy was withdrawn is not unrelated to the fact that more than 90 percent of poultry farms (producing 75 percent of poultry products) were private enterprises. In contrast, public sector farms continued to enjoy government support. The corn subsidy, it may be pointed out, was estimated at about £E260 million in 1986.[66]

The policy of subsidizing the chicken industry, which began in 1975, had run into difficulties by the early eighties. Rapid growth in the industry meant a corresponding increase in the subsidy. For instance, before 1975 domestic production amounted annually to 25 million chickens. With the participation of the private sector starting in the early seventies, production rose steadily, reaching 385 million chickens at the beginning of 1987, a more than fifteen-fold increase in twelve years. Similarly, the capital invested rose from £E200 million to nearly £E3 billion during the same period. Since more than 85 percent of chicken feed was imported, the cost to the government became substantial. By the early eighties, the government was no longer able to procure the necessary foreign exchange to import enough chicken feed, causing shortages in supply and the inevitable resort to the black market.

With the onset of shortages, allocation of chicken feed became skewed. Because some (public sector) farmers were subsidized while others (private sector) were not, production cost was no longer uniform. An unplanned balance, however, was struck between the two groups, because those who received subsidies had to deliver a quota of their produce to the MOS at controlled prices. Moreover, it seemed that many farmers cared more for the availability of feed than for subsidies. Though with the removal of the subsidy and the liberalization of imports in 1988 the availability of feed improved considerably, by that time the crisis had already claimed its toll, causing nearly 80 percent of farms to stop production.[67]

In addition to the impact of government monopoly on foreign trade, domestic price controls added to the industry's problems into the late eighties, when retail prices of eggs were still managed by the MOS. Squeezed between the purchase price from wholesalers and the low price imposed by the government, shopkeepers on more than one occasion withdrew the product. The policy of controlled egg prices was not lifted until late spring 1988. Consumer prices went up slightly in the first few months, then by fall rose to 15 piastres an egg, compared to 10–12 piastres before. In January 1989 the president called on the public sector to expand its share of the chicken industry in order to provide low-priced eggs and white meat to the public. The threat from competition by the public sector could have been serious, because with its lower-than-cost sales, the government would undermine the price structure of the industry. Expansion of the public sector in poultry at that point, however, was hampered by inefficiency and corruption in government poultry firms.

As it turned out, it was not the threat from the public sector that hurt but government trade policy. Official concern regarding the provision of food products at affordable prices resulted in imports of cheap frozen chicken meat by the MOS in 1987. The distribution of this meat at very low prices hit mainly the private producers.[68] Public sector farms of the Ministry of Agriculture were not as affected, because they already had to deliver their products to the MOS at controlled prices (1–3 piastres below market rates).[69] Moreover, their share of the market was very small, consisting of about 5 percent[70] of the egg market and slightly more for meat.[71]

In trying to justify its act, the MOS claimed that local producers were charging high prices. The industry, on the other hand, claimed the MOS had imported stocks dumped on the international market, and that their consumption in Egypt was not limited to the low-income population but included tourist hotels. Independent observers confirm that the MOS imported chicken meat whose validity date was just about to expire.

It may be noted in this regard that while the chicken industry in Egypt is still not competitive by international standards, prices of eggs and chicken meat were still reasonable, even a year after the feed subsidy was withdrawn and more than half the farms had been forced to close by the financial squeeze.

Private industry suffered in addition from the attitude of some provincial officials. In some public sector farms of the governorates, provincial authorities discriminated in their purchase practices against local producers of baby chicken, insisting that only importers need apply for tenders. Egypt now has a high production capacity of baby chickens, and could with proper encouragement reach domestic self-sufficiency. Some private sector farmers attribute the discriminatory behavior of the provincial authorities to shady deals, including commissions received from foreign exporters.

In 1987 the crisis became a cause célèbre, attracting public attention. Faced with an embarrassing situation, the MOS stopped dumping frozen chicken meat in its distribution outlets and declared an end to that policy. A blow to the industry, however, had already been struck, and the number of failing enterprises reached new heights.

It should be noted here that not all the chicken farm closures were caused by the imports policy, withdrawal of the feed subsidy, or price controls. The industry's inefficiency had also contributed to the problem in a serious way. Underfinancing and misuse of financial resources have been commonly noted. In some cases, entrepreneurs diverted their low-interest loans to other uses, did not carry out feasibility studies, or lacked expertise and management skills. This was further compounded by maturation of the debt payments of most farmers in the mid-eighties and reduction in the credit available following the 1987 agreement with the IMF. The debt owed to banks by poultry farmers was estimated at £E1 billion. Many indebted farmers were unable to pay their loans and demanded rescheduling of their debt payments.

The failing of private enterprises, especially at the beginning of such a process, is not surprising in light of market economics. The Egyptian case followed almost a textbook example, as inefficient private farmers dropped out of the picture while more efficient ones survived. The high cost of imported feed and medicine was another factor leading to business failures. Here again, government policy indirectly bears a responsibility, since its price controls on the pharmaceutical business discouraged private production. Egypt's private sector produces only a negligible portion of veterinary medications, about 5 percent of national needs. Moreover, the chicken industry is new and has not yet developed all the necessary technological advances and skills. Deficient equipment, such as refrigerators and slaughter machines, have also contributed to business difficulties.

Most serious in keeping production costs high is of course the fact that most farms operate below capacity due to shortages of raw material and, more recently, financial resources. For instance, in 1985 unused capacity in egg production reached 40 percent.[72] In 1988, a year the industry underwent severe crisis, unused production capacity exceeded 60 percent.[73]

The national government bears a major responsibility for this situation. Its policies regarding exchange rates, dumping practices, monopoly on imports of feed, fixed prices, and subsidy withdrawal contributed in a major way to lowering production below capacity.

The record of the poultry industry in Egypt shows that, though it is difficult for private business to flourish in a centrally managed economy, the task is not impossible; in fact, some businesses prospered. Moreover, government's support of production in the private sector showed, in this case, better results than in the public sector.

CONCLUSION

The auspicious beginning of land reform policies were later offset by extensive government controls and management of surplus transfers, which were based on the needs of the national economy rather than individual farmers. The benefits peasants received—low tenancy rates, small land plots to cultivate, easy cooperative credit, subsidized inputs, health care, education, moderately participatory local institutions—cannot be disregarded when evaluating financial transfers the government undertook at the expense of the countryside. The imbalance after all was small, when the total inflow and outflow of resources are compared. However, other policies reflecting the integrative approach tipped the balance moderately against the peasantry. Especially crippling was crop control, which reduced the income opportunity for peasants by forcing them to plant less rewarding crops. The loss to farmers from this policy does not show in the calculation of terms of trade. Still, on balance, the countryside must be considered to have received equal treatment, if not more generous treatment than the rest of the economy. Most disadvantages suffered by peasants were due to the general national policy of integrative development, not particular policies aimed at them or at agriculture.

The integrative approach in place by 1960 undermined the creative strategy of agrarian reform implemented during the first decade of the Revolution. By following an integrative development approach, the regime diverted resources away from growth for individual enterprises (farms in this case) to sectoral or national economies. The interdependence and mutual support of enterprises meant that successful enterprises had to sacrifice their own growth to the maintenance of less efficient enterprises. Growing of high-yield crops was officially restricted in favor of low-yield crops, like cotton. In addition, surplus-producing farms, like industrial firms, were tapped for financial support of the social order, what the regime called "equity." It did not much matter whether the enterprise was in the public or private sector. Land was privately owned, but farmers had to bear burdens similar to those of public sector firms.

Having no political means to change the situation in their own favor, agricultural producers sought to flout and evade the law. While there was a feeling of gratification, especially by landless peasants during the early period of the Revolution, this attitude gave way later on to the feeling that the government was not being fair. Peasants felt cheated and imposed on by the government, a situation which convinced them that evading the law was not only beneficial but also a matter of right. The answer to compulsion was evasion.

In this case, evasion occurred individually, not collectively; everyone used clandestine techniques at their own command. Seeking redress by clandestine means thus had the effect of stifling the spirit of collective action for reform. It generated, moreover, a sense of futility and cynicism engendered by the feeling of unfairness inflicted by a strong government.

Evading the law was a practice not limited to farmers but included wholesale and retail merchants. Efforts by the government to regulate and impose official prices created a struggle that often involved clandestine tactics, such as selling on the black market or bribing officials. Retail traders, lacking the same ability as wholesale traders to fight back, often suffered the most. Curiously enough, the press, considered by many to be leftist in political orientation, often directed its attacks against the small retail traders and attributed price gouging to them.

Rather than satisfying the low purchasing power of the consumer and increasing revenue from exports, policy controls brought on scarcity and, ipso facto, indirect price increases for consumers. Egypt's revenue from agriculture dropped, and its terms of trade in agricultural produce turned negative. After enjoying a surplus estimated at the beginning of the seventies to be about US$300 million, it suffered a deficit of nearly US$800 million in the late seventies and over US$2 billion by 1987. Part of this deficit, of course, was brought on by the high rate of population growth and by increased consumption, caused by subsidized goods and high levels of liquidity generated by the seventies oil boom. Instead of creating plenty and improving standards of living, the policy created scarcity and dependency.

The case of agriculture in Egypt illustrates the need for passing beyond the discussion of private versus public sector in development. Here is a situation where a business is for the most part in the hands of the private sector, yet was treated, because of unchecked government powers, as though it was in the public sector, its agents public officials subject to orders from above. Although in industry public sector firms were hurt by government policies, in agriculture it was private businesses that were hurt.

The description of agriculture in Egypt as private sector may be a mere formality, for in reality it was a mixed system. Land ownership, cultivation, and returns were kept as the farmer's domain. Cropping patterns and marketing, on the other hand, were controlled by the government. Should public and private character be viewed as two exclusive categories, then it would be difficult to determine the true nature of the Egyptian case. The fact is, though, that the character of a business in a modern society eludes simple and exclusive classification. The process of generating economic values is a complex one, consisting of an assortment of rights exercised at different stages by actors who have a different juridical character.

The main issue with respect to economic development, therefore, is public policy, rather than abstract ideologies such as socialism and capitalism. What really matters is how many and which title rights should be determined by which side in the equation. Policy could affect the public sector adversely or favorably, just as it could affect the private sector. The public sector, therefore, should not be considered as inherently unproductive and unprofitable. Those results are variable factors contingent on sound economic and managerial structures and policies.

In Egyptian agriculture, there seemed to be a balance struck between the two sides in the partnership—government and peasant. In fact, until 1987 the most effective rights in the business cycle—prices, crops, trade in agricultural inputs and outputs—were controlled by the government. Since these factors affected value returns more than ownership title or labor, agriculture in Egypt can be considered to have been a highly managed sector.

Central government hegemony, as I have demonstrated here, has not worked for the maximization of growth, returns, or profits, especially after 1970. Since the public sector treats an economic enterprise as if it were a nonprofit service firm, economic growth would require a greater role for the private sector. The argument for a market economy, perhaps, rests more on the need for change in this area than on a need for greater efficiency and managerial skills.

With the increasing pace of liberalization, one can look for higher agricultural growth, more efficiency, and less distortion. Early efforts at relaxation of controls in agriculture have shown encouraging signs of improvement in production, bettering the interests of farmers and merchants alike.

Chapter Five

Subsidization Policies

Implications for Growth and Welfare

Subsidies of one kind or another exist in most countries, in varying degrees of importance. In Egypt, however, their prominence is a feature of the political order that emerged under the Revolution of 1952 and led to involvement by the government in most aspects of its citizens' lives.[1]

Though subsidies may well have started in Egypt as a support system for the urban poor, they developed into a major instrument of the integrative model, which was based on direct and indirect redistribution of resources. Balance of inputs and outputs in public sector firms was artificially maintained by means of subsidies. Consumer goods were sold at cut prices to workers, but workers were given low wages in return. Factories received low-priced inputs, but then had to sell their products at lower-than-market rates. This balancing act, however, went out of kilter, as the regime found itself extending subsidies to practically everything from steel industries to movie theater tickets.

Basically, subsidies reflect distortions and weaknesses in the national economy. These include (1) low productivity of the labor force; (2) low wages; (3) a high level of unemployment, explicit or disguised; (5) inability to compete in international or regional trade; and (6) a strong tendency on the part of policymakers to use administrative means to resolve economic problems.

Types of Subsidies

Subsidies may be direct or indirect. A *direct subsidy* is the value of a commodity or service paid in full or in part by the government to consumers that represents the difference between the actual price and the price consumers pay. For example, the cost of education in Egypt is fully paid for by the government, whereas the price of bread is only partially subsidized. On the face of it, the government paid the difference in the price of a subsidized commodity as an assistance to consumers, but in fact it had already discounted the difference, more or less, from the salary it pays its employees, by keeping their wages low.

The process constitutes a series of distortions affecting several actors or agencies. For instance, in 1976 the Egyptian government paid the farmer 110 riyals (5 riyals equal £E1) for a ton of raw cotton. The farmer was not at liberty not to sell at the officially low price and, in effect, was subsidizing the government. The government then sold the ton of raw cotton to public sector spinning factories at 76 riyals per ton. Its loss of 34 riyals per ton constituted a subsidy to the spinning factories, and the loss was charged to the Treasury.

The sum paid by the government as a subsidy to spinning factories appears in the national budget account. When the same factory, however, sells the yarn at below cost to a weaving factory, the loss is not recorded as a subsidy in the government budget account. For example, when Nasr automobiles were first produced in Egypt in the sixties, they were sold to the consumer at below production cost, as has occurred later with color televisions. This is like a direct subsidy to the consumer, except that it does not appear in the budget that is submitted to Parliament for approval.[2]

A hidden subsidy, on the other hand, is the opportunity the government forfeits by not selling at international prices. In the case of cotton sales previously cited, the government sold a ton of raw cotton domestically at 76 riyals, while on the international market a ton of cotton fetched 200 riyals. Under those terms, the government's loss was 124 riyals per ton, not the 34 riyals borne by the government as a subsidy to the local spinning factory.[3] Seen in isolation, selling at less than prevailing prices is an irrational act. However, under the aspect of integrative development, the government considered that selling the cotton to local industry contributes to value added and to the sector's balance and maintenance.

Hidden subsidies are not listed in the budget and are hardly ever calculated into the figures that appear on the value of subsidies. In some countries, hidden subsidies are aimed at promoting national exports in a world market in which they are not competitive. However, this was not the case in Egypt; hidden subsidies here simply underline the grave economic conditions the official balancing act could cause.

A form of subsidy rarely discussed is the one borne by private producers as a result of officially set compulsory prices. A cotton farmer who is paid far less than the market rate for his produce is in effect subsidizing consumers or public sector firms. When the burden for a subsidy is borne by producers, such as farmers or manufacturers in the private sector, its value never appears in official accounts, or anywhere else. When all those subsidies that are not included in official accounts are considered, the aggregate figures given by officials regarding the size of the subsidies turn out to be grossly understated.

Subsidies and Revenue Transfers

When the government establishes a subsidy, a revenue transfer takes place involving three parties: the government, the producer, and the consumer. Of the three, the consumer seems to be the beneficiary, at least on the face of it. In the long run, all three end up losing since the subsidy system is inimical to growth and generates serious deficits.

The balancing act the government performs in the case of production subsidies takes the following form. The government subsidizes some production inputs such as energy or raw materials and keeps wages down; both measures are intended to artificially reduce the production cost to an inefficient producer, usually public sector firms. In return, the government sets prices of the commodities produced low to reflect the input subsidies and low wages. Consumers then gain through low prices at the store, but they indirectly lose through low wages. What cannot be determined with certainty is whether a balance or equivalence exists between low wages and subsidies as an alternate form of payment.

Consumer subsidies are a supplementary wage system; they are not gifts or welfare measures. Only a very small part of basic subsidies affect the destitute and may be considered a support system. In the government budget, increments to salaries parallel increments to subsidies. For instance, in the 1989/90 budget, increments in both wages and subsidies were set at 13–14 percent, which corresponds to the officially estimated inflation rate.

Wages lagged behind inflation. During the years 1978–88, wages increased 60 percent, while prices rose 351 percent.[4] The average wage was supposed to rise 11 percent annually during the second Mubarak Five Year Plan (1987/88–1991/92).[5] Inflation, however, had reached 25 percent during the base year alone,[6] while the wage increment listed in the budget for that same base year was 5.9 percent.[7]

Subsidies are in certain respects compensation in kind, a throwback on a premodern economic system. A government employee, for instance, is eligible to purchase low-priced commodities through special outlets. This practice was still going strong in October 1988 when it was announced that 2.5 million pieces of clothing would be made available under the employees' clothing program (kisaa' al 'aamilin bil dawlah) at half the market price. Half a million pairs of shoes were also provided for the same group at reduced prices—an indirect payment but a payment nevertheless.[8]

In yet another kind of distortion, government subsidies for production inputs fall short of what is taken away from producers. This is particularly true of agricultural production. The "value of input subsidies does not compensate for the value of product taxes," estimated by the World Bank to be, for the whole sector, 30 percent of value added.[9] The "transfers to Treasury from profits by the Cotton Organization summed to £E348 million whereas the direct producer subsidies paid by the Agricultural Prices Stabilization Fund on all crops for all purposes amounted to only £E187 million over the period extending from 1973 to 1976."[10] The statement continues, if "one adds in the exchange rate gains, the transfers out on cotton alone more than pay for all the direct producer subsidies, all public sector investment in agriculture and all the current expenditures of both the Ministries of Agriculture and of Irrigation."[11]

The input subsidy that goes to producers cannot be counted in their favor as a production subsidy, since it is passed on to the Treasury or to consumers in the form of low fixed prices for finished consumer products. Mostly, the sum transferred goes to the user—be it the final consumer or a business firm—for very little goes directly to the Treasury (see table 4.2). An example of the transfer of revenue from the producer to the consumer through the mediation of the government was seen in Chapter 4's discussion on price controls in agriculture.

The artificial values of transfers made through subsidies do not add up to a balanced transaction, though that may be the object. Somebody has to come up with the difference between cost and purchase price. When a public sector producer suffers a net loss from selling low-priced products, the Treasury will have to make compensations; if it does not, the firm's production levels will go down and it will eventually close, something the government of Egypt does not allow by law. In practice, the firm is neither fully compensated for losses nor completely starved out. Public sector industries end up facing problems of shortages, poor quality products, and low productivity. Subsidies may be a manifestation of widespread poverty, but they can also be one of its causes.

THE COST OF SUBSIDIES

The Egyptian economy is infested with direct and indirect subsidies, and it is very difficult for anyone to determine their total cost. Moreover, precise accounting is compounded by multiple rates of foreign exchange, which prevailed until the unification of rates for the Egyptian pound in 1991. President Mubarak admitted for the first time in August 1988 that the total subsidy bill had reached nearly £E10 billion out of government revenues of £E18 billion.[12] By the mid-eighties direct subsidies constituted 13 percent of the GDP.[13] When all the various implicit subsidies are added, it will be seen that subsidies eat up most of the Treasury.

The government has extended the subsidy network to nearly everything exchanged through the medium of money. In 1990, subsidies still affected bread, flour, sugar, tea, coffee, oil, soap, rice, fats, meat, imported and public sector chicken, milk, medicine, clothing, gasoline, natural gas, diesel, electricity, water, telephones, housing, rents, transportation, movie theater tickets, automobiles, air conditioners, refrigerators, education and health services, interest rates, and exchange rates. However, the pace at which the government was reducing subsidies accelerated after 1990. As of 1991, direct subsidies were reported to have been reduced from 13 percent to 6 percent of GDP.[14]

EFFECTS ON ECONOMIC GROWTH

The most serious aspect of the subsidy system is its anti-growth bias, since it deprives the producer, public and private alike, from earnings necessary for investments and renovations. Indeed, this policy has contributed in a major way to the low operating capacity of the public sector and to rampant waste and corruption,[15] as the following examples show.

Domestic Water Usage

An examination of the domestic water subsidy in the city of Cairo shows some of the difficulties implicit in the integrative approach. What stands out is the extent to which the government had lost control over the management of the economy, be it through inefficiency or waste generated by the subsidy system. The distortion in this case is multifaceted: official rates are set far below cost of delivery; no distinction is made between the needy and the affluent; and no accurate assessment of charges could have been made. Finally, water was wasted because of poor maintenance and lack of incentives for conservation on the part of consumers.

According to the head of the General Authority for Water Resources for the city of Cairo, in the early eighties it cost the government 8 piastres to process and deliver a cubic meter of water to consumers. Of that cost, consumers paid only 1.2 piastres.[16] The subsidy per cubic meter was thus 6.8 piastres, for rich and poor alike.[17]

In May 1985 the Higher Policy Committee of the cabinet raised the price of a cubic meter of water to 3 piastres for the first 30 cubic meters used per month and 5 piastres for water in excess of that amount. Still, the new rates remained far below cost, which was rising too. An accounting of the cost of providing the city of Cairo with water for residential purposes shows that until 1985, the government paid over £E89 million annually.

An especially unfortunate part of the story is that fully 50 percent of the 3.6 million cubic feet processed for Cairo everyday is lost. This waste of 1.8 million cubic meters daily occurs through leaky pipes and faucets and careless domestic practices.[18] Most Water Authority bills are based on the average rate per residential unit. This method of billing provides no incentive to the individual consumer to conserve water.

Add to this the fact that the water department collects payment for a lesser amount than it actually delivers, due to faulty meters and shortage of staff. In Cairo 85 percent of the water gauges are out of order.[19] When water gauges are not functioning, the Water Authority makes an estimate of average consumption for different-sized apartments.[20] With only one hundred employees who read water gauges, they can collect only once a year.[21]

As mentioned, domestic water use in Egypt is extremely wasteful. Anyone familiar with housing conditions knows of the constant dripping from taps and bathroom toilets.[22] One estimate has put the cost of waste in domestic water use from leaking faucets and toilets at £E26 million annually, not including the investment cost to replace the wasted volume.[23] Since consumers pay practically nothing for water use at home or in the agricultural fields, they have no incentive to conserve. The situation has endured long enough to become an ingrained habit.

The greatest amount of water wasted, of course, remains in agriculture, where methods of ditch irrigation and shifts are extremely wasteful of both water and land. In comparison, potable water constitutes only a small part of the water used in Egypt. Water for irrigation is provided almost totally free. The waste is costly not only to the provider but also to Egypt's agriculture. The water table is continuously rising, and that in turn increases land salinity. Drip and pivot irrigation systems have been introduced but still constitute a very small proportion of usage.

Water management in Egypt suggests that while the central government can bring a resource under its jurisdiction, it is not necessarily able to run it properly. Government control seems to slide in proportion to the size of the undertaking and the extent of hegemony. Water usage also shows that government management of a resource leads to impermissible levels of waste.

The Sugar Subsidy

The sugar subsidy illustrates once again how government policies encourage waste and illegal behavior. Sugar was heavily subsidized and the per capita consumption almost doubled between 1973 and 1986,[24] a period that witnessed a general expansion in subsidies. From an average per capita consumption of 17.2 kilograms in 1973, consumption jumped to 33 kilograms in 1986.[25] This amount constitutes one of the highest consumption levels in the world. Government officials have admitted that increased consumption of sugar has been largely caused by the low cost to consumers.[26] Alarmed at the rising cost of the sugar subsidy and the spiraling consumption rate, the government started a campaign in 1988 publicizing the harmful effects of consuming large quantities of sugar. Yet, the sugar subsidy continued undiminished, and the price was not raised.

The sugar subsidy affects all consumers. Ten million holders of coupons are entitled to 18 kilograms annually at a nominal price of £E0.3, while its cost to the government is £E1.05.[27] In addition to any coupon share, consumers can buy sugar at the reduced price of 70 piastres per kilogram at the MOS consumers' society (*Gam 'iyah Istihlaakiyah*). Though this rate too is subsidized, there is no limit on how much a single buyer can ask for.

The estimated import cost of sugar to the government in 1987 was £E300 million, not including capital expenditures by the MOA to increase local production. Yet, the president allowed by special action the import of an extra shipment of $50 million worth of sugar in March 1988, at the time the government was advertising the harmful effects of sugar consumption.

Shortages in sugar supply were experienced by the fall of 1987 and continued through 1988. At that time, Egypt produced locally 910 thousand tons of sugar and imported about 600 thousand tons. The MOS claimed 948 thousand tons for distribution to holders of coupons. An additional 55 thousand tons of sugar were handled by the MOS at lower-than-cost prices.[28]

Shortages plus price distortions have given rise to a very active black market and constant demands in the Peoples' Assembly that the government clamp down on merchants. The security officers of the Ministry of Supplies, though, rarely try to apprehend offenders. Moreover, much of the black market originates in government outlets, through the consumers' society.

FOOD AND ENERGY SUBSIDIES: A COMPARISON

As the role of the IMF became increasingly visible in Egypt, considerable blame was assigned to subsidies of basic foods as the major source of national budgetary problems and, ipso facto, the chronic economic crisis. Yet, subsidies of basic foods represent a fraction of the total subsidy bill. Food subsidies have gained notoriety because they are visible and affect almost every citizen on a daily basis. They are also conspicuous because of the poor quality of the delivered goods, chronic shortages, and Egypt's growing dependence on imports for essential foods. For instance, by 1981 Egypt was importing half its basic foods at great cost, with the government footing the bill for a food subsidy of nearly $1.7 billion (table 5.1).[29]

Table 5.1. Egypt's increasing food dependency

	1970 (%)	1983 (%)
Wheat	44	76
Corn	3	33
Lentils and fava beans	10	20
Frozen meat	3	28
Cooking oil	52	81

Source: al-'Isawi, *al-Da'm*.

The financial burden on the government budget has undoubtedly been heavy, despite the fact that as of the late seventies, the United States provided grain at concessionary rates for one of every three loaves of bread consumed by city dwellers.[30] Compared to energy subsidies, however, the cost of food support is small. In 1979 it amounted to about one-half that for energy.[31]

In 1974 the government decided to protect all energy users, whether individuals, industry, or official agencies, from the rise in international oil prices. The price of oil increased on the international market roughly seven-fold between 1974 and 1979, thus pushing up the subsidy cost borne by the national government. To appreciate the sums involved, it should be kept in mind that the GDP of Egypt was £E19.6 billion in 1980 and £E26.6 billion in 1985.[32] Table 5.2 gives some examples of the range of subsidies to petroleum products. Of this list of highly subsidized petroleum products, only kerosene may be said to primarily benefit needy citizens.

The estimated cost to the government in 1979 of direct subsidies on food and energy combined was £E2.9 billion; about one-third went for food subsidies,[33] while the remaining 1.9 billion was the direct and indirect cost of supporting domestic use of petroleum products and electricity. The figure for petroleum product support alone reached £E1,727 million in 1981.[34] The subsidy for other fuel products came to £E850 million. For nonindustrial use of electricity, the subsidy bill was estimated at £E222 million, and for industrial use it came to £E289 million.[35]

In 1979 both food and energy subsidies discriminated against the rural population; about 75 percent of these two subsidies (65 percent of energy, excluding kerosene, and the entire food subsidy) were disbursed in urban areas, in which lived only 45 percent of the population. Feeding the urban areas cost the government £E1,019 million. The amount spent for energy (petroleum products and electricity) in the cities came to £E1,171.3 million; the share spent in rural areas was £E725.2 million. The rural share of the kerosene subsidy is slightly larger than that for the urban sector, but almost all the butane subsidy (92 percent) went to urban areas, followed by electricity (89 percent), and gasoline (78 percent).

With respect to distribution among income groups, the energy subsidies are sharply skewed in favor of the rich. When it is also remembered that energy subsidies are twice as large as food subsidies, the discrepancy becomes more significant, and the bias in favor of the rich becomes more striking. The upper 21 percent income group received 39 percent of the energy subsidy (£E461 million), while the lowest 27 percent income group received 15.5 percent. Looked at differently, the lower half of the population received only 34 percent of the energy subsidy and 44 percent of the food subsidy.

Table 5.2. Petroleum products subsidy, 1979

Fuel	Subsidy value (million £E)
Butagas	89.5
Kerosene	339.8
Gasoline	160.3
Gas oil	478.5
Diesel	20.2
Fuel Oil	265.8
Natural Gas	85.9
Total	1,440.0

Source: USAID, Egypt's Food and Energy Subsidies in 1979.

Among the individual energy items, gasoline was the most skewed in favor of the upper income groups: the top 21 percent of the population received 70 percent of the subsidy. Butane, electricity, and the indirect energy subsidies follow in descending order. Only in kerosene did the lowest income group receive more than their share based on population: though comprising 27 percent of the population, they received 33 percent of the kerosene subsidy. This represents almost a 7 percent increase in household income to the poor, whereas the electricity subsidy represents only about a 3 percent increase in their income. Other related subsidies are used almost exclusively by the rich: for instance, telephones, air conditioners, refrigerators, washing machines, color television sets, and automobiles.

Compared with energy, distribution of the food subsidy was more equitable.[36] The top 21 percent of households received 27 percent of the food subsidy, accounted for mostly by their greater consumption of high-cost subsidized products like meat, fats, and oils. The poorest households, 27 percent of the population, received 22 percent of the food subsidy. The remaining 52 percent of the population, in the middle, received 51 percent of the food subsidy. In comparative terms, this is as close to an equitable distribution of income support as can be found anywhere in the world. Nonetheless, the most needy are still not the main recipients of the food subsidy.

In terms of per capita shares of the food subsidies, a person in the lowest income group received £E35, whereas a comparable person in the top income group received £E54. For per capita shares of the energy subsidy, an individual in the lowest income group received £E29, compared to £E90 for a member of the highest group. It is clear from these figures that the subsidy system reflects income differentials and thus constitutes an alternate wage system rather than a shield against deprivation.

Universal application, maladministration, and the wasteful distribution of some food items reached such proportions in the eighties that the situation became ludicrous. Bread, for instance, was being fed to animals and chickens, and flour was smuggled from government warehouses to be sold on the black market.

In short, the date on the distribution of the subsidies show that in fact the wealthy receive a share disproportionate to their size in the population. Even with a regime committed to equality and to the welfare of the poor, those who are advantaged in some respect will also be advantaged in the reception of government largesse.

THE SUBSIDY SYSTEM DURING THE TRANSITION PERIOD

The extensive expansion of the subsidization system during the open-door policy period continued in the early eighties under Mubarak, before restraining measures were taken. This may be because liberalization policies are associated with a rise in the cost of living, which prompts the government to increase subsidies.

Energy

The cost of the energy subsidy to the government of Egypt rose from £E1.9 billion in 1979 to £E4.7 billion in 1986; these figures are estimated at the then prevailing free-market rate of US$1 to £E1.9.[37] The 1986 USAID study maintains that the prices of energy to the consumer had declined greatly in relative terms over the previous ten years. During that period, "the nominal price of electrical energy was about 50 percent higher in 1984/85 than in 1974," whereas the wholesale price index tripled over the same period, "implying that the price of electricity to the consumer declined by 50% relative to the prices of other goods and services."[38] There was an average increment of about 37 percent in nominal electricity tariffs announced in July 1985 but no other increase until 1987, which again led to erosion of the increment relative to the annual increase in the prices of other goods and services.

Electricity was sold in 1985 at 20 percent of its market price. The long-run marginal cost price of electricity was estimated at 10.4 piastres per kilowatt-hour with the nominal price of electrical energy in 1985 at 2.1 piastres per kilowatt-hour, making the subsidy an estimated £E2.8 billion annually.[39] At those rates, consumption was rising at 11–12 percent annually.[40] Nearly half (45 percent) of total electric power produced in Egypt goes toward home use, a ratio higher than anywhere else in the world. The moderate increases in energy prices in 1985 and 1986 remained far below the rise in the cost of living price index.

Charges for electricity continue to be low and vary according to consumers: rates for domestic consumption differ from those for industry, and rates vary from industry to industry. Public sector firms, investment companies operating under public law number 43, and companies operating under law number 159 pay different rates, a situation which causes confusion and difficulties for industry.

As of 1987, the brakes were beginning to be put on the rise in the subsidization bill. Charges for domestic use were made progressive—the greater the amount consumed, the higher the charge. A price floor has been maintained for low-income people which keeps their bills practically unaffected by the price rise. Gasoline prices were also increased in July 1986 from 20 to 25 piastres per liter for regular and from 25 to 30 piastres for premium gasoline. In the spring of 1988 an increase of 10 piastres on each kind was made. Though this last increase is relatively sharp, it is still very low in absolute terms; when one accounts for an inflation rate of about 25 percent for that year (Central Bank estimate), plus deflation, which raised the price of the dollar by nearly 22 percent, the gasoline price increment almost disappears.

Energy subsidies in Egypt have also contributed to waste, deprived the national budget of an important revenue in hard currency, and given the wrong signals to industrial and commercial establishments. They have caused inefficient production processes and contributed to the slowing down of the economy.

Attempts at Reform

The years 1990 and 1991 witnessed the last stages of long and arduous negotiations between the government of Egypt and the IMF regarding economic reform. In May 1991 Egypt signed the reform package negotiated with the IMF and the World Bank. In the period leading to the signing of the agreement, the government had raised the prices of gasoline, butane gas, electricity, medicine, and a number of food items, including basic staples such as fava beans and lentils. It had, moreover, freed almost all agricultural products from compulsory price controls, except cotton, rice, and sugarcane. However, the increases in energy prices, though more substantial than at any other time in the past, were still short of a free-market rate. For instance, gasoline prices were raised in two stages: from 25 to 40 piastres a liter, then to 70 piastres. Premium quality gasoline was raised to 80 piastres. Energy prices, though, remained about 45 percent of the international market value. Moreover, government-owned enterprises continued to receive energy at subsidized prices even after rates had been completely freed.

Two other important reforms, the unified exchange rate and interest on bank deposits, affected subsidies. For all practical purposes, the exchange rate was unified and the pound floated. Money changers were authorized to function legally after securing a license, and foreign currency could be sold and bought freely. However, in practice purchase of foreign currency remained circumscribed, and the government continued to interfere in setting currency prices.

Food

As for food items, the burden on the Treasury continued to grow unabated until 1986, and at a faster rate than the energy subsidy. The rapid increase in the cost of the food subsidy relative to energy during this period was due to the steep rise in food prices internationally and the decline of oil prices in the eighties. In 1986 growth in the wheat subsidy was contained, partly because the price of bread was increased to 2 piastres a loaf and partly because international prices dropped.[41] However, it rose again sharply in 1988 due to a drought in the United States. In fact, the wheat and flour bill exceeded £E2 billion, according to President Mubarak.[42]

Five basic commodities, sugar, rice, edible oil, tea, and soap, were subsidized to the tune of £E1,390 million in 1986/87 (table 5.3).[43] Ten million Egyptians, nearly the whole population, held family coupons (bitaqaat tamwiin) from the Ministry of Supplies that entitled them to a fixed quota at subsidized prices.[44]

The gap between subsidized and market rates is considerable (table 5.4). Moreover, when the various exchange rates used to calculate the value of subsidies are considered, the heavy burden on the government appears in its real magnitude (table 5.5). It is clear from table 5.5 that the government's policy of manipulating currency prices to maintain an equilibrium in the transfer of values was actually leading to greater distortions and loss of control.

Waste in distribution occurs at the numerous official outlets (gam'iyaat) because shortages, plus the very low official prices, have given rise to a thriv-

Table 5.3. Rations and subsidies of basic consumer goods, 1987

Item	Monthly share (kg/person)	Subsidy (£E/person)	Cost/family (£E)[a]
Sugar	1.50	0.75	3.75
Oil	0.55	0.36	1.85
Rice	1.40	0.37	1.82
Tea	0.08	0.35	1.60
Soap	2 pieces	0.52	2.60
Total	11.59		

Source: Minister of Supplies, Al Ahraam, 2 August 1987.
[a]Average family size is five members.

Table 5.4. Comparison of actual to subsidized prices of selected basic commodities, 1986 (piasters/kg)

Commodity	Subsidized price (I)	Avg. actual price	Difference (II)	Ratio (II/I)
Lentil	35	275	240	6.86
Rice[a]	14	105	91	6.50
Sugar[a]	10	70	60	6.00
Edible oil[a]	10	65	55	5.50
Tea	138	800	662	4.80
Ful	15	70	55	3.67

Source: GOE, al Siyasaat al Si'riyah, vol. 1, p. 28.
[a]Represents the ration coupon price.

ing black market. When a shipment of rice or sugar arrives at the gam'iya, a horde of hawkers known as *dallaalaat* line up, get more than their share, and sell it on the black market. Aside from corruption, a study by a World Bank specialist found these outlets least efficient.[45] Corruption and waste are pervasive in the distribution of nearly all subsidized consumer commodities.

As we have seen, in addition to loss of control, unequal distribution, adverse effect on productivity, and waste, the subsidy system has contributed to the expansion of the black market, an illegal activity. Thus, the subsidy system has proved to be a contributing factor in the establishment of an uncivic culture.

TRANSFER POLICIES AND LOSS OF CONTROL

The arbitrary system of assigning responsibility for paying the public's bill has had several serious effects on Egypt. In terms of equity, it has victimized certain economic groups for no fault of their own except that they were within the reach of the sharp knife of governmental institutions. Second, the unreasonable burdens placed on some productive forces, private and public, proved to be anti-growth measures that undermined the general good, including those for whom it was meant to satisfy.

To illustrate the endemic problems attendant with creating a balanced economy using the integrative approach, I shall examine the case of the bread industry during the transition period of the eighties.

THE BAKERS' DILEMMA

In May 1986 the Ministry of Supplies decided to reduce the amount of wheat flour made available to privately owned bakeries, who produce most subsi-

Table 5.5. Subsidy cost of five basic food items under different exchange rates, 1985/86

Exchange rate	1£E = $0.70	1£E = $1.35	1£E = $1.90
Wheat	279,130	533,565	750,944
Flour	154,053	294,160	414,003
Sugar	33,180	17,376	12,346[a]
Edible oil	170,374	325,326	457,366
Tea	49,149	93,849	132,083
Total	685,886	1,264,276	1,767,242[b]

Source: GOE, Ministry of Supplies, List by Items.
[a]The decline in value in this case is due to the fact that most sugar was produced locally, not imported.
[b]Corrections in totals have been made by the author.

dized bread exchanged on the market. The measure was an effort on the part of the government to regain control over the spiraling wheat flour subsidy. "Suddenly, wheat flour disappeared from the market," wrote one weekly magazine, "and long queues were formed in front of bakeries in search of bread. ... Black market prices of flour were 40 percent higher than the official rate."[46] All flour received by bakeries came from public sector mills of the Ministry of Supplies, which produced 90 percent of flour consumed.[47]

Here we have a supply crisis, a drama of sorts. The actors were bakers, black marketeers, detectives, and officials of the Ministry of Supplies. The stage is the greater Cairo area, which enjoys the lion's share of the flour allotments and subsidy.

The Bakers' Story

"Yes we are thieves," said one bakery owner to a correspondent, "and the reason is the Ministry of Supplies." Not quite a cops and robbers scenario, but rather a game played by the government and the bakers, the object of which was to load more of the burden of subsidizing bread on the other side. Two reporters from the journal shuffled between the parties, seeking to uncover the sources of the crisis. Though they uncovered nothing new in the twenty-year-old bread financing crisis, their stories portray massive problems, caused, among other things, by the illusion of power.

In 1987 private sector bakeries produced 90 percent of bread on the market. Public sector bakeries, constituting only about 6 percent of the industry then, produced about 10 percent. Private bakeries remained small and traditional, due to lack of incentive to make capital investment improvements.[48]

As the private sector bakers told their story, they related that the Ministry

of Supplies regulated the bakery business by a number of decrees and decisions (the latest being law number 516 in 1984), thus creating most of the
problems faced by bread producers. The weight, size, price, and composition of
a loaf of bread were specified.[49] Producing according to these specifications,
the bakers claimed, would mean operating at a loss of 300 piastres for every
flour sack of 100 kilograms provided by the ministry at an officially subsidized rate of 1,200 piastres (£E1 equals 100 piastres). In 1987 bakers estimated
their loss at 1 piastre for every 2-piastre loaf.[50] Further, government specifications do not account, bakers claimed, for the costs of labor; other inputs such
as electricity, water, salt, yeast; depreciation; and distribution. Some bread industry experts in the Ministry of Supplies and in the public sector admitted
publicly in 1988 that the official specifications were impossible to put into
effect and that conditions under which bakers operate constitute a disincentive.[51]

The bakers made the case plainly that they could not operate at a loss, nor
were they allowed to close up shop and cease working. The government has
repeatedly warned bakers against closing their shops; the latest warning happened in October 1987. The detectives of the Ministry of Supplies watch the
bakeries very carefully.[52] Bakers have admitted that they pass on expenses to
the consumer in two forms, both of which constitute cheating. First, they violate the specifications decreed by the ministry for making a loaf of bread, mix-
ing it with inedibles and adding too much water. Second, they sell a portion of
the flour allocated to them on the black market, where they make a profit of 8
pounds per sack, nearly 67 percent. In contrast, the government allows each
baker a profit of £E0.47 per sack.[53]

The bakers also complain of government control of labor and say that the
government does not allow them to raise wages because production costs would
go up, thus affecting prices. Labor has been fleeing the bread industry due to
the low wages and hard working conditions. The bakers charge that the Ministry of Supplies does not take into account inflation and how it affects production costs over time.[54]

Officials in the public sector and Ministry of Supplies have admitted the
connection between negative incentives and the production of a bad loaf of
bread. Because of these conditions, bakers tried to discourage demand in order
to reduce the pressure on their time and resources.[55] All this results in evasions of the law—for example, the diversion of flour to other uses, such as
unregulated high-priced bread, sweets, or the outright sale of flour on the
black market.

Policing the bakeries is not practical, nor are bakers expected to honor the
allotment under the conditions of their employment. The black market is a

firmly established business that seems to flourish despite police surveillance. Officials at the Ministry of Supplies have estimated that bakers manage to save from five to ten sacks of wheat flour from their daily allotment of twenty-five sacks for sale on the black market.[56] The usual practice was to smuggle the commodity from Cairo to the provinces, where much of the flour was fed to animals. This occurred because a ton of animal feed in 1987 sold at £E80 more than a ton of flour.

The ministers of both Supplies and of Agriculture appealed in 1987 to the public not to waste bread or feed it to animals. When a journalist asked the former how would he resolve this dilemma, the minister stated that there must be a solution, though he failed to specify one. Then he turned the question back to the journalist, asking, "Do you have a solution?" The journalist put an interesting twist on the matter and said that maybe it is all for the better, for had chicken not been fed bread at a subsidized prices, poor people would not have been able to buy chicken meat. "A point of view!" responded the minister.[57] Have bakers discussed the matter with ministry officials? Yes, but as the bakers explained, it was them versus the decision-making power of the ministry.

What prompts officials to act so arbitrarily? The bakers answer that the ministry is itself in a bind and knows not how to solve the problem. It must either increase the amount and subsidy of wheat, or increase bread prices. Severe budgetary strains preclude the first option, and political considerations discount the other. Consequently, the ministry prefers inaction, leaving the burden to fall on bakers. In keeping with the tradition of the regime, the government opted to pass on the burden to someone else, preferring increased tension in the industry and greater costs for police surveillance to steps that would lessen tension and unrest.

The government has in the last ten years tried to avoid some problems by having the public sector assume part of the responsibility for making bread. Mechanized bakeries, in full or in part, were introduced in the late seventies, and the process was speeded up in 1981. They have thus far succeeded in raising the public sector's share of bread production from 1 percent of total bread output in the seventies to about 10 percent in the eighties.[58] The military forces have been deeply involved in producing and running mechanized bakeries. Most public sector bakeries have been active in the greater Cairo area. Public sector bakeries, however, have not operated at a profit.[59] Their losses are covered by the Treasury. They also have had technical problems and have proven to be less than an unqualified success.[60]

Having obtained as much as it could from foreign aid, the government had no one on whom to pass the buck except local revenue makers, such as bakers.

The punishment, consisting of fines and jail, would be severe for those bakers who failed to deliver honestly. Bakers tried but did not succeed to limit the punishment to pecuniary fines.[61]

The bakers' dilemma is thus not an easy one. As they complained to the press, they could not produce under present conditions, could not disobey the laws without punishment, and were not allowed to go out of business. The only answer was to cheat, selling flour to dealers in the black market. "We are not responsible for the black market. The responsibility falls squarely on the government," they assert. "When a kilogram of flour sells for 12 piastres and a kilogram of animal feed for 30, then one should expect a black market and cheating on our part." The bakers showed that they were not entirely helpless; they would not put up with policies harmful to their interest.

If the bread issue is a chronic problem, why then did queues not appear until May 1986? That is when the government decided, in order to prevent black market dealings in wheat flour, to reduce the quota of flour allotted to bakeries. This caused a reduction in supply and a shortage of bread available for the public. It may be added here that the problem of reducing the allotted amount of flour to bakers recurred in the fall of 1987 and produced similar protests and work stoppage.

The Government's Story

The undersecretary of the Ministry of Supplies was indignant when told of the bakery owners' charge that the ministry had reduced the bakeries' flour quotas. "I refuse to hear the word reduce," he retorted. "The decision was made after careful and extensive study by experts of the ministry. We discovered that the average production capacity of a bakery was 22 sacks of flour, whereas we had been dispensing to each 35 sacks. This means that the bakeries have been letting the [surplus] flour reach the black market to the benefit of the owners."[62] The same charge, it may be added, was repeated by officials a year later.

His indignation did not cease at this point. He added: "I refuse to hear the word bread crisis, or a crisis in the supply of wheat. I have wheat reserves sufficient for 3.5 months. There is no wheat crisis, but rather *a moral crisis*. Those who have an interest in the continuation of the black market put up resistance to the decision of the ministry and slowed down bread production, thus creating a crisis atmosphere, whereas in reality there is none" (emphasis added). He went on that the reduction of the flour quota was a blow to "flour thieves and black market dealers."

After he cooled off, the official added that in response to the production slowdown, the ministry had promised to restore quotas to what they had been in the past, on condition that "there be a program and a plan to limit the flow of flour [to the black market]. Black market dealers are realizing big profits," he complained.

The undersecretary then made an about-face: "But then we should stress that this problem will not go away unless there is a price adjustment somehow or another." Evidently, and on second thought, the crisis was not to be considered entirely a moral one. He continued, "Consider that a ton of flour sells for £E100 [actually £E120], while a ton of animal feed sells for £E180. Who would believe that the peel of the fava bean sells at a higher price than the officially fixed price of the bean itself. We do not live in a society made up of prophets!"

Finally, the undersecretary admitted that wheat and wheat flour find their way to the black market not only from bakeries but directly from the ministry's depots and mills. He added that the price distortions make smuggling possible from every imaginable place. As for bakeries of the public sector under the ministry's direction, he admitted, they experience severe losses, which are made up from the general bread subsidy.

From October 1984 to December 1988, the price of a loaf of bread remained unchanged, but bakers were allowed in 1988 to produce a 5-piastre loaf in limited quantities. In terms of quality, the 5-piastre loaf has registered a modest improvement. It may be recalled here that inflation in Egypt runs high (25 percent annually is the official estimate) and is not reflected in the price of bread. The government continued to resort to official measures to overcome the problem, and police surveillance was increased. Touring the provinces in July 1987, the Minister of Supplies declared in Beheira Province that "if the bakers do not abide by the production specifications set [by the ministry], their bakeries will be closed and they will be prosecuted."[63]

Waste at the dining table is variably estimated by different sources. On the low side is the estimate by the General Organization of the Public Sector for Mills, Silos, and Bakeries, which puts it at 10 percent. On the high side are two survey studies that put waste at the dinner table at around 15 percent of bread purchased per capita.[64] In short, there seems to be agreement that total waste of bread as a finished commodity amounts to 30–40 percent.[65] Experts in the Ministry of Agriculture estimate that 4 million tons could be saved by controlling waste and nonhuman use of wheat. Though these points are sometimes discussed in the Peoples' Assembly and in Majlis al Shura, no steps have been taken to cut waste or change the picture.

One minor change in the bread question has been government tolerance in 1988 of the new 5-piastre loaf (named *al raghif al tabaaqi*, after the straw cage on which bread is displayed for sale on the streets). The Minister of Supplies rationalized his acquiescence by saying that if some people want to pay that price, it is their business. The number of 5-piastre loaves sold, though, is very limited. No bakery can convert to tabaaqi bread unless approved by the Ministry of Supplies, which has defined production of this kind of bread at 9 percent of total production. The head of the public sector for mills and bread in the Ministry of Supplies, Ahmad Abd al Ghaffaar, admitted that "for the first time the Ministry of Supplies acts realistically and gives the producer and the distributor a reasonable margin of profit and does not tempt one to cheat."[66]

Finally, it may be observed that official policy regarding bread, its production and distribution, has been seriously flawed for the last twenty years. The policy has caused considerable waste, unnecessarily high consumption, chronic shortages, poor quality bread, and intense black market activities and other forms of cheating. It has also required the employment of a large number of police and civilian officials for surveillance and administration of the industry. In effect, the government has leaned heavily on a private sector industry, attempting to force it to carry out an official task under extremely unfavorable conditions. This course has resulted in a decline of the industry and tension with the government.

Conditions for Regime Change

The chronic flaws in the patron state have all manifested here: that is, inability to deliver the promised objective, at least adequately; shifting of the burden of the subsidy to the producer; loss of government control; and a counterproductive policy of transfers of burdens and favors. In addition, it is clear that the private sector in the patron state is not free.

The question of why reforms been avoided or overlooked so far is difficult to answer. It is worth examining, though, the conditions under which officials will introduce economic policy change in the patron state. First, any change must be of a partial nature and not undermine the entire edifice based on the integrative development model. Second, officials have responded to external pressure from aid donors and international financial institutions like the IMF, though these pressures had only made a dent in the patron state edifice by the end of the eighties. Egypt, like some other LDCs, tried to respond to the IMF's suggestions in the mid-seventies, and the officials who took that step were burned out by the destructive riots that followed. Since then they have become very careful of, and indeed resistant to, the IMF. In those cases when Egyptian officials responded to IMF recommendations, the situation had reached the disaster point, as was the case with the devaluation of the pound that followed depletion of foreign exchange reserves in 1987.

Third, reaction to a Malthusian-type situation seems to be an impetus for policy changes in the patron state. Corrective action does not take place until the limit is reached and disaster threatens. One may refer to this as the *Malthu-*

sian impetus; one waits until the condition of the sick person becomes intolerable, then calls the doctor. Most economic reforms undertaken by Mubarak were of this sort.

Government fears of social unrest may have been exaggerated in response to the 1977 riots. The reactions of the masses in January 1977 should have been predicted. The policy of raising prices of essentials such as sugar, tea, bread, and kerosene, all used heavily by the poor, while leaving subsidies of gasoline and telephones used by the rich intact, was intolerable. Moreover, the Egyptian population did not then enjoy the liquidity that existed in the eighties. In 1987 and 1988 many prices rose sharply, including those of meat, vegetables, and fruits, without the population registering the mildest tremor. The cancellation of the return-to-school grant, however, did produce limited demonstration in some labor-concentrated areas.

CONCLUSION

The tendency of the patron state to be responsive to the basic needs of the masses, and its ideological commitment to relative equality, allayed the harshness and rigidity of policies emanating from an authoritarian government. Meeting basic needs is a program supported by the populist nature of the patron state and is consistent with the integrative development model. Central planning is perceived as an effective strategy for reducing waste, avoiding exploitation, increasing productivity, and introducing an equitable distribution of wealth. Had the planning model lived up to its promises, there would have been no need for subsidies.

The model, however, failed in two critical areas: it did not increase productivity, and it did not reduce the need to transfer resources extensively from one economic enterprise to another. Those on the receiving end of the transfers did not consider them enough, while those on the losing end considered them extractive. Thus, subsidies may be considered as one of the policy mechanisms that have contributed to the failure of the national design, symptomatic of the complicated economic arrangements created by the integrative model. Low levels of wealth generation and an inability to meet adequately the basic needs of the people brought into question the rationality of the central planning model and government hegemony over the economy.

The paradox of the integrative model is that though economically speaking it did not function as expected, administratively it did. The less adequately the model performed economically, the more reliance was placed on administrative measures and on coercion. Thus, the rational economic model was transformed into a powerful tool for artificial economic manipulation. What constituted an administratively rational decision, however, was economically irrational, as the administrative control of wages, prices, investments, and employment demonstrate. Hence, there came the serious economic distortions that made ad hoc measures such as subsidies necessary.

One suggestion for reform, made quite often by officials and observers alike, is to free public sector firms from direct government intervention and remove subsidies and price controls. Recommendations for autonomy of government-owned enterprises have been publicly voiced by most leaders, including the president, the prime minister, parliamentarians, and Ministers of Finance, the Economy, and Industry. Indeed, according to government books, public sector firms have been under an autonomous regime for more than a decade. Autonomy cannot be achieved, however, without transforming the economic system, if not the political regime itself. Naturally, that is not in the cards for the Mubarak regime. Indeed, autonomy never materialized, despite numerous claims and plans.

Given autonomy, an executive of a government-owned firm would make investment, employment, and pricing decisions on an economic basis; that would undermine the principal tenets of the regime, which are to provide jobs, to shield the salaried population from high prices, and to make sure that all government-owned enterprises continue to function regardless of their economic viability questions. It would also change the commodity mix in industrial production to meet market rather than regime priorities. In addition, salary scales, especially for executives, would run out of line with the salary scale in the civil bureaucracy. Such a development would not be looked at kindly by administrators. Moreover, autonomy would make superfluous many of the higher structures and echelons of government. These thresholds are difficult to cross for a regime bent on preserving itself.

The policy of economic transfers soon moved beyond the original objective of creating relative equality and punishing political opponents. The victims of official transfers were not necessarily a politically or ideologically targeted group, as in the early years of the Revolution, but anyone who happened to generate material values, namely producers, private or public.

The bill for the extensive subsidy network was not borne by the Treasury alone; a considerable part of it was passed on to producers in the form of controlled prices. This caused considerable damage to economic growth and was unfair to many producers. None of this, of course, contributed to the development objectives of the Revolution. Private producers who found themselves subjected to unfair practices preferred to cut back on their operations rather than function under unprofitable conditions.

Government subsidy of production inputs for both public and private sector producers did not and could not compensate for the losses. The input subsidy to public sector firms is in the last analysis a value transfer diffused in a variety of economic channels. Neither the beneficiary nor the victim are easy to define in an integrative development system. Lowering the cost of production to a government-owned firm did not mean a larger margin of profit on the sale of its products. To the extent that the prices of some private sector goods have at various times also been officially set, they too did not profit sufficiently from input subsidies.

The complications generated by the integrative economic model put the leaders of the regime in a position of immobility. The regime has been trapped by its past actions. Once it committed itself to, say, free education or low food prices, the government could not easily pull out of its commitments without creating social upheaval and economic crisis. Government subsidies have created accelerated demand for resources the government does not have. At the same time, public resistance to official retreat increased as did the number of dependents, thus the combined power of these dependents, increased.

Here the regime was trapped. It was able neither to acquire the necessary resources nor to stem the rising demand for its largesse. As a way out, the gradualist approach has become the preferred avenue of reform, and in Egypt this means prolonging the crisis. In countries where there has been radical political change among the elites—such as in Poland, Turkey, Chile, and Argentina—reforms have been sweeping and fundamental. Egypt, Syria, and Algeria, on the other hand, have had changes in personnel but not in political regime. Hence, reform moves at a snail's pace.

Economic retrenchment partly means slow price increases, implemented by stealth and by psychological conditioning of the public to decreasing returns from subsidies. In recent years, the Mubarak regime has started to increase prices of subsidized goods and services in small increments. They have allowed the 5-piastre loaf, while phasing out production of the 2-piastre loaf.

Perhaps the most effective means in the regime's possession for limiting public dependency on the government has been conditioning the people to the futility of continuing reliance on subsidies. Failure to deliver the goods or to deliver products and services of acceptable quality are tools of psychological conditioning. As delivery of subsidized goods and services deteriorates, the public loses hope of acquiring them, and those who can afford it turn to goods exchanged on the free market. The cases of poor quality bread and of education are relevant examples. However, this type of psychological conditioning, whether in the bread industry or higher education, has the effect of corrupting and lowering standards rather than diverting the public to other suppliers. It has generated an uncivic attitude, evident where subsidies have contributed to smuggling, cheating, and the underground practices of the black market. Success of such policy evasions should not be considered as a sign of strength on the part of social forces or as an alternative to development.

Rationalization of subsidies is one of the reforms most often suggested by

Egyptians and international observers alike. A World Bank Report written in 1987 makes the following comment:

> The challenge before the Egyptian government is to identify and to eliminate "redundant" subsidies: i.e. subsidies that do not improve the welfare of the poorest members of the society. By better targeting the subsidies to low-income groups, a reduction in the deficit can be achieved without affecting the redistribution objectives of the existing policy.[67]

While rationalizations of the subsidy system are widely discussed, it is overlooked that subsidies are not only a result of a welfare system gone wrong by maldistribution but an artificial mechanism to maintain some semblance of balance between wages and prices and assuring the survival of inefficient public sector enterprises. Subsidies are supplementary wages and cannot be removed or reformed without overhauling the whole structure of prices and wages and the type of management the government has used to run the economy. Prices and wages, in turn, cannot be adjusted without providing conditions necessary for economic growth.

Subsidies are not welfare policy measures but a wage system of a distorted and archaic nature. They have served as a major mechanism of the integrative development model and account in large measure for the indifferent performance of economic development in Egypt since the early sixties.

Chapter Six

Foreign Exchange Controls
Counterproductive Policy

Foreign exchange has been a chronic problem in most Third World countries. The push for rapid economic development, building of infrastructure, and greater food production for rapidly increasing populations has meant escalating demand for goods and services from the industrial world, the price for which had to be paid in hard currencies. Most Third World countries relied primarily on the export of raw materials to industrialized nations to secure the necessary foreign exchange. The demand, however, remained in excess of the supply. Problems then arose with respect to the balance of payments and the governments' share of the foreign exchange revenue.

Chronic shortage of hard currency in LDCs led governments to decide who could use it and to institute official controls. In Egypt, foreign exchange controls became one of the major mechanisms for distribution of resources in accordance with the integrative economic development approach. Controls enabled the government to transfer resources through privileged allocations and multiple foreign exchange rates. The value of national currency was set by administrative means at a favorable rate vis-à-vis foreign currencies, and access by private users was restricted.

The restrictive foreign exchange model in Egypt was primarily based on external trade considerations, which were no longer the major factor in determining equilibrium in the balance of payments. Capital from such sources as remittances from expatriate workers, tourism, foreign investments, and various dues had become a prominent feature in the balance of payments picture. The failure of the regime in the seventies and eighties to adjust to this development proved very costly.

Manipulating foreign exchange rates and its administrative allocations was a major way by which the regime sought to create equilibrium in the various sectors of the economy. As this chapter will show, rather than create balance, foreign exchange policies have caused serious distortions in the national economy and in foreign trade in particular. Moreover, the restrictive policy model shrank rather than augmented foreign exchange revenue in general and the government's share of it in particular.

The ineffectiveness of administrative controls had been a prominent characteristic of the basic development design of the regime. This is because the objective of achieving economic self-sufficiency underplays exports, which are one of the major sources of foreign currency. In addition, heavy investments increased the demand for the import of capital goods, intermediate goods, and raw materials, all of which had to be paid for in hard currency. As a result, demand for foreign exchange increased. Finally, the transfers policy of the regime had the effect of reducing incentives for exporters and driving foreign exchange dealers underground. These observations will be discussed in more detail in this chapter.

A Brief Historical Account of Policy

Egypt's policy of foreign exchange controls was a response to scarcity of supply and relative weakness of the export sector. Currency controls go back to the year 1947 under the constitutional monarchy, subsequent to Egypt's exit from the sterling area. The tendency to resort to administrative measures to resolve economic problems can also be traced back to that period. When the value of the Egyptian currency fell in 1951, the government introduced two rates for the pound, one for general transactions and one for foreign trade.

At that time foreign exchange controls consisted of the following regulations: (1) transactions in foreign currency could be made only through authorized banks; (2) residents of Egypt had to turn over their acquisitions of foreign currency for sale to the authorized banks; (3) revenue from exports should be turned over to the authorities within a period of no more than three months; (4) transfer of foreign exchange outside Egypt was prohibited without authorization; and (5) all transactions in foreign currency were prohibited except under conditions determined by ministerial decrees. A special arrangement, the own-exchange system (istiraad bi dun tahwil ʿumlah), was created, whereby businesspeople could secure the foreign exchange needed for imports outside official channels.[1]

These stringent rules were later adopted by the regime that followed the 1952 Revolution, with a few subsequent modifications. In 1953, for instance, the government introduced what has become known as special accounts (hisaabaat al tajnib), whereby imports could be partially paid for from the revenues earned by exporters. This system was briefly interrupted in 1955, then resumed in 1958 under the condition that the National Bank (al bank al ahly) henceforth would buy the foreign exchange designated in hisaabaat al tajnib with a premium. Banks were given limited rights to sell foreign exchange in external trade at a premium, thus creating a new rate of exchange.

The depletion of Egypt's foreign exchange reserves in the early sixties forced leaders of the Revolution to turn to the international money markets for loans. The crisis began in 1961, and Egypt resorted to the IMF for the first time in

1962 and accordingly devalued the pound. The value of the US dollar was raised from 35.2 to 43.5 piastres for all transactions except revenue from the Suez Canal toll and students' scholarships abroad.[2] A black market rate continued to exist despite the devaluation. The financial crisis reached an acute state in 1965[3] due to extensive government borrowing and expenditure on the first Five Year Plan and because the United States refused, for political reasons, to continue to accept local currency for wheat sold to Egypt.

A number of other factors contributed to the foreign exchange crisis: compensations for stockholders of the nationalized Suez Canal Company (1956), compensation for sequestrated foreign businesses, and the Yemen war (1962–69). By 1966 Egypt found itself unable to pay back its debts and resorted to short-term borrowing from European commercial banks at very high interest rates, which Khedive Ismaʿil would not have accepted, according to Hansen and Nashashibi.[4] Egypt's involvement in three wars—the Yemen war, the 1967 war, and the war in 1973—contributed to the worsening of an already critical financial situation but was not the main cause of it. Foreign currency revenue from exports was depressed, due in good part to import-substitution policies, which were intensified with the socialist drive that started in 1958.

After 1975, Egypt's hard currency revenue started to improve markedly as a result of a number of factors: the opening of the Suez Canal; resumption of oil production combined with the spectacular rise in its prices; and increased remittances from expatriate workers, foreign aid, and tourism. Income from these sources peaked by 1981/82, when the domestic market was saturated with liquidity. The volume of dollar accounts in local banks, for instance, was estimated at $8 billion.[5]

Arguments for Control

The enormous volume of foreign exchange flowing to Egypt after 1975 did not lead to a change in the foreign exchange control policies, as one would expect. Foreign exchange policy based on the trade model continued as before, though it was clear that the main source of hard currency was no longer foreign trade. Egypt continued to be guided by ideas that considered strict foreign exchange controls necessary in a weak economy. One reason for failure to shift policy was the fact that controls continued to be necessary for distribution of foreign currency in accordance with the government's transfer priorities. The flow of currency would have taken a different course under a liberal policy. Another reason was that controls served as a source of revenue for the government. It forcibly acquired incoming foreign exchange at lower-than-market rates, sold it at a profit, or used it to finance government activities and public sector enterprises.

A third reason for controls is that in a poor and unstable economy, flight of capital is one of the most serious causes of economic strain. Flight of capital, which occurs because of political and economic instability, is a serious threat to financial security in LDCs.[6] Political instability, an almost universal feature in LDCs, makes businesspeople nervous and insecure. They hedge their bets by maintaining accounts in foreign countries, often receiving higher returns on their deposits than they would get at home. Economically, capital flight is caused by low returns and lack of opportunity for investment,[7] which was the case in Egypt.[8] Capital movement across national boundaries accelerated rapidly all over the world after the United States and Europe abandoned the gold standard and floated their currencies.

The following discussion shows that the use of such fiscal mechanisms to realize national development objectives has proved to be self-defeating and counterproductive. Excepting their role in preventing the flight of capital, exchange controls constitute a major source for value transfers in the patron state. Moreover, it will be shown that foreign exchange policies were less relevant to fiscal management issues like the balance of payments and more related to domestic affairs like subsidies and official revenues.

HISTORY AND CONSEQUENCES OF DIVERSE RATES

By the beginning of the eighties, several legal rates of foreign currency were used in Egypt in conjunction with the black market rate. These different rates developed over a period of more than two decades. In 1962 the official rate of the Central Bank for the US dollar was raised from £E0.35 to £E0.43, then to £E0.70 in 1979,[9] where it remained constant at that level until May 1987. This rate was separate from the one used exclusively in bilateral trade agreements with Eastern bloc countries, which was valued at £E0.40 to the dollar.

To increase its revenue of hard currency, the government reintroduced in 1967 the incentive value to the dollar, which was higher than the official rate. By 1969 the incentive rate value was about 35 percent higher than the official rate.[10] In 1971/72 the premium was raised to 50 percent and extended to foreign exchange returns from tourism, hotel services, and few other transactions.

In September 1973 the incentive rate was developed into what was called the parallel market in foreign exchange (al suq al muwaaziyah), with the hope of increasing foreign currency revenue from remittances, tourism, and nontraditional exports.[11] The Central Bank, according to a cabinet decree, was to officially set the value of the incentive rate and to name the commercial banks that would be authorized to carry out foreign exchange transactions. Designated uses of foreign exchange revenue from the parallel market were the following: invisible expenses of individuals and the private sector; authorized travel money; and private sector imports of inputs for crafts, industry, and for the tourist business, whether private or public sector. Exporters were allowed to finance imports within six months after payment was received but not to sell their earned convertible currency to other importers.

Despite the creation of a parallel market in foreign exchange, the divergence between the Central Bank and the incentive rates continued to increase during the open-door policy period; by 1976 there was a 70 percent difference between the two. Shortage of hard currency had become a chronic problem, causing the main pressure for devaluation of the pound.

At this time also, the own-exchange system was revived. Under prevailing conditions, the own-exchange system meant tacit official acceptance of the use of the black market. In 1976 a law was passed making it legal for individuals to hold accounts in foreign currency provided they declare its source, but the law continued to prohibit its conversion outside official channels.

The incentive rate became the basis for transactions covering all revenues from the remittances of expatriate Egyptians, tourism, returns from nonconventional exports within limits of the law, transfers from citizens of Arab countries, and part of the returns of conventional public sector exports. In turn, authorized banks were permitted to use the incentive rate to finance private individuals and businesses, imports of spare parts, inputs and capital goods for the private sector, imports of the tourist industry (private and public), other specified imports, and (within a designated allowance) Egyptians going on travels abroad.[12] In 1974 another ministerial decree expanded the uses of the parallel market and established that the incentive rate would henceforth be determined in relation to supply and demand.

At times, the incentive rate and the free-market rate became close, even identical, as in the period from March to October 1981. Law number 242 of 26 July 1981 brought the two prices together at the rate of 84 piastres.[13] The rates then split again; one remained at £E0.84 (the authorized banks' rate) to be used for limited purposes, while the incentive rate continued to change in a race with the black market. By 1983 the difference between the two had grown wide again, and the black market rate reached a range varying between 110 and 120 piastres to the dollar,[14] or a 30 to 43 percent difference with the incentive rate. Thus while the Central Bank and the authorized banks' rates remained constantly low until May 1987, the gap between the incentive and the black market rates of the US dollar varied from time to time, though it widened considerably in the eighties.[15]

The multiple price exchange system was developed to meet separate situations that could not be dealt with by means of the artificially set rate alone. The different rates as they stood in 1985 are listed in table 6.1.[16] Those vari-

Table 6.1. Value of U.S. dollar under different systems of exchange, 1985

	£E/US$1
Bilateral trading agreements	0.40
Central Bank	0.70
Authorized banks pool	0.84
Incentive rate	1.12
Free market (black market)	1.60–1.85

ous rates served the manipulative transfer strategy of the regime in a variety of ways. The Central Bank rate was used primarily for settling interdepartmental accounts. Its main purpose was to maintain the subsidy system by providing the Ministry of Supplies with foreign exchange at a low rate; then basic foods such as wheat, flour, cooking oil, fats, meat, and other consumer goods could be imported cheaply and sold at a very low price to the consumer.

The Central Bank rate also served as the basis for imports of industrial inputs and machinery at an artificially low price for government industrial firms. The Treasury, of course, absorbed the difference. The authorized banks pool rate was introduced to facilitate the acquisition of hard currency by commercial banks and to provide businesspeople with their foreign exchange needs. The incentive rate was of course introduced to encourage Egyptians, mainly expatriate workers, and foreigners in Egypt to change their money through official channels. However, the persistent gap between the incentive and black market rates clearly indicated that the juggling of various stratagems was not successful.

The black market was in an odd way informally recognized by the Ministry of National Economy as the means of exchange in the free zone areas, where it was designated as the "free-market rate." Businesspeople in free zone areas, such as that of Port Sa'id, could legally buy and sell dollars at the free-market rate. Anywhere else, the practice was illegal and labeled black market. The free-market rate, however, was often used by the government as a reference price, as for instance in import law number 121 (1986), which considered the free-market rate as the basis of accounting and price setting.[17]

COMPLICATIONS OF MANAGING MULTIPLE RATES

The multiple rates of foreign exchange posed a problem to authorized banks. They had been committed by the government to provide hard currency to the public sector at the official authorized banks pool rate ($1 equals £E0.84) while they had been receiving dollars from expatriates at the higher incentive rate.

Not to be shortchanged, banks imposed fees on such transactions to make up the difference.[18] As a result, government-owned enterprises had to pay fees called charges for finding hard currency (*masaarif tadbiir ʿumlah*) imposed by none but the government banks. Sometimes banks charged more than the difference in value, thus making a profit. One executive of a public sector trade company declared in 1983 that his company had to pay extra fees to government banks upwards of 50 percent of the official authorized banks pool rate. Officials in the ministries of National Economy and Finance knew about this illegal gimmick but overlooked it out of necessity. As they explained, they were unable to enforce the official rate that they declared, nor were they able to declare the actual rate at which they operated. This attitude is commonly known in Egypt as management by *al taghaadi* (deliberate oversight).[19]

In effect, the government had passed impractical rules, then was obliged by the facts of the situation to tolerate violation by its own agencies, suggesting through example that the people do the same. The irregularities in this sphere of activity were quite extensive, and the range of the black, or undeclared, economy was nowhere as serious as in the area of foreign exchange.

As the gap widened between the incentive rate and the black market rate, the government stepped up the use of punitive measures against black marketeers, especially when Mustafa al Saʿid began his tenure as Minister of the National Economy in 1983. He passed measures freezing the accounts of money dealers, a step many experts thought illegal. Foreign currency police (*shurtat jaraaʾim al naqd*) became very active.

During the sixties, the overpriced pound did not cause a great inconvenience, as only tourists and Egyptians who needed to travel abroad had some reason to use foreign exchange. Import-export trade was already nationalized, while in 1963 small private businesses were deprived of the right to import materials needed for their own businesses and therefore were not pressed for foreign exchange. They continued, however, to need small amounts to finance the black market trade in spare parts, much of which was channeled through Beirut. Government industrial firms also made use at that time of the black market to obtain spare parts.

The foreign currency law thus presented a problem for all prospective users and/or earners of hard currency. Going through official channels was legal and safe but financially a losing proposition. Going through the black market, on the other hand, was the way to obtain a fair price, but at the risk of embarrassment, fines, and possibly jail. Still, no one who otherwise was able to change money in the black market resorted to a bank. Government holdings in foreign currency dropped to a dangerously low level of more or less $500 million in 1987, according to the Minister of the National Economy.[20] During this whole period, the government demonstrated once again that it could not live with the consequences of its own policy. Government agencies, including the Ministry of National Economy, became leading customers of the black market.[21]

Shortages of hard currency in the Central Bank and public sector companies were the main reasons for government tendencies to bow to black market practices. Some, if not most, products of government industrial enterprises contained a high ratio of imported inputs. Those inputs were paid for with hard currency. The necessary foreign exchange needed to pay for raw and intermediate materials was obtained from the Central Bank. The Central Bank, however, was chronically short of foreign exchange and proved not to be a reliable provider. Companies found it necessary, therefore, to either generate their own hard currency or slow down production. Both possibilities were realized, and production cost went up because companies operated below capacity. In sum, such twists and turns leave no doubt that, willingly or not, the government condoned and even encouraged departures from official policy, including the black currency market.

In addition, because public sector companies were short of needed foreign exchange, they resorted to charging hard currency for their products locally, by orders of the Minister of Industry. The practice was, furthermore, recognized by the cabinet, including the Central Bank. Relative liberalization of the exchange rate in the late eighties resulted in complications for the transfer mechanisms on which the system rested. In May 1987, when the so-called free market in foreign exchange was instituted, a conflict developed between the prime minister and the Minister of the National Economy on one side and the Minister of Industry on the other over the practice of charging hard currency for products of public sector industries in the domestic market. The first two wanted the practice stopped in order to reduce demand for foreign exchange on the black market. The Minister of Industry, however, wanted to wait until he was sure the government could honor its commitments to provide the needed currency to public sector firms. At any rate, the mandatory payment in dollars for public sector products had nourished the black market with the tacit understanding and approval of the government for a long time and did not entirely cease with the May resolutions.

The multiple rate generated other complications and distortions in the economy. Consider for instance the financing of imports. The government sold foreign exchange to legally designated clients, such as importers, at below its own cost. An importer was entitled to obtain needed foreign currency from the authorized banks pool at the officially set rate, if available. That rate, however, was less than the actual value of the dollar. For example, if the rate of the authorized banks pool was £E0.84 to the dollar and the free-market rate £E0.90

to the dollar, then the government was losing 7 piastres for every dollar it sold to an importer. After the institution of the free exchange market, public sector importers continued to receive foreign exchange at below the free-market rate: £E1.89 as compared to £E2.32. Referred to as the customs dollar rate (*al dolaar al gumruki*), it was the subject of criticism, but a year and a half after the institution of the free exchange market it was still unchanged.[22]

Another area where government policy reflects elements of economic irrationality in the management of foreign exchange is customs duties. Until 1981 customs duties were paid in dollars, which increased the demands of businesspeople for hard currency from the black market. After 1981 businesses did not have to pay custom duties in dollars anymore, but the value of imports paid for in dollars abroad was assessed at the dollar's official rate, which was lower than the market rate. In effect, the government opted for lesser revenue from customs duties on imports than it was entitled to. Excessive controls resulted in a proportionate disability to enforce these controls, thus proving them counterproductive.

Exchange Controls and the Inflow of Currency

Historically and until the last few years, no foreign currency enters or leaves the country without passing directly or indirectly through checkpoint controls of the government. Foreign aid, export returns, fees from the Suez Canal, tourism, business or personal transfers—they all pass directly through official channels. Egypt's revenue of hard currency witnessed a dramatic increase since the mid-seventies, as Egypt's became a rentier economy, receiving most of its hard currency from sources not related to the domestic productive process, such as fees from the Suez Canal, foreign aid, tourism, and remittances of expatriate workers.[23] Oil may also be included in this category, since it is mainly an extractive industry. Cotton, once the leading export and source of foreign exchange, was relegated to a fifth rank.

All sources of foreign exchange continued under infitaah to go directly through government agencies. However, since returns from tourism and remittances passed through private hands first, the black market and other concealment opportunities made it possible to partially avoid official channels. Indeed, vast sums of foreign exchange from tourism and from expatriate workers found their way into the black market and never reached the pool of the Central Bank or that of authorized banks.

Every time the government tried to divert revenue from tourism and remittances to official channels by compulsory means, it obtained the opposite effect. For instance, under Minister al Sa'id's stringent measures of 1984–86, hard currency revenue from expatriate sources dropped to $350 million from previous highs of over $1 billion. Money dealers were very active inside and outside Egypt, and many had established direct contact with expatriate workers in host countries, mostly in the Gulf states. Islamic Investment Funds (*Sharikaat Tawzif al Amwaal*, henceforth STAs) were started in the early eighties, mostly by such money dealers. Over and above that, capital generated by expatriates found its way into banks in foreign countries. Holdings of Egyptian nationals in foreign banks and other financial institutions are variably estimated at $80 billion and at over $120 billion.[24] Had these funds found their way into Egypt, the complexions of the Egyptian economy would have looked quite different, and it could have made the difference between successful development and chronic economic crisis. At any rate, such massive capital flight shows that in this case, currency controls failed to realize one major objective for which they were introduced.

There are several reasons for the "flight" of capital from Egypt. The term flight, however, needs some qualification. The deposits of Egyptian nationals in foreign banks hardly ever originated in the domestic market; they were mostly generated abroad and are considered in flight because they were not channeled to Egypt. Major exceptions to this are illicit transfers by individuals for personal use, and investments made overseas—where the economic climate is more favorable and profits are higher—by Egypt-based commercial banks.[25]

One reason for avoiding repatriation of earnings or limiting their amount is the absence of a free exchange market at home and the low official rate of the United States dollar, which to expatriates means a net loss of income for every dollar transferred home. Capital flight has also been caused by the inheritance laws, which claim more than 40 percent of the estate of the deceased. Expatriate workers are thus wary of establishing large deposits in Egyptian financial institutions. The absence of lucrative investment opportunities in an environment considered difficult for business has contributed as well. Moreover, the stock market remains very small, having been reopened only in the late seventies. Most stocks are of the closed type, not open for trading.

Remittances from expatriate workers started to have an impact on the foreign exchange system in Egypt as of 1968[26] and were perhaps the single most important factor affecting that system since the early seventies. In order to encourage the inflow of foreign exchange from remittances, the Nasser regime decided to add a 35 percent supplement over and above the official rate of the dollar, later to become known as the incentive rate (*al si'r al tashji'i*). Three years later the supplement was extended to returns from hotels and tourism in general.

To avoid losses from changing currency at the rate designated by the government, many expatriates brought back with them valuables in kind. The law permitted the entry of property purchased abroad for personal use upon return, a privilege that was liberally used and abused. From 1975 to 1978, currency remittances through banks ranged between 52.5 and 78.5 percent, while the rest were in personal imports of commodities. As of 1979 the cash to commodity-transfers ratio dropped to 40 percent. The share of commodity transfers increased due to the widening gap between the black market rate of the dollar and the incentive rate in the early eighties (table 6.2).

Disappointed for not getting its share of foreign exchange revenue from expatriates, the government followed its normal course of action, which was to impose sanctions. Thus, it introduced decrees requiring expatriates to change 10–25 percent of their foreign income through official channels. Custom declarations were required, and this discouraged expatriates from making direct money transfers. The government also required tourist agencies, transport agencies, and hotels to charge in foreign exchange and deliver the hard currency to authorized banks.[27] Then the government decreed that every foreign national entering Egypt should change $150 (or equivalent foreign currency) at ports of entry.[28] In a way, the government hoped by these two measures to be a partner, if not the sole recipient, of hard currency from tourism.

The restrictive foreign currency measures imposed in 1984–86 by the Minister of the National Economy, Mustafa al Saʿid, and the repressive moves against money dealers had the same effects on tourism as on remittances. Foreign currency that was generated by tourism and passed through official channels did not exceed $330 million in 1984, despite the fact that the number of tourists reached 1.6 million that year. On the basis of these figures a tourist spent on average no more than $206. Needless to say, this low per person return suggests that considerable sums changed by tourists remained undeclared. Removing foreign exchange restrictions, or most of them, as was done

Table 6.2. Remittances by expatriate Egyptians (in million £E)

	Cash (%)	Commodities (%)
1975–78	32.4	13.0
1979–85	32.7	22.5

Table 6.3. Ratio of remittances to current revenues, early 1980s

	1986/87	1987/88	Change ratio (%)
Transfer in cash	1035.6	5223.8	211.3
Transfer in kind	4316.8	2396.7	-21.3

Source: Al Ahraam, 8 November 1988, quoting official figures.

in May 1987, showed immediate improvement in the inflow of remittances. It by no means attracted all or most of the earnings of Egyptians working abroad, but it did improve the situation (table 6.3).

When devaluation of the pound brought the value of the United States dollar to near parity with the free-market system, expatriate workers lost the reason for commodity transfers and shifted to cash transfers. However, transfers through official channels remained less than what had been hoped for. Uncertainty as to the future behavior of the government and the possibility that it might not adjust the exchange value regularly inhibited many from using official channels and prompted them to keep their links with money changers.

Cash returns from tourism also improved after the May decrees. Tourism in 1987/88 was on the upswing, as were foreign currency returns through the banking system. Foreign exchange that passed through the official banking system reached $950 million, up from $450 million. This increase is more than 100 percent, whereas the number of tourists increased only by 28 percent.[29]

The Decrees of 1985

Conflict over the acquisition of foreign exchange generated by expatriates went through a dramatic phase in January 1985. The January decrees by the Minister of the National Economy, Mustafa al Sa'id, clearly illustrate the economic disruption and business distress that resulted from attempts to solve economic problems by legalistic rather than economic means. Frustrated by the inability of the authorized banks to attract foreign exchange, which existed in abundance in the market, Minister al Sa'id decided to strike at the money dealers soon after taking office in 1983. He accused money dealers of speculation aimed at pushing the price of the dollar up, and he put a freeze on their bank accounts. Then he began a harassment campaign and played their Arab competitors abroad against them.

The minister's next step was to implement a wedge separating the dealers from their major customers, the importers. On 5 January 1985 he issued decrees that in effect abrogated the own-exchange financing of imports, added new limitations, and tightened the screws applied by the committees controlling imports (*lijaan tarshid al waridaat*). According to the new rule, once importers secure permission for import of an item, they must obtain the needed foreign exchange by applying to the authorized banks. In effect, the measure cut out the main sources of hard currency for foreign trade by excluding both the black market and offshore banks. Under the own-exchange practice, offshore banks, which by law were limited to dealing only in foreign currency, were a source of foreign trade financing. Under al Sa'id's measures, importers had to buy needed foreign exchange from authorized banks with Egyptian pounds, a restriction that automatically excluded offshore banks. To put teeth in the new decree, the minister clamped down on money changers, arrested some, and froze their bank holdings for the second time.

The minister's orders to the merchants and other businesspeople seem on the surface simple enough: buy hard currency at the official agencies in Egyptian pounds. The hitch was that the authorized banks did not have the foreign currency reserves necessary to meet newly created demand, and neither did the Central Bank. Importers were in danger of forfeiting their business orders abroad, and industrialists could foresee the stoppage of their projects for lack of imported inputs and intermediate goods.

An open battle raged between the Minister of the National Economy on one side and the money dealers and importers on the other. All the money dealers actually needed to do was sit back and let the government broil in its own stew, for the parties adversely affected by the minister's policies were legion—namely, merchants, industrialists, public sector firms, expatriates, and consumers. The outcry was sure to reach members of the Peoples' Assembly. The opposition took advantage of the unpopularity of these measures to denounce the government, while members of the ruling party, upset by the embarrassing position in which they found themselves, joined the chorus of critics.

In the face of the uproar, the cabinet failed to back up the minister, despite his claim that the measures were approved by the prime minister before they were issued.[30] As expected, the government backed down, and amends were made four months later. The new rulings introduced in April 1985 returned the own-exchange financing of trade and a limited devaluation of the pound. In 1986 the rulings of Minister al Saʿid were officially abolished, long after their sting had been taken away. Money dealers were released and resumed their normal black market activities.

Al Saʾid's measures were yet another attempt on the part of the government to solve an economic problem by administrative rather than economic means. The minister acted in the manner expected from a member of the authoritarian patron state, and in that spirit he failed to provide alternatives to those who depended on money dealers. Again, legalistic and punitive measures were tried to solve actual economic problems, and once again these measures proved wanting.

Export Trade and Foreign Exchange

It is possible to argue that socialist Egypt had never been export oriented but rather followed a nationalist economic course, aiming at self-sufficiency through import-substitution policies. Efforts at promoting export were made in the fifties and sixties as a means to deal with the crunch of shortages in foreign exchange, not as an impetus for growth and integration into the world economy.

In 1959 the Nasser regime extended some subsidies to the export of manufactured products; this included raw cotton and onions but excepted cement and textiles.[31] These incentives, though, were offset by the export tax.[32] Perhaps the most significant improvement with respect to foreign trade during the Nasser period was the diversification of Egyptian exports and an increase in the use of manufactured components. It may be noted here that Egypt's exports were some of the least diversified in the world when Nasser came to power.[33] Due to his import-substitution industrialization policy, however, the consumer needs of the domestic market commanded first attention. It was in 1959/60, under his regime, that the concept of exporting the surplus and only the surplus was introduced.

The export business remained unattractive to the private sector because of the advantage merchants had in a protected market,[34] the adverse rate of foreign currency, production hardship, and bureaucratic considerations. In 1961, however, the nationalization wave encompassed foreign trade, and exports became a public sector business in which countertrade deals prevailed.

By the end of the sixties exports were at a lower level than a decade earlier,[35] and the regime's export record was described as "far from being remarkable."[36] Rather than showing improvement ten years after the infitaah, exports declined in the early eighties. It is noteworthy to mention here that the concept of exporting the surplus remained in effect under President Mubarak.

Between 1975 and 1988 industrial exports declined 700 percent for semimanufactured products and 200 percent for other products. The ratio of industrial exports to total exports in 1970 was 30 percent; this ratio declined in 1980, during the Sadat period, to 13 percent, then rose slightly by 1986 to 15 percent. The value of manufactured exports also took a serious plunge in the early eighties, primarily because of the drop in international oil prices, which constituted about 67 percent of exports. The share of primary materials, especially oil, in exports rose to over 80 percent in the late seventies and eighties, after dropping considerably. Not until 1987–88 did signs of amelioration and of improvement in the volume of nonconventional exports appear.

Import substitution, restrictions on use of foreign exchange, taxes, export licensing, price controls, excessive regulations, and the structure of production have all had adverse effects on the export record of Egypt. International constraints on foreign trade, of course, are a factor affecting export volume, but that effect is limited in the case of Egypt[37] and goes beyond the scope of this study. Various restrictions and obstacles to exports were reduced in 1983, and many were restored in 1987.

The Mubarak regime reasserted the principle of self-sufficiency (*al iqtifaa' al dhaati*) as a priority. Restrictions on exports were confirmed, official rhetoric notwithstanding. Government regulations limited exports to quantities that exceeded the needs of the domestic market. Only after the domestic market had been fully satisfied was export of a commodity permitted. In 1987–88, the authorities seriously considered a change in policy toward what they called exports by targets (*bil-ahdaaf*), that is, the singling out of a certain volume of a commodity for export even though the domestic market had not been fully supplied. Not until 1991 did the government meaningfully liberalize the export trade, removing restrictions on a large number of commodities. Included in the list of permissible exports were some food products.

Aside from lack of opportunity for export under Egyptian socialism, official attitude toward exporters was unfriendly. Exporters were not only paying taxes and fees, but the prices of their goods were set by a regulatory agency, a practice not removed until February 1987. Also onerous was the government's rule that exporters must surrender their foreign exchange earnings from exports to the government, a practice common in many LDCs. The exchange value by which they were compensated was below the free-market rate, constituting an indirect tax and outright loss to exporters. Exporters were also penalized for delays in turning over their earnings to the government; in case of default by the foreign importer, the Egyptian exporter was nevertheless obligated to turn over to the government the value of the aborted deal in foreign exchange. Needless to say, very few merchants remained in the export business. As will be discussed, the foreign exchange earnings rule was relaxed in 1983, then tightened again in 1987.

Official currency controls had very adverse effects on the Egyptian export business and ipso facto on the national economy. First, an inflated value of the pound made Egyptian goods costly and hence less competitive in foreign markets.[38] Second, exchange controls served as a disincentive against exports, because exporters were by law supposed to turn over hard currency revenue to banks within three months. In certain businesses, such as book publishing, the rollover is very slow, taking more than three months. Often in case of default, Egyptian exporters would be forced to buy hard currency from the black market to pay the government what was supposed to be their earnings in hard currency. Though Egypt had a great advantage in the publishing and export of books, especially in the Arab world, book publishing declined and did not begin its slow revival until 1987.

Countertrade, which was gaining increasing acceptance in Egypt and Third World countries in general during the eighties, added another disadvantage to private exporters. Countertrade is basically a public sector reserve in which private producers are invited to participate. According to the foreign exchange regulations, the government pays private exporters for their share in countertrade deals in pounds at the customs dollar rate, equivalent as of 1987 to £E1.89, compared to £E2.3 for the free-market rate.

A 1983 decree allowing exporters free use of their hard currency earnings[39] was reversed a few years later. In February 1987 a decree by the Minister of National Economy (*qaraar*, number 273) restored some previous restrictions on hisaabaat al tajnib by limiting their use to one's own business: the business from which the hard currency was earned. Thus, those traders whose business was limited to export and who were not manufacturers or farmers could not benefit from the hisaabaat al tajnib. Similarly, one could no longer use the currency to import for other businesses, such as small manufacturers. Amounts in hisaabaat al tajnib not used for the designated purpose would have to be sold to the authorized banks at the free-market rate. Businesses, moreover, had to apply to the Ministry of National Economy for permission to use part of an account in hisaabaat al tajnib for business travel, marketing expenses abroad, or fees for consultants.

These restrictions were not applied to the public sector, whose companies could continue to exchange among themselves some of their hisaabaat al tajnib freely. In response to strong criticism from businesspeople, especially the Businessmen Association, the minister issued instructions to authorized banks to permit exporters to retain 25 percent of hisaabaat al tajnib for business use without seeking authorization from any official body. This was, in effect, a modest but helpful concession.

Restrictions against carry-on goods for travelers were another product of foreign control rules detrimental to exports and the economy in general, especially to small businesspeople in the arts and crafts. The Ministry of National Economy stipulated that anyone leaving the country could not carry goods exceeding £E100 in value if the individual was Egyptian, and £E250 if a foreigner. The measure was intended to limit the amount of foreign currency a person could change on the black market. An opportunity for export was therefore missed for no reason other than a desire to maintain control over foreign exchange. Not until August 1988 was the measure annulled.[40]

Contrary to some claims, private businesspeople were not given a free hand in foreign trade under the infitaah.[41] For instance, the private sector was forbidden to export major agricultural crops, including citrus fruits, the ban on which was not lifted until February 1987. The public sector continued to have a monopoly over trade to Eastern bloc countries and to discriminate against the private sector in trade with Arab countries. All this explains why the export share of the private sector was still below 10 percent of all exports in 1988.[42] In view of these business regulations, it should not be surprising to see that while imports flourished under the infitaah, exports remained stagnated.

The bias against exports continued into the late eighties, despite official promotion efforts. For instance, in 1988 formal measures for processing exports were still three times more difficult and complicated than those for imports.[43] Exports were subject to the authority of nine different governmental agencies,[44] necessitating about a week to fulfill all official requirements to export an item. Exporters continued to speak of their travails completing export requirements as the journey of sorrows (*rihlat al 'adhaab*).

THE ISLAMIC INVESTMENT COMPANIES

Unlike government-owned firms, private sector importers under the infitaah were allowed to furnish their own hard currency using the own-exchange system.[45] Aside from the few offshore banks, the black market was the main supplier of the own-exchange system. Those few importers who were also exporters could use part of their share of export earnings for the purpose by virtue of the principle of *al tajnib*, their foreign exchange earned from exports. In effect, through the own-exchange system, the government indirectly opened the door for dealing with the black market—no declarations required, no questions asked. In 1983 government-owned firms were allowed to use the own-exchange system of imports like the rest.

The relations between the government and money dealers in the black market, nevertheless, remained cautious, and at times tense. Though dealers suffered from occasional clampdowns by authorities, the major confrontation occurred in 1983–85, as has already been discussed. The prize to be won was expatriate earnings in foreign exchange, which had risen in volume to become one of the four major sources of foreign currency in the land. The authorized banks received the minimum that expatriates were required by law to transfer to Egypt. The rest went through unofficial channels.

The relevant issue here is the underground channels through which foreign currency entered Egypt. One tactic chosen by some expatriates to preserve the value of their earnings was to finance Egyptian importers overseas with foreign exchange, then receive payment in pounds in Egypt at the free-market rate. Egyptian money dealers who handled these operations realized early in the game that financiers in Gulf countries had already turned the handling of savings and money transfers of Egyptian workers into big business. Egyptian dealers quickly cut into that market and became a financial force to be reckoned with. In effect, the newly created Egyptian "transnational" money dealers succeeded in drying up the Egyptian government's revenue of foreign exchange at the source. What became known as the Islamic "Investment Companies" (STAs) originated in that business in the late seventies and early eighties.

Most of the 104 STAs, eighteen of which were sizable and five of which

were truly large, started out as money dealers[46] before expanding into overseas speculation in metals, currencies, and other activities.[47] Their enterprises
within Egypt consisted at first mostly of services such as finance, tourism,
trade, transport, and real estate. Their most significant activity, however, has
been raising capital, not only from expatriate workers abroad but also from
small savers at home; they do so under the claim that they deal with *halaal*,
that is, they operate according to Islamic law. They were also attractive because of the high dividends they gave on deposits. The STAs in effect beat the
authorized banks in the competition for the savings and foreign currency re-
ceipts of Egyptians at home and abroad.

Encouraged by increasingly protectionist economic policies and pressured
by the government and the media to show "patriotism" and become "productive elements," some STAs started to form manufacturing companies and increase their investments at home. Not taking kindly to the stiff competition,
the government's attitude toward them vacillated between harassment and
acceptance. While some officials indulged in attacking them, others of high
rank appeared with STA executives in photos displayed on the front pages of
newspapers.[48] Moreover, some government agencies sought their assistance
in obtaining foreign exchange, imports of essential commodities for which the
government had no hard currency, and for joint ventures with the government, like the Daqahliya Apparel Company, in which the al Saʿd STA acquired
a 38 percent share in 1987.[49] The attitude of the official press was divided vis-
à-vis the STAs; some supported while others attacked vehemently.[50]

Veiled threats against STAs from official and quasi-official circles started
to appear in 1985 and reached a crescendo in the spring and summer of 1988,
when the government finally issued decrees regulating them. They were accused of being pseudolegal in status; acting as banks, which they were not;
speculating in currency against the national interest; not paying taxes; and
cheating customers. This last accusation was based on a claim that the high
dividends paid by STAs were actually from new subscriptions rather than from
actual high STA returns and profits. That is, disbursements were made from
capital rather than profits. The failures, starting in 1986, of a number of STAs
gave strength to this claim. The core of the matter, though, was that STAs
attracted billions in foreign exchange while the government's coffers were near
empty, a situation that explains in part the leading role played in 1986 by
Central Bank governor Ali Nagm in opposing them.

To a certain extent, the ability of STAs and other large black market money
dealers to siphon off hard currency from official financial institutions contributed to the failure of the government to pay back interest and principal on its
mounting international debt in 1987 and 1988. It is thus understandable that
international financial agencies dealing with Egypt were in favor of regulat-

ing the STAs. When the government eventually acted to regulate the STAs, however, its measures were structured as punitive actions rather than legislation intended to protect depositors, as the government had claimed.[51]

A new law (number 146) was issued 9 June 1988 giving STAs the option of submitting to the law or liquidating their companies and returning deposits to customers. The new law stipulated very difficult terms especially designed for STAs and not applicable to other businesses. It required, for instance, that STAs limit their capital to a maximum of £E50 million, that they submit to supervision by the Money Market Authority (hay'at suq al maal), and that they apply for approval from the Ministry of National Economy and the Central Bank for any transfer of funds abroad. The law was criticized, moreover, for its concern with the mobilization of funds by those companies rather than the question of investments. Some feared that the rule would be applied in the future to limit other business activities and discourage the private sector.[52] The harshness of the new law was admitted even by leftist commentators such as previous Minister of Planning Isma'il Sabri 'Abdallah.[53]

In response to initial criticism of the law, the government moderated the tone of the executive order (al laa'ihah al tanfidhiyah) issued 7 August 1988 and gave STAs three months to decide whether to liquidate or reorganize. In the meantime, publicity and official proceedings destroyed al Rayyaan—one of the largest, most defiant, and least savory among the STAs.

The reasons for the official clampdown and virtual destruction of STAs may be summarized by the fact that in addition to being tough financial competitors to government banks, they constituted a potentially serious political contender to the regime. They were extremely wealthy and, at least in appearance, took on an ideological character—an Islamic one. They were associated rightly or wrongly with extremist fundamentalists, some of whom were conducting a campaign of violence and thus who came under the heavy hand of the Minister of the Interior. Growing official fear of the political role played, or that could be played, by such a financially strong group as the STAs was a factor in the government's final move.[54] Moreover, the government apparently had reason to believe that some STAs were financing radical Muslim activists,[55] especially university students. Another aspect of the economic power of these groups was the large number of clients who were small depositors and were dependent on them, a fact which gave STAs a popular base both economically and politically.

This Egyptian episode makes it clear that stringent controls against the free use of foreign exchange cannot function properly when there is great demand and equally great potential supply. Creating a small opening to release the pressure, as the government did with the own-exchange measure, proved to be like opening a hole in a dike. Apparently the lesson was learned, and the regime took steps in 1987 to reduce if not eliminate distortions and contradictions in the foreign exchange market.

THE FREE EXCHANGE MARKET (*al suq al masrafiyah al hurrah*)

It was partly to undercut the hold of the STAs on foreign currency that the government devalued the pound on 10 May 1987 to approximately the black market rate. The mounting financial crisis also contributed to the government's corrective action. As the prime minister, Dr. 'Atif Sidqi, stated in a major interview with the editor of the leading national paper, *al Ahraam*, the foreign currency crisis had a strangling effect on the country that threatened to bring all economic activities to a halt: "I had before me one of two courses of action: let factories and farms stop functioning . . . or find a way to increase the supply of foreign exchange."[56] He naturally opted for the second course, setting up a committee under his leadership whose deliberations reached the conclusion that

> the only solution was to enter the market [of foreign exchange] as a competitor, because we knew the extent of the volume of funds of the expatriate Egyptians and of their savings in overseas banks. We thus started thinking that in fact we had prohibited our own national banks from entering the money market except at the rate of £E1.35 to the dollar at the time the dollar was worth in the black market £E2.00 or £E2.10. As a result everybody used to resort to the black market.[57]

Thus, on 10 May 1987 the Minister of the National Economy issued a long-awaited decree (number 222) that devalued the pound by some 60 percent, to the level of the then prevailing black market rate (£E2.16 to the dollar). The regulation allowed authorized banks to buy and sell foreign currency in accordance with the law, for purposes and to parties specified in the law. The government set up an official body, the Managing Committee for the Free Foreign Currency Market, to determine the price of foreign exchange on a daily basis. The committee was made up of eight representatives selected by the governor of the Central Bank and included representatives from the authorized banks and the ministries of Economy and Trade.

The Central Bank rate of the pound (£E0.70 to the dollar), however, was not affected by the new measures, in order to preserve the basic goods subsidy. The Central Bank rate, though, was purely administrative, regulating interdepartmental accounting. It enabled the Ministry of Supplies to obtain the necessary dollars from the Central Bank for imports at the officially low rate. The customs dollar rate was also preserved, but raised in value from 135 to 189 piastres.

Technically, the new decree had done away with the own-exchange system of financing imports. The Central Bank issued a decree on 11 May specifying that private sector importers should pay the cost of their orders at authorized banks in Egyptian pounds, based on the rate declared by the Managing Committee for the Free Money Market. Though this step was not welcomed by importers, it was not onerous, since the free rate then was almost identical with the black market rate. Moreover, in case of failure by authorized banks to provide foreign exchange, which occurred to a certain extent, importers could secure their own foreign exchange and ask the bank to cover the sum needed from their own accounts, after performing the official conversion.

Whatever the result, the government devaluation and liberalization policy was a daring and necessary move, proving that the national decision makers were still able to make radical policy decisions. It also meant that they had to scale down some terms of the integrative model, though they hedged their bets by maintaining the two rates of the Central Bank and customs.

The initial results of reform were rewarding. Government revenue from the free exchange market jumped to nearly $1 billion in about three months, a range of $8–12 million a day; formerly it had ranged from $.75–1.0 million per day.[58] The flow continued at the same rate, and by June 1988, after thirteen months, the volume had reached $3.6 billion, according to official sources. Remittances by expatriates reached £E2,733 million eleven months after the introduction of the free market, compared to £E431 million for the previous twelve months.[59] Thus, the government made in one month what it used to make in one year.

The Sidqi government, however, was unable to float the pound and unify its value after an eighteen-month period, as promised in the May decree. Nevertheless, the free-market policy remained the basis of most transactions and was regularly adjusted to the extent that the difference with the black market remained negligible. In October 1988, less than eighteen months after the free exchange system was introduced, the two rates were about 6.4 percent apart.[60] However, businesspeople in need of large quantities of foreign exchange in the fall of 1988 had to pay a higher black market rate than the one mentioned here. The battle between official and black market operators, however, has not totally subsided, for demand is still greater than the official supply.

Fears that prices would rise sharply with devaluation of the pound proved unfounded. The reason is simply that most actual transactions involving foreign exchange were already based on the black market rate, rather than the official one. It was even made formal a year earlier when the Minister of Supplies and Foreign Trade, Galaal Abu-al-Dahab, issued decree number 121, setting the profit margin for imports of consumers goods on the basis of the free (black) market rate. The official rate was mostly for interagency accounting purposes and other balancing activities within the government that are not reflected immediately in prices. Price hikes in the second half of 1988 were not caused by the liberalization of foreign exchange rates but by marked increases in international prices of grains and by production shortages.

Offshore banks, indebted businesspeople, and black market dealers were adversely affected by the freeing of the price of foreign exchange. Offshore banks were by law limited to foreign exchange transactions, but with the new measures opening up the field for the rest of the banking system, their share of the market was reduced. Above all, they used to be a major source of foreign currency to businesspeople, and termination of the own-exchange system cut them out of the market. Their request to carry out transactions in local currency was denied. Businesspeople who had taken bank loans in dollars saw the premium on their loans going up sharply as a result. As for the black market dealers, the government clamped down on them and threw the leaders in jail, some 320 of them. In July 1987 it started to release them in phases.

The banishment of the black marketeers, however, was not totally successful. Egyptians who needed hard currency for personal purposes, such as travel, study abroad, or for medical reasons, were not officially eligible to benefit from the free-market holdings and found it necessary to resort to the underground and buy from black market dealers. Even some legitimate demands for hard currency were not satisfied. Though the government claimed that all import requests for hard currency were met, some businesspeople insisted three months after the implementation of the reform measure that this was not the case. They charged that the government entered the exchange market as a buyer, not as a seller. The fact that major industries such as al Nasr Auto Company continued to find it necessary to charge for a portion of their products in dollars, even after the May 1987 reform measures, confirms the persistent shortage of officially available foreign exchange.[61]

CONCLUSION

Manipulation of foreign exchange by various official stratagems was a characteristic of the integrative approach. Currency values were artificially determined and their flow controlled with the express purpose of diverting foreign exchange from where it tends to flow to other desired uses. It was important for the government to mobilize foreign currency holdings to make possible imports of raw materials and intermediate and capital goods for agriculture and industry, and to meet the food imports bill. In so doing, as in all other control mechanisms discussed in this study, the government infringed on the fair share of those who generated hard currency, found it necessary to use police force to secure conformity, contributed in a major way to the flourishing of an uncivic culture, and created shortages instead of abundance. More-over, though the redistribution was supposed to conform to the artificial price system prevalent in the entire economy, the desired effects failed to material-ize. Instead, economic distortions became widespread.

Policy controls tend to develop escalating consequences, demonstrated in almost all measures discussed in this study. In order to make it possible to implement one restrictive measure, additional regulations would have to be introduced. For instance, to obtain conformity to the rule of changing hard currency only in authorized banks, the government had to restrict the amount of goods travelers could take out of the country. The volume of exports was thus reduced and, in effect, the volume of hard currency flowing into the country.

The obverse side of the escalating effect of controls is also true. There is a tendency when excessive controls are imposed to have a descending order of compliance. The more excessive the controls the greater the tendency for them to be ignored or violated by the public, as well as by government officials. This response is at the source of the black market, in effect, an undeclared economy. As a result, a clandestine business environment emerges and blunts the effect of most financial and economic instruments designed by the government. The development of an undeclared economy is an indication of a loss of govern-ment control over public affairs, a phenomenon manifested in a variety of ways in the authoritarian patron state. Excessive controls reduced the inflow of foreign exchange and increased the outflow, despite strict rules made to force compliance in the opposite direction. When the Minister of the National Economy created the free money market in 1987, he partially justified it by saying, "There has been an increase in the financing [of imports] outside the banking system. That led to the loss by the relevant authorities of control over one of the instruments of managing the national economy."[62]

In addition, excessive controls are associated with excessive abuse. The freer the hands of the government to make binding rules for the disposal of mate-rial values, the more likely it is that power will be abused. For controls are not necessarily used to fulfill rational economic objectives but other objectives of the power holders, such as patronage and self-enrichment. A corollary to the free-hand proposition is that autonomous governments tend to be insensitive to rights of property. They make value transfers that cut deeply into the rights of individuals and corporations, regardless of whether the latter were public or private. Thus, the price of foreign currency was set officially below its real value for the purpose of giving the government revenue it was not otherwise entitled to by the fair play of economic exchange. Under such circumstances, intended victims naturally seek their own rescue and select defenses with which to elude the official threat to their rightful share of property. Not only do producers try to evade the law, but they also cut back on income-generating activities.

Distortions lead to gradual decline in the level of government control over policy, as the Egyptian economist Mahmoud Abdul-Fadil has explained:

> Control over the aggregate quantity of money and currency issues in the Egyptian economy has become an extremely difficult process since the middle seventies. This is linked to the fact that the authorities in charge of currency (and at its head the Central Bank) have been gradually losing their control over the conventional instruments of financial policy such as interest rates, exchange rates, domestic credit and the means of payments.[63]

Foreign exchange generation activity, such as exporting, was discouraged by controls in more ways than one. Artificially set prices of foreign exchange pushed the price of Egyptian goods up and made them uncompetitive in world markets. Exporters were deprived of part or all of the hard currency they earned from sales abroad, thus limiting their ability to promote their exports in foreign markets. They were also cheated financially when they were given less for the hard currency they turned in than its true value, often making their enterprise unrewarding. These disincentives discouraged Egyptian exports, which dropped to a very low level.

Foreign currency regulations also generated losses to the Treasury. During the infitaah, when the regime partially opened the doors to private sector importers, these importers bought hard currency from the government at the official rate, which was very cheap. Here the story is reversed. Instead of buying cheap and selling dear, the government bought hard currency dear and sold it cheap. One Minister of Finance, who during his tenure in the seventies could not change this strange practice, never stops marveling in his private conversations about the absurdity of government behavior.

As this discussion has shown, reform may sometimes prove less difficult than originally assumed. When Egypt liberalized its foreign exchange policies in 1987, the feared consequences did not materialize.

Chapter Seven

Education Policy
Idealism, Scarcity, and Civic Culture

DEVELOPMENTAL DILEMMAS IN EDUCATION

Nowhere is the clash of values and hard reality more evident than in the policy toward education. A country full of national pride and aspirations to achieve equality with advanced nations is yet shackled by poverty and an enormous illiterate population. The principle of nationalism, moreover, expressed in the takeover of most foreign schools and the downgrading of foreign languages during the Nasser period clashed with the need for students conversant with modern technology and scientific findings.

Stressing a policy of equal educational opportunity for all in a country with limited resources meant the primacy of quantitative considerations at the expense of quality. Progress made in higher enrollments was offset by the declining quality of education in general. The problem was further aggravated by the determination of policymakers to have full control over education. General policy, curricula, teacher training and recruitment, salaries, access, holidays, and exams were determined at the level of the Ministry of Education. Not until the eighties under President Mubarak did the university achieve relative autonomy, though national security considerations continued to take precedence over freedom of education and university autonomy.[1]

The regime's basic strategy of establishing control over services in the same way as it did over productive activities strained an already narrow resource base. Despite mandatory transfer of resources in the integrative development approach, expenditure on education fell far below needs. Policymakers thus had to distribute a limited budget across an extensive system, paying for salaries of nearly half a million teachers and for school infrastructure, without being able to satisfy either undertaking. A disturbing pattern of public and private behavior marked by frustration, cynicism, and law violation followed from the resulting untenable conditions. Egypt shares such tribulations with many, if not most, of the Third World countries.

EDUCATIONAL EXPANSION AND THE BUDGET

Rapid expansion in education was an opportunity and a risk at one and the same time—an opportunity for those who had no means of their own to go to school, and a risk that the limited facilities available might render their education inadequate.

The fifties and the later decades witnessed very rapid growth in the number of students. Tuition-free public education at the elementary and secondary levels was first introduced a few years before the Revolution of 1952.[2] From there on public schools became the main source for education in the country. Private schools, which were dominated by foreigners, suffered a major setback subsequent to the Suez invasion of 1956. The 300 foreign schools were either nationalized or put under strict government controls in the fifties.[3] The small number of private schools run and owned by Egyptians were not nationalized, though official ideology created an adverse climate for them. The main exception was the small and elite American University in Cairo, which continued to function with hardly any obstruction.

At the primary level, the number of school-age children enrolled in school rose to 90 percent in 1988. Actual attendance, however, was lower, and the dropout rate was estimated at about 40 percent.[4] There is a tendency among school administrators to inflate enrollment figures in order to obtain better allocations from the government for practically everything, from meals and supplies to teachers.[5] Adjusting the figures for such inflation would put Egyptian enrollment in primary education below the average of other middle income LDCs, and a little above average for secondary school enrollment.[6] The enrollment ratio of secondary students officially reached 69 percent of eligible youth in 1988, a sharp increase from 26 percent in 1965.[7]

Opening university education to all qualified students swelled the numbers in a very short time, from 91,300 students in 1961/62, the year tuition was made free, to 169,500 ten years later, an 86 percent increase.[8] The seventies, however, witnessed the greatest increase in the number of university students, from 152,200 in 1970 to 544,200 in 1980, a 258 percent increase.[9] Eight new universities have been added in the provinces since 1958, of which five were opened in the seventies to take the pressure off the Cairo and Alexandria universities. Growth in the number of university students slowed in the eighties relative to earlier periods, perhaps due to reluctance by the government to give ready employment to all graduates.

Free and equal educational opportunities have been guaranteed by all the constitutions promulgated in Egypt since 1956. This makes it practically impossible to charge tuition fees in public education,[10] though many educators at the university level feel that a change is necessary to keep up with mounting costs and to weed out unqualified students.[11] In addition to free tuition, the government makes contributions toward the general living expenses of students, plus insurance. Out of town students are provided with full room and board at a fraction of cost, £E11 per month.[12] A student who can prove financial need, moreover, is entitled to assistance in the range of £E25–30 for clothing, a monthly stipend of £E10–20, and three free textbooks. In addition, special assistance is extended to the handicapped. The total cost for support of these various needs came to £E30 million in 1987.[13]

Permissive university regulations added financial burdens to an already strained educational budget. The gratuity rules made no distinctions between rich and poor students. Moreover, university students were allowed a longer than normal stay before graduation. A failing student, for instance, had the right to get reexamined nine times in the span of four years.[14] Student failure rate was quite high. In 1986, for instance, 53 percent of all fourth-year students in the College of Arts failed to graduate.[15] In pre-university education, the law of 1981 stipulated that a student who fails in two consecutive years is terminated. However, the Minister of Education admitted that the law was not respected, and cabinet decrees made it possible for students to repeat a year for a third and even a fourth time.[16] That same cabinet adds 20 percent more students to university admission lists every year.

Allocation increments for education lagged behind student population growth. Official expenditure figures on education are scarce and often contradictory, nevertheless a careful perusal of these figures will show that government expenditure on education fell way short of the rate of expansion of student enrollments. This was true during the Nasser period, too. In 1951, for instance, the Ministry of Education budget was £E40.2 million; after thirteen years it had increased to £E96.5 million. Though inflation was low at that time, the increment was still small.[17] Nasser maintained that in the first ten years of the Revolution (1952–62) his regime spent twice as much on education as had been spent in the previous ten years. He also stated that the student population in general rose from 1 million to 3.3 million during that same period.[18] In effect, enrollment more than tripled while the budget only doubled. The budget for universities alone during the same period rose from £E4 million to £E13.5 million, while university student population rose from 15,000 to 100,000.[19] The budget thus increased by 338 percent, while student enrollments increased by 667 percent. The expenditure share per university student did not go beyond £E135.[20]

The education budget continued to lag behind during the Sadat period, to the extent that in certain years it fell below the inflation rate. In 1979 the education budget rose to £E407 million, from £E235 in 1975.[21] This constituted an annual increase of 18.3 percent, whereas inflation hovered around 20 percent or more. When accounting for the increase in student enrollments during those four years, it becomes clear that expenditure on education in 1979 fell below the 1975 level.

Two sets of data are given for expenditures on education during the Mubarak years; both put public expenditure on education below the rest of the African continent but above that of Asia. In the first scenario, based on a statement by the Minister of Education, Dr. Fat/hi Srour, the government's total expenditure on education in all its levels and forms came to £E1.3 billion in 1986/87, £E1,250 million for pre-university education and £E50 million for university.[22] Taking the budget of 1979 as a base year, the increase would amount to about 27 percent annually, barely keeping up with inflation. However, figures from the same official sources sometimes differ substantially.[23] If the true figure is indeed £E1.3 billion, then education would have received 7.2 percent of government revenue and 3.25 percent of GDP.[24] In low-income countries such as those of South Asia, it was 3.1 percent of GDP in 1985, while in Latin America (including the Caribbean) it was 4.4 percent.[25]

The second set of figures cited in the UNESCO statistics raise the perceived level of expenditure for 1987 to around £E2.3 billion and 5.9 percent of GDP.[26] The latter figure is comparable to that of 6.6 percent for the total continent of Africa and 4.4 percent of GDP for Asia. If those figures are correct, then the Mubarak years would compare favorably with the past. Still, comparative figures from the World Bank and other sources place Egyptian expenditures on education at the lower end of the scale.[27] It may be noted here that the shortfall in the financing of education has occurred despite large sums in aid given Egypt for this purpose by the USAID since the mid-seventies.[28]

Considering, however, that the national revenue of which the education budget is a part is itself low, expenditure on education turns out to be quite inadequate. According to Egyptian sociologist Madiha al Safty, the expenditure share per student has been going down steadily,[29] possibly as low as £E120 ($36) per student in 1987 according to the low scenario, and £E209 ($63) according to high estimates.[30] The lowest estimate comes from the National Planning Institute (NPI), which puts the figure for the official expenditure per student at £E26.8 in 1970/71 and £E52 in 1983, at the constant prices of 1970.[31] Other estimates maintain that the government spent about £E90 ($28) per student in the mid-eighties.[32] The comparable figures are $39 for Africa, $71 for Asia, $90 for Latin America, and $124 for the rest of the Arab states. The figure for North America is $1,349.[33]

It is not surprising, in the light of the low expenditure figures, to see that the ratio of teacher to student at the university was low and declining, even lower than for pre-university education.[34] In the humanities at Cairo University, Egypt's best, it deteriorated from 1:89 in 1967/68 to 1:180 in 1974/75.[35] In business schools in the late eighties the ratio was 1:294, while in law it was 1:140.[36] Only in the sciences (1:28)[37] and in medicine (1:13)[38] were the figures reasonable, though in both cases it was lower than the ratio in industrialized countries. In 1987 the ratio for all universities in general was 1:46, reflecting a marked increase in the number of university teachers in the first period of President Mubarak's term.[39]

Per capita expenditure on education has been declining steadily since the early sixties, and has in general fallen drastically below levels reached in the late fifties. However, some individuals remain more deprived than others, since more of those who are socially less advantaged never reach the university level.[40] In contrast, a large number of students from well-to-do families are being educated free at public expense over many years, including into the doctoral level. Still, opportunity for education since the Revolution has expanded markedly for less-advantaged students.

Figures on enrollments and expenditures show that the number of Egyptians getting to school increased dramatically at the same time expenditures on education lagged behind. The discrepancy has resulted in a lowering of education standards on all levels.

ENDEMIC PROBLEMS

Though education was made free for all at all levels, Egyptians ended up paying a supplementary tuition fee for private lessons. Because of the deterioration in the quality of education, parents had to pay for special lessons to make up for what their children did not receive in the classroom.

By the late sixties the claim that education in Egypt was free of charge and provided equal opportunity for everyone in the school-age bracket had already become a myth.[41] The wealthy and the poor alike, but to a different extent, were paying for special lessons, possibly in excess of what they would have had to pay in a private school system. One estimate of what Egyptian families were paying for private lessons in the late eighties came to nearly a billion pounds annually.[42]

The introduction of a nonofficial pay system through the necessity of private lessons reflected the wide gap between teachers' salaries and the cost of living. The public schools, moreover, failed in the following important areas: teacher training, textbooks, compensation, classroom space, and maintenance.

Aware of these problems, in 1988 the Minister of Education, Dr. Fat/hi Srour, set two objectives to his policy: (1) reconfirmation of the existing policy of democratization of education, and (2) the raising of standards in the quality of instruction. By democratization he basically meant reaffirming the principle of free and universal education. At present, access to elementary school is indeed almost universal but does not necessarily provide equal opportunity, nor is it adequate. Many schools have overcrowded classrooms, and some hold classes in shifts, generally two or three a day.

Teachers' Salaries

Low education budgets translate into a low salary scale for teachers at all levels, a fact at the root of the degeneration in the educational system. Pre-university teachers have been known to be the lowest paid of all government and nongovernment employees. The basic monthly salary of a starting primary school teacher is £E95 (£E1 equals about 30 US cents).[43] One should add to this about £E30 in supplementary payments and social security. In contrast, the annual salary for a third rank (al darajah al thaalitha) employee of the Ministry of Education, according to the 1986/87 budget, ranges from £E576 to £E1,608.[44]

University professors are also underpaid. A starting assistant professor begins at about £E120 per month. With the passing of time, however, a professor's personal enterprise may grow, and he or she may make a reasonably good living on supplementary pay and commissions, which can more than double the basic salary.

When one takes into account that in the late eighties a shirt cost no less than £E12, a pair of shoes £E15–25, and a kilogram of meat £E8–12 (with coupons it was about £E2, if one could find it and accept the quality), one realizes the odds against which schoolteachers had to fight. Rent for an average apartment in the distant and less desirable parts of Cairo was not less than £E50 a month during the eighties. A taxi driver stopped on a city street may well turn out to be a moonlighting schoolteacher. Taxi driving and other odd jobs are usually performed by those unfortunate pre-university teachers who do not succeed in cutting a lucrative share of the private lessons market.

In none of Minister Srour's reform plans of the late eighties does the cost of education come up as a serious measure under consideration. When asked during a panel discussion in 1988 what would be the best way to combat private lessons, improving the teacher's social conditions or prohibiting private lessons, he answered that one should start by improving instruction methods first. The only financial plan during his tenure to ameliorate the material condition of teachers was a decision to provide £E25 million to correct the situation of some 140,000 elementary school teachers whose promotion had been put off for a number of years. While on occasion admitting, at least in principle, that reform starts by improving the material conditions of teachers, the minister nevertheless has not taken or announced any steps to raise the salaries of nearly half a million teachers in charge of the education of nearly 11 million students.[45] He has, however, shown interest in building more new schools and in improving their design.

The extent of deterioration in teachers' salaries makes it very difficult for the government to correct this situation overnight. All the same, evidence that it tried is lacking. For their part, teachers are not agitating for salary increases. Many of them are doing well in the undeclared economy with extralegal activities and would rather stay with it. Many teachers successful in the art of private lessons have made fortunes and have bought private automobiles and apartment buildings. Improved official salary scales would be less lucrative than functioning in the undeclared economy. Thus, the absence of a reform movement within teachers' ranks is no surprise.

The Undeclared Economy

In the last three decades, a clandestine, or what might be called the undeclared, economic system in education has sprung up in conjunction with the regular school system. The undeclared economy in education includes private lessons as well as unethical examination management and fraudulent trade in textbook writing. Technically, private lessons are not illegal; they are, though, more or less a fraudulent practice, bearing the same stamp of the black economy we have already witnessed in other spheres of contemporary Egyptian life. Private lessons have had the effect of subverting the constitutional provision of free education and equal opportunity. This is because most public school students now pay for private lessons, and the rich can buy the services of the better teachers. The phenomenon has spread to university education, especially in recent years.

Since teachers find themselves paid almost a subsistence wage by the government, they have sought to raise their income by their own devices. There is no law against it, but the way the phenomenon of private lessons has developed in practice has to a large extent rendered it a corrupt operation. The private lesson phenomenon is not limited to Egypt, of course, but it has reached unprecedented proportions there.

Though known in earlier times,[46] private lessons started in force and on almost all educational levels during the seventies. The conditions leading to the thriving of private lessons have probably been summed up best by the Minister of Education himself: large classroom size, short school day, and low socioeconomic standards of teachers.[47] One should add also poor training of teachers and low quality of textbooks.

This extralegal system of private lessons, functioning as it does outside the regular school program, is expensive and yields disappointing results. Crowding at the university has contributed greatly toward the spread of private lessons, especially in professional schools, where large numbers make access to laboratories practically impossible. The high fees charged by the higher-ranking teachers have given an advantage to wealthy students over others.

In fact private lessons constitute a parallel system of private education on which millions are spent. A so-called middle-class family in Cairo with three children in school could pay over £E200 monthly in private lesson fees. Some low-income people in popular quarters of urban areas have been paying up to £E50 per month per student, and fees that low are possible only when the students are assembled together in groups of five to ten per teacher. Sometimes as many as twenty students were put together for a private lesson. In more recent years, numbers of students into the hundreds have been assembled for that purpose in one place, usually the premises of a private school building during off hours. The number of hours during a week that a student takes varies, but it could reach as many as four in some special subjects.

Private lessons are least expensive in rural areas, where school attendance is also not universal. However, according to one survey, the phenomenon is more widespread in villages: 71.5 percent compared with 63.5 percent in Cairo.[48] In a village in Kafr al Shaykh in the eighties, a private lesson cost £E0.5. Thus, a family with three children in school, two of whom are taking private lessons once a week, could pay a minimum of £E8 per month. It is a question of market conditions, commented one teacher in a rural area of Kafr al Shaykh province. "People here cannot afford more nor would they pay more than £E0.50 a lesson." Similar rates are paid in Cairo, where private lessons are organized by mosques at £E0.50 a lesson.

Community standards and the economic level of the individual are not the only factors determining the price. Teachers favored for their skills could charge as much as £E15 pounds and more per hour. With the approach of the opening school day, the rush to reserve the important teachers starts. "Important" here means either an effective instructor or one who sits on the examining committee. The subject matter of the lesson also makes a difference. Mathematics and foreign languages are more expensive than other courses.

Though the phenomenon has spread to some private schools, one finds the largest ratio of students enrolled in private lessons to be in public schools. The smallest ratio of students who take private lessons is to be found in the best schools, such as those known as private language schools. Private schools known as Arabic schools are generally considered weak, and among them one finds the highest ratio of students enrolled in private lesson programs.[49] Those schools have catered particularly to the needs of the nouveau riche students, who have low aptitude levels and cannot make it in public or private language schools.

Teachers have developed certain tactics, most of which are ethically questionable, to increase the number of students demanding their services. One approach is to deliberately avoid proper instruction in the classroom to create a need for their extra services. Another, flagrant method is to explicitly designate students who should have lessons. On the first day of class, teachers size up their students, figure out who among them enjoys the means to pay, then make their selections. Some families have complained that their children were given low grades though experiencing no difficulties. Those grades, however, were raised retroactively upon starting private lessons.

Another tactic used by teachers to compel students includes intimidation. From the first day of school, a teacher may declare: "I am not responsible for those of you who fail the course," meaning that the sure way to earn a passing grade is to take a private lesson with the respective teacher. Soon enough, students become convinced that there is no alternative, if success is to be achieved, but to enroll in a private lesson group. Since members of the graduating class (in primary, preparatory, and secondary levels) are examined at the end of the year by external committees, parents do not have to employ the same classroom teacher. Nevertheless, teachers of the graduating classes still have a leverage over students in that they determine 40 percent of the final grade. In his reforms of 1987/88, which will be discussed further, Minister Srour cut back on the teachers' leverage power, reducing their responsibility by half for determining the final grade a student receives at the end of the year.

Examiners have enjoyed a strong advantage for extraction. Some of them have gone as far as making it known to students and their parents that they could make examination questions available to them. This revelation, of course, makes the value of such a teacher's services very high.

The Minister of Education went public in 1987 against private lessons as well as the use of supplementary books. Realizing how powerful the hold of teachers on students and parents had become, he bypassed the usual practice of enforcing the formal prohibition on private lessons. His campaign was as much of a show as a moral stand, for it is known within his own close circle that he does not believe it possible to put a stop to private lessons. However, he proposed to combat the phenomenon by what he called "competition with private lessons."[50] First, he encouraged officially sanctioned private lessons to be given on school premises. These sanctioned lessons were referred to as "supportive lessons" (*durus al taqwiyah*, or *majaami' al taqwiyah*), one of the many official euphemisms. The idea was that a number of students could take private lessons taught by the teachers on school premises; the students would pay fees, but in reasonable sums. This legally sanctioned practice had been known for some time but had little popularity; only students who could not otherwise manage to pay for a private lesson attended these sessions. They were crowded, met at a very inconvenient hour before regular classes, and were associated with low social status. The government-sanctioned rate for a lesson was £E2–3 per hour, which was less than the market rate.

The minister's other propositions were not very practical, except perhaps those concerning the use of audio-visual aids. Inexpensive educational cassettes were made available to students and instruction programs on TV were strengthened. None of the measures taken apparently made a dent in the irregular system, and private lessons continued to flourish in the nineties under Srour's successor, Dr. Husayn Baha'-al-Din, another reformer.

The undeclared economy in education is, of course, an evil growth resulting from the shortcomings of the public instruction system: classroom overcrowding, inadequate teacher training, poorly written texts, an outdated educational curriculum, methods that require cramming of enormous quantities of educational material, and a short school day.

Classroom Overcrowding

School buildings have been in short supply, while school population has been expanding rapidly. In some city schools, a classroom may include as many as 110 students, especially in certain quarters of Cairo.[51] The range in 1987, according Minister Srour, was between 30 and 110 students in one classroom.[52] Elementary and preparatory classes meet only for half a day in 50 percent of the cases to make room for other students. Two shifts, morning and afternoon, constituted a normal load. In some cases, three shifts was the usual practice.[53] It has been estimated that in 1985/86, 40 percent of schools had more than one shift per day.[54] In Cairo alone, 50 percent of elementary schools held two or more shifts.[55] Schools lacking basic facilities were estimated at 36 percent, and those unsafe at 7.7 percent.[56]

A related problem that should be mentioned here is the insufficient time spent in class. The short school day is understandably the product of a space shortage, but the short school year is another matter. A long summer vacation, frequent holidays during the year, and a prolonged examination study break are responsible for a short academic year at all levels. The curriculum is designed for an eight-month school year, while officially it is only six months long and in practice even less.

Minister Srour has tried since 1986 to grapple with the problems of space and time spent at school, with little results. He first tried to extend the academic year as of 1987/88 by starting a few days earlier than usual. Then, the school day for elementary and preparatory school students, which started at 8 A.M. and lasted until 11:30 A.M., was changed in the fall of 1987/88 to start at 7 A.M., and last until 12 noon. The academic year remains, however, much shorter than it should be. In effect, short school hours and poorly written texts make it difficult even for capable students to succeed on their own.

Another measure introduced by Minister Srour to cope with overcrowding was to reduce the period a student spends in basic education from nine to eight years. It was hoped that the plan would reduce the number of students presently enrolled in the basic education level and create more classroom space for the rest. The result, as feared by parents and other critics, was a deterioration in the performance of basic education students, as indicated by a drop in the success rate in exams.

Teacher Recruitment

Teacher recruitment for elementary and middle levels constitutes another serious problem. The downgrading of schoolteachers starts at the very beginning of their preparation, when the weakest graduating students are sent to teacher training schools to train to take charge of educating Egypt's children. The government determines broadly who studies what subject at the university, using achievement scores as the criteria. The lowest on the totem pole are assigned to schools of education. Moreover, most elementary level teachers are not university graduates but hold teaching institute certificates. They are admitted to these institutes before graduating from high school.

In an effort to upgrade teachers' levels, the Ministry started in 1985 requiring that all new teachers have a high school diploma and be graduates of a school of education at one of the various Egyptian universities. The system of the Ecole Normale (*Dar al Mu'alimin*) has also been abolished in favor of a single, university system of teacher training.

In 1989 the Ministry started, with USAID assistance, to train adult teachers already in the system. The project was entrusted to schools of education, who created year-long classes for teachers to take after school hours. Lectures were also given on TV twice a week for this group. Those enrolled had very little incentive, however, to show up for class. They managed to pass exams by a variety of means, including permissiveness on the part of the program directors and cheating.

The recruitment and promotions system makes schools top heavy with administrators. Teachers are promoted on the basis of seniority. Thus, many become entitled to an administration poition such as principal or superintendent in a short period of time and start teaching less. Since there are not enough positions for higher administrators, many teachers end up drawing salaries, teaching short hours, and giving private lessons.

Texts

In 1987 the Minister of Education sought to improve the quality of textbooks. The required texts at pre-university levels are prepared and made available to students almost free of charge by the Ministry of Education. The writing and the production are of low quality, and students find them unappealing and difficult to use. They contain too much material and very few exercises and questions. Texts written in a foreign language tend to be full of glaring errors. Most students shelve them and buy supplementary texts at much higher cost, often written by their own instructors but more helpful than the official texts.

The widespread use of unofficial supplementary texts occurs in open violation of a law prohibiting the writing and use of textbooks that are not officially sanctioned by the Ministry of Education. Those complicit in ignoring the law include officials of the ministry, teachers, authors, and students.

Some corrupt practices have found their way into the textbook-writing business. Authors are often found to be in league with printers and sometimes officials to delay official texts from appearing on time, according to the Minister of Education. Delays in the date of publishing give a sales advantage to unofficial texts, which are made available from the first day of school.

In 1987 the Minister of Education waged a campaign against the use of supplementary texts, prohibiting their use. He insisted that the official texts were adequate and that improvements were being made. During that same period in which the minister made his statement, the leading official paper, *al Ahraam*, published a full-page feature with photocopies of material from official textbooks showing blatant errors.[57]

Needless to say, the minister's campaign had hardly any effect, and external books continued to be used and advertized on television, an official medium. Some education experts attribute the popularity of external texts to the fact that they are usually written by those teaching the subject matter, whereas the responsibility for writing an official text has shifted to ministerial committees of experts, who are somewhat removed from the scene.[58]

Before Srour's term as Minister of Education ended in 1989/1990, he had made some progress improving official texts. The competitive element he introduced into the system plus his personal involvement contributed to a measure of progress. The success of this system, it is clear, would depend on the alertness of both the minister in charge and the minister's assistants.

Cheating on Exams

Private lessons are no guarantee of success for a student. To secure a passing grade at the end of every educational level, starting with the passage from elementary to preparatory, many students have had to resort to cheating. One must cheat, and cheat with the help of parents, teachers, proctors, and officials. The process often takes a group form and therefore has been called by observers "collective cheating" (*al ghush al gamaa'i*). The practice had been prevalent for years when Minister Srour admitted in 1987: "I have even heard it said by teachers that photocopying machines were brought to the vicinity of schools in Kafr al Shaykh to copy exam questions and answers for distribution to students, not to mention loudspeakers [which announced questions and answers]."[59] He added that he was going to put an end to the common saying, "to pass an examination one studies, to pass with distinction one cheats."[60]

The forms of cheating varied. In some instances, schoolteachers or administrators would literally sell examination questions to students in advance. In one school in Sharqiyah Province, the superintendent of the school opened the envelopes containing the examination questions and held meetings in the theater hall of the teachers' club, where he divulged the questions in return for £E10 from each student.[61] The infraction was concealed under the pretext that the session was held for pre-examination orientation.

The power of the minister to stop irregularities was limited, for the administration of examinations was the responsibility of provincial government. Minister Srour publicly admitted his limitations. "At first," he said, "I tried to contain this phenomenon with a number of administrative measures. Regrettably no one responded. I therefore decided to face the situation and seek the assistance of public opinion. I held a press conference and put the facts before the public eyes."[62]

The case of al-Husayniyah Joint Secondary School in Sharqiyah Province in 1986 illustrates the advanced stage of degradation education had reached. Here, parents were the active perpetrators, driving a bulldozer through the school wall fence and into a classroom window. With the wall fence broken, these parents were simply able to reach through an examination room window, obtain a copy of examination questions from a student, write and photocopy the answers, then return them to the students. Yet, no action was taken by any of the parties concerned—not the governor, school administrators, teachers, security forces, or the deputy Minister of Education. Efforts on the part of teachers to stop that operation were neither serious nor successful. On the second day, the same drama was played out, again successfully. In one instance, a parent announced the answers through a loudspeaker. The minister admitted that year that the level of cheating had reached 73 percent.[63]

While other violent incidents were also reported in other provinces— Miniya, Fayyum, and Damietta, among others—the al-Husayniyah case was undoubtedly the most extreme, and the one that attracted national attention. Other forms of cheating-related violence included throwing stones and bricks at teachers and administrators if they interfered with parents' efforts to help their children cheat.

Eventually, the minister was able to stop cheating in the al-Husayniyah School, though provincial authorities were not willing to annul the examination results of 1987. In the country as a whole, the minister's efforts to contain the cheating wave apparently had some effect. The rate of success in the 1987 exams was lower than in the previous year, and, assuming that meant a reduction in cheating, the minister was able to take pride in that fact.

The preferred and more common method to ensure the passing of a student is usually handled with more subtlety. This practice involves extending favors to proctoring teachers, both locals and outsiders. Favors are also extended to school administrators to secure their cooperation. External proctors are hardly paid enough by the ministry to cover travel costs, let alone room and board. Local people made sure that they were well treated, to make their cooperation worthwhile. While conspicuous incidents of cheating were more or less put under control in 1987, these subtle and more common methods have hardly been touched.

A contributing factor to the ease with which cheating takes place is the reluctance of government officials to prosecute, or at least investigate, known cases. Reluctance to punish or reward is a behavioral pattern within the Egyptian bureaucracy. Government officials and policymakers are loath to put other officials on the spot. As Minister Srour put it: "In fact, we always tried in the past to conceal this phenomenon which has occurred more than once in fear of attributing wrong doing to an official."[64]

The subtle methods for cheating continue, however, and so do leniency traditions. The leniency system (qawaaʿid al-raʾfah) is organized through official committees, who find circumstantial evidence in favor of borderline failures. Even after the much-heralded educational reform conference of July 1987, allowances were made to permit low-achieving students to get into universities.

The attitude of those concerned—parents, officials, teachers, and others—is the most curious aspect of this situation and indicates the extent to which respect for the law and faith in the system had declined. Cheating has been tolerated as not only acceptable but as something really necessary. Parents were not apologetic. On the contrary, they acted as though it was their right to help their children pass by whatever means possible. As one source commented, cheating "is a matter which has almost become conventional and acceptable. It is thus no longer considered strange or as something new to see school administrations collect annually large sums of money from students before the examination dates, especially for this purpose [facilitating cheating]."[65]

The collusion of schoolteachers and administrators is in part prompted by the desire to obtain a high record of performance for their schools. The Ministry of Education rates schools on the basis of the number of students who pass the general examinations, and therefore school officials find it in their interest to increase the reported cases of success, even if it means inflating the numbers artificially.

By its inability to provide adequately, the government, in effect, transferred revenue away from teachers and academic administrators, whose numbers had risen to nearly half a million by the late eighties.[66] The benefits they received in the form of subsidies did not make up for what they lost in salaries and better teaching conditions. When one takes into account inadequate school facilities, it becomes clear that the integrative strategy of artificial transfers was not working.

Thus, failure to maintain adequate educational services resulted in widespread cynicism, corruption, and extralegal behavior on the part of all involved in the educational process. Establishing policies aimed at lifting the poor from the depressing condition to which they had been condemned for as long as one can remember is one thing, making such policies work was another.

Expansion of education leads to occupational transformation of the economy by increasing the supply of applicants for jobs requiring education faster than the economy can generate them. This tendency has created imbalances in the economy of many developing countries, Egypt among them.

PRIVATE SCHOOLS

While the Egyptian constitution guarantees free education for all, it does not prohibit private schools that charge fees. However, private schools came under stricter supervision as a result of the laws passed after 1952. Admission, fees, curricula, texts, and examinations were placed and continue to function under the supervision of the Ministry of Education. While some older private schools survived under the Nasser period, there was no growth in their numbers during his term.

Under the infitaah, the role of private schools remained quite limited. Moreover, they grew less rapidly than government schools in both number of students and number of schools. The ratio of student enrollment in private schools declined from 10.7 percent of total enrollments in 1975/76 to 6 percent in 1986/87. The same decline is reflected in the number of schools, where the ratio dropped from 17 percent of the total number of schools in 1975/76 to 8 percent in 1986/87.[67] By 1987 private schools enrolled 5.5 percent of all elementary students, 1.7 percent of all preparatory students, 14.3 percent of all secondary students, and 14.6 percent of business secondary students.[68]

Except for what is called language schools, many private schools have low standards and charge high fees, through both direct and indirect means. Many emerged to meet the educational needs of weaker students whose parents, mostly the nouveau riche, were willing to pay to keep them in school. Some went there to avoid a social atmosphere in public schools not to their liking.

Language schools, in contrast, enjoy a high reputation. It is interesting to note that the Ministry of Education itself has introduced similar schools for pay called Experimental Language Schools (*Lughaat Tajribiyah*), where foreign language instruction is offered. When accused of introducing an unconstitutional practice, the Ministry of Education replied that the constitution guarantees education to everyone but does not prohibit providing extra or special education such as foreign languages. Some critics respond that this argument glosses over the issue of equal opportunity, which is guaranteed by the constitution.[69] The number of these schools, of course, remains negligible.

Many Egyptian educators see in private schools a means to relieve the financial pressure on chronically strained government budgets and a way to provide a choice to those who could afford quality education. This is not, however, an unchallenged view. Others, some of whom are in high official places, see in the development of private schools the encouragement and deepening of social class differences.

The phenomenon described here is but one aspect of the dilemma of private versus public development options. Those private schools that offer superior or above-average instruction are few and cannot meet the rising demand for their services. Official restrictions have, moreover, discouraged a free-market response to educational needs.

According to the logic of private competition, shortages in services demanded would raise the price and stimulate supply until a balance between supply and demand is reached. After that point, fees start to go down as a result of excess supply. However, in practice supply has not been rising to the point expected—first, because of the small number of able and available agents who could offer quality education; and, second, because of competition from tuition-free government schools. Added to this are government disincentives, like official restrictions and interference in private schools.

Private schools operate under numerous official constraints. They have for decades been under the direct supervision of the Ministry of Education in matters pertaining to admission, promotion, fees, teacher recruitment, curricula, and examinations. Their students must pass the standard national examination in order to graduate. This last requirement by itself is not an onerous burden and is known in many other countries, developed and underdeveloped. The main problem they face, however, is constant interference from the Ministry of Education, which increased under the reform-minded Minister Fat/hi Srour. The fees they charge are regulated by the Ministry of Education, which has been allowing them a meager 2–3 percent annual increase. At the same time, in 1987 the government decreed that private school employees be given a 20 percent pay raise, far more than the increment made by the Ministry of Education for government schools.

The Ministry of Education put ten private schools under its direct financial and managerial supervision during the period 1986–88.[70] The minister also dismissed the school boards of several private institutions and appointed superintendents of his own choice. These schools took their case to court and lost.[71] The association of school owners held several meetings and conferences in 1987/88 in order to discuss the minister's policies.

Private schools have no protection against the arbitrary behavior or biases of officials. When managers of these schools tried to avoid the minister's order not to raise fees by requesting contributions from parents, the minister issued another order prohibiting all contributions to private schools. In so doing, he inadvertently deprived some private schools from charitable contributions for school buildings, land on which to build, or for aid to students from poor families. Protests by those affected were to no avail, and the web of bureaucratic controls closed more tightly on those who were in a position best to serve the educational needs of the country.

The Ministry claims that it is protecting citizens from grasping owners of schools. The evidence, however, shows a tendency for officials to interfere under the slightest pretext. Protest by parents against high tuition fees has encouraged official interference. Fees at private schools are high considering the standard of living and could go much higher. The irony is that many private schools offering education of average or below-average quality follow the example of the better schools in setting their tuition fees high.

Faced with official controls on tuition fees, private school owners and administrators have resorted to methods known since the Revolution started to interfere in the marketplace. School owners find extralegal gimmicks to make it possible to stay in the market. Not able to raise fees freely, they institute other pecuniary impositions on students. In short, they go underground and develop those clandestine tactics known throughout Egyptian society and designated here as the undeclared economy.

The Ministry of Education refuses to let private schools hire foreign language teachers or import texts, insisting that they use official ones, when it is well known that government school texts are deficient. Teachers and educators pointed out in 1987 flagrant cases of errors to the Minister of Education in a public meeting during which the minister was flaunting his achievements.

Though stripped of cash, national leadership continues to discourage nongovernmental actors from playing a role in education. Instead the government prefers a system in which parents pay low administrative fees and buy low-cost texts, then pay dearly for private lessons, external books, and cheating. "The country is all 'mixed-up.' We pay for corruption, but for the whole-some (*al khayr*), we do not." This statement is made, not by a critical parent, but by none other than Minister Srour,[72] the same minister who showed a negative attitude toward private schools throughout his career and who opposed the establishment of a private university.[73] Yet, he was frustrated with the system over which he presided, with its corruption, improvidence, and ineffectiveness. Both the minister's statement and his record clearly show that by trying to establish total hegemony over education, the regime's ability to control in fact declined.

The Private University Project

Nowhere is the clash of cultural values as evident as in the ambiguity expressed toward the establishment of a private university. The subject has been on the government agenda since the early seventies and as of 1992 remained unresolved, though millions in contributions have been promised by individual Egyptians and by corporations.[74]

After initial resistance, the principle of a private university was accepted by the Minister of Education in 1988, but disagreements persisted regarding practically every aspect of the project. The main divide has been between the old Revolutionary values of equal opportunity and elimination of special privileges on the one hand and freedom and pragmatism on the other.[75]

The educational debate in Egypt is imbued with a class and cultural bias. Those from the "refined" social groups, such as university professors, intellectuals, and the socially prominent, have, since the Revolution, become people of modest means. They have witnessed as of the mid-seventies the emergence of a class of nouveau riche who lack their own level of culture. This latter group includes craftsmen, traders, and people in various business pursuits who have prospered in oil-producing countries, through smuggling, or in the import business. The nouveau riche are able to send their children to private schools, driving them in and out in Mercedes Benz automobiles. University professors, in contrast, are obliged to chase taxis to reach their numerous moon-lighting jobs, day in and day out. The resentment against the nouveau riche by the "cultured" classes has therefore spilled over to the phenomenon of private schools and private enterprise.

The effect of the downward mobility of the cultural and social elite can be noticed clearly in their steadfast resistance to change. Some university faculty critical of the poor conditions of education and the results of the shortage of revenue, including poor salaries, oppose the introduction of tuition, and often even the establishment of a private university. They are also critical of private schools. For instance, the man who did the most in the eighties to defeat the

idea of a private university was the late Dr. Rif'at al Mahgoub, a career professor at Cairo University and speaker of the Peoples' Assembly.

Consider the argument raised by Dr. Rif'at al Mahgoub in the Peoples Assembly against the position advanced by some deputies who proposed instituting tuition and a merit system at the university. On the face of it, he said,
this suggestion seems to be a measure of compassion, but in reality (*baatinuhu*)
it is sheer misery. His reasoning is that in a pay system, wealthy students will
always be able to find a place, even if their scholastic record is below that of
the socially less advantaged. The wealthy with their power will take the place
of the poor, he argues, hence violating the principle of equal opportunity. In
short, Mahgoub's main concern was that he did not trust his countrymen to
respect the merit system.

The very same distrust was presented in a more explicit way to this author
by another influential academic at the University of Cairo, an individual often
found in the advisory councils of the ruling party. He argued vehemently
against introducing a system that charges tuition fees in general or for the
rich only. Because of the corruption and favoritism in this society, he said, the
wealthy will always be able to get into any system, fee-based or free, but not
the poor. In the current system, he argued, the rich and the poor are equal,
even though in mediocrity. Introduce a merit and pay system, and the only
ones able to get in will be the wealthy and the powerful, whereas the masses
will be left out. "I want to enjoy the favors of the present system, which makes
me equal to them; in mediocrity or not, it is equal." He continued: "The problems of the present system are more tolerable to me than the alternative." In
short, if he could not enjoy the advantages of the wealthy, then he wanted
them to share his disadvantages.

Many Egyptians have given up on the possibility of change in view of the
magnitude of the problem and have instead started to maneuver for advantage within the existing system, everyone for themselves. Individualism and
cynicism have replaced collective action and reform.

A variant of Dr. Mahgoub's argument is one that stresses the principle of
equal opportunity. We shall raise here the case of two scholars whose work I
used to prepare this chapter: Dr. Madiha al Safty, a professor at the American
University in Cairo, a privileged position; and Dr. Kamaal al Minufi, a professor at Cairo University, also in a way a privileged position.[76] Both have studied the serious shortcomings of the present system of education in Egypt. Yet,
when it came to the question of charging tuition for education or establishing
institutions in which the few could distinguish themselves, they showed outright opposition.

Commenting on the distinctions enjoyed by students of the American University in Cairo, Dr. al Safty stated the following about the institution at which she was employed:

> The very existence [of the American University] can be considered a violation of the principle of equal opportunity among Egyptians and creates distinctions among members of the same society, not only because it charges very high fees but because it enables its students to have better jobs than their counterparts in Egyptian national universities.[77] Moreover, the conditions under which instruction is done are far better than at national universities. With higher fees, the American University in Cairo can afford to provide better services.[78]

Dr. al Safty is critical also of private technical institutes and considers all institutions of higher education that charge fees as in "violation of the constitutional right of free education."[79] It seems that the cultured and the so-called middle class would rather have equality, even when it means mediocrity, than see educational distinction associated with privilege.

Dr. al Minufi also does not hesitate to criticize the principle of fee-based education, though he is very aware and critical of the existing system, in which everyone pays to sustain a corrupt system. In his comments on the educational policies of Minister Srour, he states: "obtaining education of distinctive quality in return for pay means making financial ability the criterion of differentiation between one student and another, and is an admission of the low standing of free public education. This constitutes a failure to comply with the principle of equal opportunity."[80]

One can hardly deny the merits in this argument, though in practice a viable alternative has not been offered. Dr. al Minufi is clearly opposed to private education, including the establishment of a private university.[81] His interest lies first with making tuition-free public education in Egypt respectable and distinguished. He does not think that expanding private education would solve the problem, since the majority of Egyptians will continue to depend on public schools. His argument, however, does not conceal a negative attitude toward private schooling, reflecting a deep-seated cultural norm pertaining to equal opportunity. Considering the financial disabilities of the Egyptian government, his views may in practice lead to the preservation of the same deteriorating conditions of the educational process.

Others have shown less sophistication than al Minufi in rejecting the association of educational distinction with privilege. In stating his reservation vis-à-vis the establishment a private university, Minister of Manpower ʿAsim ʿAbd al Haq warned that graduates of such a university may turn out to be more qualified and find greater demand for their services in the labor market. That would have an adverse effect on graduates of government schools in the employment market.[82] In other words, Minister al Haq prefers to leave everyone equally mediocre in order to prevent advantage and privilege for the few. Though views reflecting the other side of the argument have also been expressed, the position of Minister al Haq and others still reflect the dominant culture that has prevailed now for four decades.

CONCLUSION

The educational policies of the 1952 Revolution are expressions of ideals generated by the fighting spirit of young Egyptians who refused to accept injustice, the misery of poverty, and subordinate status for their country. Out of that spirit came such ideals as the right to education and to equal opportunity.

Their idealism, however, bears the seeds of its own frustration. In the complex set of ideals borne by the rebels of Egypt at midcentury, we can detect two sentiments that have had destructive effects on the progress of education and equal opportunity. The first is nationalism. Since the Revolution had to cope with the last vestiges of colonialism, its policies inadvertently contributed to the diminution of the right to an education. While Egypt gained control over the inculcation of values in the younger generation, the curtailment and loss of foreign educational institutions brought on a decline in the quality of education.

The second sentiment undermining education and equal opportunity is an overdrawn aspiration for collective responsibility. This principle, which in effect gnaws at the ideals of the Revolutionary spirit, states that only those who explicitly work for the "national community" were selfless and honorable. Those who began a private enterprise, say a private school, were acting out of selfish motives inconsistent with the good of the country. Those motives may be personal profit or the promotion of segmentary rather than national advantage. Hence, it was concluded that education should be carried out by the selfless agents for the nation as a whole. The fact that "public" means in effect the government, whose control and management have not proven to be either selfless or competent, is not considered. Moreover, the central question of how to pay the bill for a gratuitous and expanded system of education was not given sufficient attention, indeed, hardly any consideration at all. Moreover, the priority placed on expanding access to education was associated with a tolerant attitude toward mediocrity. Hidden under the ideal of equality, educational mediocrity became palatable to government leaders and many others throughout the period discussed.

Official educational policy has, since the Revolution, given rise to a number of tendencies adverse to development. First, when the financial cost for a public service assumed by the patron state is beyond its financial capacity, one or both of the following tend to occur: (1) the service offered falls below acceptable standards, (2) the government resorts to mandatory resource transfers to make up for the shortfall. Both occurred in Egypt.

Second, under conditions of slow or negative economic growth (or insufficient revenue in the Treasury), resource transfers are made at the expense of the producer and other earners of revenue. In this case, it is the teacher and adminstrator, the productive factors in the educational process, who are the victims of the integrative development strategy.

Third, when the government offers a free or subsidized service to its citizens across the board, regardless of need, the wealthier strata in society receive a greater share of government expenditures than their numbers entitle them to. This is as true in education as in other cases of subsidies. Moreover, the opportunity cost of education to the poorer segment of the population proves to be too high. Some among the poor may find that it makes more economic sense to put their children in the workforce than in school.

Fourth, when the decline of a service offered is deemed adverse to the vital interests of those receiving the service, they will buy additional units of the service outside official channels, making the gratuitous nature of government services a matter of appearances, not reality. Moreover, when private expenditure goes to support the official structure that delivers the deficient service, it prolongs the life span of the inadequate system. The paying customer's behavior precludes reform of the educational system as well as the emergence of a substitute delivery system. Hence, the extra cost for education paid by the client should be viewed as a hidden tax that maintains an ailing official system of education.

Fifth, when the government transfers resources from one individual or group to another, the party negatively affected, in this case the teachers, finds an irregular way to make up for losses incurred by the transfers, totally or partially, and at the expense of the system. By relying heavily on private lessons and moonlighting, Egyptian teachers made up for what they had been denied in fair compensation by the system. The effect proved detrimental to education.

Sixth, the policy of integrative development in the form of official resource transfers created a sense of victimization and contributed to the generation of devious public conduct. It engendered a culture in which disrespect for the law became a general rule, in effect undermining civic norms. Most disturbing is the feeling by citizens that evading or violating the law is a legitimate act and an unquestionable personal right to be claimed. Public policy that is perceived to be unfair generates anti-legal attitudes and corrupt behavior, in short, a socially disintegrative culture.

Seventh, particular policy biases, in this case against the role of private actors in education, has aggravated the patterns of behavior already observed.

Once again, we find that the artificial transfers of resources of the integrative approach have led to distortions rather than balance. Insistence on excessive controls by the central government has, as in other areas, resulted in a sliding scale of actual control and increasing irregularities. Subsidies did not sufficiently compensate teachers and administrators for the low salaries they received from the government. Moreover, not enough transfer of resources was made to cover the cost of building the educational infrastructure. Not being in a position to stand up to the regime, teachers and administrators resorted to individual devices to correct their situation. The undeclared economy in education partially compensated for the inadequacies created by official policies and contributed in a major way to prolonging the life of a deficient system of public education.

Chapter Eight

Housing Policy

The Limits of the Possible

MARKET-RESISTANT ENVIRONMENT

The story of housing under the Revolution and its successive regimes is again one of progressive government intervention coupled with comparable decline in the ability of officials to remain in control of the course of events. In a major way, shortages and irregularities in housing were due to the intractable nature of urban growth in the midst of an economically underdeveloped environment. This was in turn compounded by government intervention. The premium placed on land in strategically located zones, such as urban centers and port towns, created serious distortions affecting opportunity cost that drove land and housing rates up, while the purchasing power of salaried workers failed to keep pace with rising cost.

Government regulations, on the other hand, offered mostly an artificial solution, aggravating problems further. This incongruous situation and the subsequent rent-control policies are not, however, particular to Egypt and other LDCs; American cities such as Boston and New York have experienced similar problems and have had rent controls for decades.

Government regulation in this particular arena stems from familiar economic activities of the free market, particularly imbalance between opportunity cost and salary scales. Paradoxically, business establishments that fuel high opportunity costs in urban centers become the main victims of their own success. By driving housing costs up, they reduce the power of their employees to pay for housing; hence, rent controls, which rely on artificial nonmarket rates, are instituted.

Many managers of private businesses, usually at middle or lower levels, tend to approve of government regulation of urban rent, an attitude they share with politicians. Lower housing cost, whether real or artificial, helps the business community cope with the housing needs of its employees and with the high cost of real estate in the center of town.

The question here is what kind of regulation will reduce the intensity of the imbalance between opportunity cost and the purchasing power of tenants.

What we see in Egypt is regulation that stifles growth, creates shortages, and breeds subterfuge in the civil order. Moreover, government rent policies, in a vain attempt to create equilibrium, have in fact victimized one group of citizens while aiding or extending favors to another. To many of those adversely affected, such policies can only be described as extractive.

Government Intervention in Housing: Background

Egypt's economic problems are originally the product of scarcity, inadequate entrepreneurial base, low productivity, low-level technology, isolation, and grave income disparities. The disparity between the high opportunity cost at the core of urban centers and that of the outlying parts of the cities and the countryside is only one of the prevailing cleavages. These developmental problems and imbalances are not necessarily correctable by the mechanism of the free market, any more than by the heavy-handed interventionist approach of government. Both systems in Egypt, the liberal system and that of central command, resorted to futile juridical and administrative solutions.

Housing problems first surfaced in urban Egypt in the forties under the liberal regime of the constitutional monarchy, almost a decade before the Revolution. The value of land and construction material was going up much faster than wages and earnings, a disparity primarily caused by interrupted world trade during the Second World War. In the face of an economic imbalance, the constitutional regime under the monarchy sought a legalistic solution. First, rents were frozen in 1944 by military decree as an emergency matter, and landlords were forbidden from evicting tenants, a measure that gave the latter a right to the rented property for life. After the war, in 1947, the government made the order permanent by passing law number 121, whose effects are still felt to this day.

The first prominent venture of the Revolutionary regime into the housing issue was in 1952, at the outset of the takeover. Housing rents in urban areas were reduced by decree, a measure repeated several times during the first decade of the Revolution.[1] Rents were reduced first by 15 percent, then again in 1958 by 20 percent. In 1961, when socialism had reached its peak as an official government ideology, law number 168 reduced rent for residential buildings by another 20 percent.[2] Real estate tax on housing units was abolished after the Syrian secession in 1961, for imagined or real political causes.[3] This was followed by the sequestration of apartment buildings of politically undesirable elements. Large contracting companies were nationalized, and a ceiling of £E30,000 was placed on investment capital allowed to private contractors.

The last time the government lowered rents on housing units was in 1965, when apartments not affected by previous reductions were subject to a 30 percent decrease in rent. Furnished apartments remained exempt from those legal stipulations. Only foreign residents, though, rented furnished apartments.

The rent reduction measures affected all tenants across the board, including those in luxury units. Thus, the rich availed themselves of choice apartments at ludicrously low rents. It was not unusual in the eighties for one to find tenants of luxury apartments on the Nile paying an extremely low monthly rent of £E50 (about $16), while the market rate was over £E3,000. Tenants in older rentals in middle- or lower-middle-class neighborhoods were paying £E2–5 a month. Still, government rent policy continued to ignore changes resulting from inflation and from deflation of the currency, until the point when most older rentals lost all value.

As for developmental considerations, the regime took the position early in the fifties that too much private capital was going into construction and not enough toward industry. Accordingly, it created disincentives and limits on capital investment in housing to divert capital to other pursuits. In 1956 a cabinet committee on housing placed a ceiling on the amount of national capital that could be invested in housing at £E30 million, down from an actual outlay of £E70 million annually.

In 1962 and for the first time, the government established a criterion for determining the value of rent in newly constructed buildings. Though not to be applied to older rents, law number 46 stipulated that rent should be equivalent to a combined sum of 5 percent of the value of the land and 8 percent of the construction cost. These percentages were raised to 7 and 10, respectively, in 1977. Thus, returns were set low, and as of 1988, officially permitted returns from property rent had not exceeded 7 percent, though they could reach 10 percent when the law was successfully evaded.[4]

The sweeping socialist measures of the early sixties left no doubt among would-be investors in the housing sector that government intervention had tipped the scales radically against their interests and made housing a nonlucrative enterprise. Private involvement in housing, however, did not cease completely. Lack of alternatives in a government-dominated economy, the low cost of living due to "repressed inflation," and subsidized construction inputs kept it going, albeit slowly.

Apartment houses built and subsidized by the government did not exceed 5 percent of all housing units built during the Nasser period.[5] This was not the first attempt at government-initiated building for the poor, though; the last Wafd government during the monarchy period had started the practice by building two housing settlements in greater Cairo—one in Halwan and one in Imbaba—for laborers. The same regime also encouraged cooperative housing ventures through subsidies and land grants. Then, in the late fifties, the military, the police, and professional groups such as engineers and journalists, all possessing clout in the new order, formed government-supported housing cooperatives, each for its own profession. Intensive building was started by these cooperatives, especially the politically favored ones. They acquired choice government-owned land on the west side of the Nile, which is now a middle- to upper-middle-class housing settlement known as Muhandisin. The cooperatives also benefited from building subsidies extended by the government. The whole settlement, which constituted the major portion of new housing construction during the Nasser period, was built by private contractors.

Nationalization of the major real estate and construction companies in the sixties coincided with an emphasis on the role of the public sector in housing construction. After 1961 the weakening of the private sector in this area was carried further by politically motivated punitive measures against some owners of furnished apartments, whose property was put under the administration of government overseers.

The limited role of the private sector in housing started to change slowly after Sadat inaugurated the open-door policy. The private sector was urged to step in again, and entrepreneurs were encouraged by such measures as a raising of the ceiling on investment, first to £E100,000 and then to £E500,000. Foreign contractors were also allowed to bid in the Egyptian market with no limitation on the size of the undertaking, which made them the winners of very large construction projects.[6] Later, in the seventies and early eighties, the private sector was allowed to enter into trading and production of some building materials, along with the public sector.

The open-door policy represented a formal invitation by the government to the private sector to become active again. Housing—along with tourism, land reclamation, and poultry farming—were areas where the private sector developed the larger share of the business. However, old ills and new legislation continued to cause distortions and serious problems for investors.

Though promulgated under the Infitaah policy, the 1977 law continued in the same spirit of the previous regime. The law kept rents low, including new ones, despite the fact it was intended to encourage private entrepreneurs to invest in housing construction. The old rule of valuing rent at 7 percent of cost remained in effect. However, to provide some incentives to the private sector, the new arrangement stipulated that above-average and luxury apartments would be exempt from rent controls.

A new law instituted in 1981 to improve the conditions of the private sector did not make much of a difference in resolving the distortions. This law (number 136) maintained the same limitations on rents and stipulated that rates on already rented unfurnished houses and apartments could not be raised, regardless of inflation. Newly built units, furnished or not, were allowed higher rates, in recognition of changes in incomes and the inflation prevalent at that time. But once a rental agreement was reached, the rate became frozen again.

This freeze on rentals continues to the present, though projects to change the law are always on the floor of Parliament.

The government determined what kind of housing will be built annually, and both private and public sector companies had to abide by the official ratios. In the early eighties, the regulations specified that 55 percent of housing built nationally should be economy apartments, 37 medium, and 8 percent luxury apartments. As we shall see, those specifications were successfully flouted.[7]

The official restrictions imposed on rental property gave rise to a new phenomenon, as sales started to replace rents. This added a new burden on most Egyptians, whose incomes did not permit them to purchase apartments. To resolve this problem, the government as usual resorted to new legalistic measures and passed a law in 1977 prohibiting entrepreneurs from selling more than 10 percent of the units in an apartment building. In 1981, as a gesture of goodwill toward the private sector, the government raised the sale ratio to one-third of all units; the rest were to be designated for rent, provided they were not intended for private use by owner.

The new laws did not lead to a solution of the real problem of disparity between income and housing cost; on the contrary, they added new distortions. The disparities in rental rates under those laws ranged from £E3 to £E65 for the same type of apartment in the same area (table 8.1). The disparities were seen as unjust by investors and as a disincentive to growth.

In effect, the rent policies of the socialist regime subjected urban landlords to the same rule imposed on agricultural land since the fifties. Land rents were lowered and frozen too, but in agriculture the policy did not have an adverse effect on production, for reasons relating to the government's comprehensive package of agrarian reform.[8]

Table 8.1. Rent variation values for a medium-priced apartment in Cairo according to year of construction

Construction year	Monthly rent (£E)
Before 1944	2–4
1945–1958	4–8
1958–1963	5–10
1963–1973	7–12
1973–1977	15–20
1978[a]	40–65

Source: Hanna, Uridu Maskanan, p. 199.

[a]Rents in the late eighties for the same apartment listed here would be in the vicinity of £E70 to £E100.

By giving tenants and their rightful heirs, including close relatives, a life-long right to hold onto a rented property, the housing laws of Egypt practically allowed tenants to share in property rights, especially if property is thought of as a bundle of rights, rather than a single one.[9] Freezing rates in turn led to serious distortions, where rents paid on housing had no semblance to the cost of living. In short, serious distortions remained a major feature of the housing policies under the infitaah and on into the nineties.

A curious social phenomenon could be detected here, suggesting a reversal in the order of social asymmetry. Property owners, who are classically considered to be in the more dominant position, if not the exploitative one, become in this case the ones under duress who receive less than their rightful share of returns. In Egypt, it is preferable to be a tenant, in agricultural land and in housing, because of frozen rent rates. What originally started out as an official intervention to introduce fairness between parties resulted in stacking the cards against property owners and business entrepreneurs in order to satisfy a national plan.

Another interesting aspect of this reversal in the order of social asymmetry is the fact that in agriculture, many landlords who put their land under tenancy were themselves small owners. Thus, disputes between owners and tenants occurred among parties who were of the same socioeconomic levels.[10] Exploitation was not necessarily practiced by the rich but sometimes by the poor among themselves. In housing units, one could also witness the deprivation of those individuals in the middle class who invested in housing only to lose the expected returns for reasons beyond their control. Here again, not all landlords were rich families, though some obviously were.

FLAWED ENTREPRENEURIAL STRUCTURE

Leadership in the housing sector has functioned under crippling formal constraints and weak formal structures since 1961, when the government nationalized large construction companies and assumed the major responsibility for housing activities. Public sector companies were overstaffed, underfinanced, and lacked autonomy in making decisions. Like most other public sector companies, incentives to succeed were not evident and punishments for failure nonexistent. Thus, the flawed entrepreneurial structure aggravated the housing crisis in more ways than one.

One would presume the Ministry of Housing and Construction to be the authority in charge of housing, but in fact it shares these responsibilities with the Ministry of Planning and a host of other ministries, and with local government. Public sector housing companies, thus, are not all under the Ministry of Housing but follow different ministries and agencies. Not only does the ministry not have control over all the public sector housing companies, but it has little control over its own business. In the matter of hiring, for instance, the Ministry of Labor Force decides on a quota of workers to send to the Ministry of Housing, whether needed or not. In addition, the Ministry of Housing has no power to turn down a request from another ministry or government agency to have one of its companies undertake the construction of a project. This is referred to as *amr al-taklif*, a command system in which there is no bidding and prices are determined by representatives of the concerned ministries. If the Ministry of Industry, for instance, needs to build a storage depot, all it needs to do is request that the Ministry of Housing and Construction designate one of its companies to do the job. The difficult part, however, is handling payments for tasks performed. Government agencies in Egypt are notorious for being in arrears with one another. Various government agencies owed the companies of the Ministry of Housing about £E890 million pounds in 1987.[11] Cost overruns and chronic shortages in funds have aggravated this situation in the government apparatus.

The *taklif* system was terminated by the Council of Ministers in 1985, but not before it had done serious damage. By then, public sector companies were already on the decline and struggling to survive the best they could. The problems of delayed payments and cost overruns have not ceased, though.

In addition to the inability to collect money owed, these companies suffered from underfinancing, mismanagement, and underpricing. By means of the taklif system, high officials in the concerned ministries determine the rate for a service, which is usually set at lower than the going rate, especially because it is calculated on the basis of subsidized supplies. Those, however, are not always available, except at the higher, free-market rate. Since government allocations are fixed annually, a company that runs short of funds resorts to borrowing from banks at very high interest rates. The rating of some companies has been so bad that neither the banks nor suppliers would extend them credit.

Public sector companies did not necessarily execute their functions by themselves, and they may not execute them at all. In the first case, the company would resort to subcontracting in order to stay in business. It would outbid its competitors in the private sector by committing to a bid that is clearly unprofitable, then subcontract out to private companies. It is a step equivalent to deficit financing, but without the possibility of making a profit, only of going further into debt. Ultimately, it was the government, not company managers and employees, who had to pay. In effect, public sector companies played a middleman's role, the very same role advocates of government involvement in the economy attributed to the private sector and criticized as parasitic.[12] The public sector, evidently, does not deserve immunity from the same charge.

The other case worth noting would occur when a government-owned company would seek a contract for a project it had no intention of executing. The contracting company would outbid its private competitor, then distribute the advance money it received as salaries for its employees, who had not been paid for months. The work would not be completed, and the client would lose out. Any client who obtained a court ruling against the public sector company would not be able to collect, considering the company's connections and that the company was as good as bankrupt.

The private sector contractors, especially in joint ventures with the public sector, were not immune from some of the ills common to government-owned companies. Shortages in financial liquidity adversely affected joint investment companies and all-Egyptian private companies. To begin with, many of these companies started with disproportionately small capital, overextended themselves, and borrowed heavily from banks. Some borrowed ten to fifteen times more than their working capital.[13] It was a time of cheap credit, and they abused it.

Though the integrative development model is highly centralized, authority remains ambiguous at the ministerial level, leaving the question of responsibility vague and precluding efficient execution of policy. Moreover, as an entrepreneur, the government had assumed more responsibility than its resources or ingenuity prepared it for. It resorted to the force of law and to prohibitions to remove competition in housing. Its structure lacked unity and provided little incentive for officials in charge to succeed. The ability of officials to take the initiative and to adjust to changing situations was taken away from them by stifling bureaucratic rules and by the reluctance of the regime to delegate real authority.

HOUSING POLICY CONSEQUENCES

The effects of the measures introduced by the Revolution on housing availability were not felt until 1960, when shortages gave rise for the first time to the key-money phenomenon. A prospective tenant had to pay a certain fixed sum in advance, unrelated to the actual monthly rent, in order to acquire living quarters. Key-money was a sort of opportunity cost paid by the customer. The government tried to stop this irregular arrangement by passing a new law (number 52) in 1969 prohibiting side payments or key-money. Though this made it legally risky, the practice did not disappear.

The government strategy of the fifties to divert capital away from housing resulted in a drop in the number of units constructed. During the first Five Year Plan, the average number of housing units constructed annually dropped to 30,000, far below the 1950s figure of 56,000.[14] It continued at a low level until the mid-seventies. The average number of housing units built annually from the period of the nationalization decrees of 1961 to 1972 remained at

30,000. The government, whose role in housing increased, maintained low investment levels in construction in general.

The actual record of the Revolution in construction and housing shows that its leaders were groping in the dark without much understanding of the economic resources under their command, or of the results of their actions. One instance is the first Five Year Plan, in which national construction needs were grossly underestimated. In the Plan, growth in the construction sector was set at 0.4 percent, the lowest of all sectors, due to the regime's strategy of diverting investment away from housing and construction. Though in practice, growth in construction reached 11.1 percent during the Plan period,[15] the major portion of this increase went into the building of the High Aswan Dam and into industrial plants, not residential units.

In as far as housing is concerned, socialist measures led to a drop in housing investment levels in both public and private sectors, in line with the strategy set in the fifties. The rate of government investment in housing in relation to total government investment dropped from 10.5 percent in 1969/70 to 8.8 in 1973 to 5.9 in 1979.[16] Investment by the private sector shrank to a fraction of its previous size, and government investment failed to make up the difference (see table 8.2). For twenty years, 1960–80, investment in housing never reached more than 66 percent of its 1955 level. The data make it clear that during those 20 years, the private sector was discouraged and the public sector did not commit sufficient resources to make up for sluggish private investment.[17] Although by 1982 government investment in construction reached almost half of total government investments, much of this was for large infrastructure projects.

Table 8.2. Total investment in housing sector, 1955–1980 (in million £E at the 1967/68 constant value)

	Private sector	Public sector	Total investment[a]
1955–1960	328	40	368
1961–1965	89	114	203
1966–1970	139	78	217
1971–1975	78	68	146
1976–1980	89	101[b]	190

Source: Adapted from Mostafa El Araby (unpublished document, Winter 1991), who drew from the following sources: GOE, Ministry of Planning, Housing Plans; GOE, Ministry of Housing; USAID, "Immediate Action Program for Housing in Egypt" (Cairo, 1976); and Muhieddin, Income Distribution.

[a]Includes rural housing.

[b]Includes investment in the cooperative sector.

On the whole, during the period 1960–65, the public sector built 93,725 housing units for urban and rural residents, or less than 20,000 units annually, compared to 81,366 units built by the private sector.[18] Moreover, housing units built by the government in the period 1960–65 cost more than those built by private entrepreneurs.[19] On the basis of these statistics and the data provided in table 8.2, it can be concluded that a housing unit built by the public sector cost £E1,216, in comparison to £E1,094 for the private sector. Considering that the major share of housing construction undertaken by the public sector was for the poor, the cost should have been less than in the private sector, which built for the middle class.

There are several reasons why housing units built by the public sector cost more. First, public sector companies have larger overhead, due to overstaffing. Second, considerable waste results from negligence and theft, in which employees are deeply involved. Third, there are long delays in completion, because of administrative routine and lack of funds. Fourth, cost overruns and operating under capacity raise the cost of work done. Finally, public sector companies resort to subcontracting to avoid some of these problems. They generally make low bids in order to keep their employees and organization in business and then hope the government will eventually cover their losses.

THE NEW POLICY OF GROWTH

The growth-oriented policy in housing started in the late seventies and early eighties; it was in part a reflection of the government's decision to free the private sector and rebuild Canal Zone cities destroyed in the wars with Israel. More housing units were built (table 8.3), and they were larger in size. This development might have been caused by the 1977 legislation that freed quality and luxury apartments from legal restrictions to which other apartments were subject. Ordinary citizens in need of modest housing facilities continued to suffer, though, from chronic shortages and inadequate housing.

The first Five Year Plan instituted under President Mubarak (1982/83–1986/87), saw a sharp rise in government investment in construction, which reached almost half of all government investments. Not all of this went into housing; rather, much went to rehabilitate dilapidated infrastructure—bridges, highways, sewers, and so forth—in addition to building a subway for Cairo. Still, on the average, the number of units built during the eighties is superior to any previous record.

The total number of units built during the six years listed in table 8.3 is 928,146. However, for the first Mubarak Five Year Plan, which overlaps with five of the years in table 8.3, the number of housing units built was, according to official reports, 812,000, exceeding the planned number by 12,000 units.[20] Observers, however, maintain that the actual figure of units completed was not more than 650,000,[21] which makes sense when one figures in distortions due to official manipulation of data and inaccuracies. Whatever the figure may be, the effort cost the government about £E5.5 billion.[22]

The cooperative sector was the recipient of generous financial help from the government, but actual construction was done mainly by private companies. The government, for instance, financed only 20 percent of the total housing bill for the Mubarak Plan directly; the rest of its contribution went into indirect financing such as subsidies and low interest loans.

Taking the figures in table 8.3 on their face value, these figures show that by the beginning of the eighties, the number of housing units built had increased almost three-fold over the mid-seventies. However, while the Mubarak Plan targets were realized, the quotas established for different categories of housing were not. The ratios shown in the table differ considerably from the distribution designated in the Plan.

The Mubarak Plan stipulated that, of the 800,000 units to be built, 55 percent should go for low-income housing, 37 percent for medium, and 8 percent only for quality and luxury units.[23] Based on the data in table 8.3, the actual distribution would be as follows: low-income, 60.4 percent; medium, 24.7 percent; above medium, 10.3 percent; luxury, 4.6 percent.[24]

In effect, high-quality housing, which is exempt from rent controls, comes to almost 15 percent, whereas 8 percent was the figure designated in the Mubarak Plan.[25] Some go as far as to assert that the actual number of luxury housing units built is higher than declared, due to the practice of applying for licenses in other categories to avoid various impositions and disadvantages and then building the type desired.[26] At any rate, expenditure on luxury housing consumed the largest share of funds invested in housing: 55 percent of total investment, compared to 25 and 20 percent for low and medium housing, respectively.[27] The biggest loser in actual numbers is medium-level housing.

Private involvement started to assume a major share of housing activities in the late seventies. By the eighties, the formal private sector assumed the leadership role in the housing industry. In four years, 1982/83–1985/86, the private sector invested £E3,373.4 million in housing, or 74 percent of total housing investment at current prices.[28] Much of this, however, came from easy loans extended by the government to local government units and to cooperatives, who in turn commissioned the private sector for the actual execution of projects.[29] Thus 73 percent of the 445,500 units built between the years 1977 and 1982 were undertaken by the private sector.[30]

The growing volume of activity by private sector companies was in part due to the increasing reliance on subcontracting. In the interest of saving time and money, the government started to rely increasingly on the private sector

Table 8.3. Number of dwellings built by the formal sector in urban areas, 1981/82–1986/87

Type of dwelling	1981/82	1982/83	1983/84	1984/85	1985/86	1986/87	Change ratio (1981/82–1986/87)
Poor	96,334	92,841	88,739	83,830	89,547	109,329	13.5
Medium	36,707	46,622	35,710	28,827	34,493	47,937	30.6
Above medium	14,717	20,783	17,954	7,965	17,451	16,800	14.5
Luxury	3,411	8,331	7,550	9,042	7,009	7,217	111.6[a]
Total	151,169	168,577	149,953	128,664	148,500	181,283	19.9

Source: CAPMAS, Al Kitab al Ihsa'i al Sanaway, 1952–1987 (Cairo, 1988), p. 173.
Note: CAPMAS table measures the ratio of change starting in the year 1982/83; here the figure for 1981/82, the first year of the first Mubarek Five Year Plan, has served as the base year, hence the differences between the two tables.

[a] A drop in the number of units in 1981/82 from 6,748 in the prior year exaggerates the change ratio. Actually, luxury housing started to go up in numbers a few years earlier; the figure for the year 1980, 6,748 units, would provide a more realistic 6.95 percent increase.

in executing its own housing projects. Since the same housing unit built by the public sector cost more than one built by the private sector,[31] the government's tendency to subcontract to private companies is understandable.[32] The work value of subcontracts to private sector companies increased from 31.2 percent in 1974 to 56.2 percent in 1979.[33] Subcontracting contributed in a major way to driving the cost of housing up and increasing the financial burden on the government.

The private sector's lead over the public sector in actual construction activity increased during Mubarak's first Five Year Plan. While private companies completed 477,000 units during the first three years of the plan, the public sector produced only 15,000.[34] The public sector thus achieved only a little over one-half its projected target under the Plan. The private sector, in contrast, realized a little over 100 percent of the target assigned to it. This trend continued into 1990, when the private sector's share of housing reached 80 percent.

Considering market conditions, an explanation of the leap in building units in the eighties is in order. First, the government itself sharply increased investments in housing; that amount reached £E1,100 million in 1981.[35] Other factors included the incidence of high liquidity levels in the country and limited investment opportunities in other areas. Expatriate workers invested some £E700 million in housing by 1981.[36] The liberalization of import policies have also contributed by reducing chronic shortages in building materials.

Moreover, housing, along with food industries and land reclamation, was an area in which investment was encouraged by the government. Rates on loans for building medium- and low-income housing were set far below commercial rates; the difference was paid by the government. The government extended credit to local housing projects and cooperatives in the form of long-term loans: £E8,000 per housing unit at 4 percent interest, repayable in 20 to 25 years.[37] In all, the amount allotted by the government to cooperative housing construction was £E150 million per year,[38] or £E750 million during the Mubarak Plan period.

Housing cooperatives were thus the main beneficiaries of the subsidized interest rate, though they have been taken to task for increasingly engaging in land speculation rather than in low-income housing.[39] The middle class rather than the very poor have been the main beneficiaries of cooperative housing activities, being the ones able to organize and take advantage of favorable credit terms.

The government continues, however, to turn to the cooperative sector in housing and local government housing agencies to provide medium- and low-income housing. In 1987, the sum of £E450 million in low-interest loans were allocated to the cooperative sector, government-owned companies, and local governments to build 120,000 low-cost housing units. Only the cooperative sector received loans in time to build the 30,000 units under its charge,[40] which amounted to 10 percent of the housing units planned for 1988. The government in addition extended the grace period for repayment from 30 to 40 years for a large number of units built by cooperatives in six provinces. Similarly, interest on loans for production of building materials was set low, at 8 percent. The annual average of easy loans was £E445 million in the eighties.[41] The subsidy, which was borne by the government, reached £E10,000 per unit,[42] while total subsidy for housing was estimated at £E300 million in 1987.[43]

Providing incentives without being directly involved in business enterprise seems to have worked in this case, for cooperatives did produce positive results in the housing sphere, better at least than government building companies. Inevitably, however, when there are two price rates, irregular behavior ensues. In this case the lure of speculation eventually engulfed cooperative societies. The extent of the damage, though, is not clear.

The Undeclared Economy in Housing

Much of what goes on in building activities in Egypt ignores the law. It is the type of irregular activity in which perpetrators make no declaration, and thus, by not informing the government of their plans, avoid its sanctions. When such acts become widespread, the cost of undoing them becomes prohibitive and the will to do so dissipates.

Extensive government regulations and restrictions have contributed to irregular behavior of entrepreneurs within the housing sector, public and private alike. As a result, Egyptians have developed the tendency to circumvent the law by all sorts of subterfuge, and they behave as if the government and its laws did not matter. A great deal of housing activity was concentrated in the informal sector and undertaken by small entrepreneurs, who could not or did not want to abide by government laws. Building activities that ignore the law are referred to in Egypt as unorganized housing (binaa' 'ashwaa'i), because they violate building and zoning codes and are mostly unlicensed.

The undeclared economy is the product of the integrative development approach of the patron state, which by its excessive resort to legalistic and administrative measures to solve problems has driven people outside the law. This in turn led to government loss of control over policy and over the conduct of individuals, including government employees. To avoid onerous regulations and what was viewed by some affected parties as extractive official measures, many resorted to underground practices. Most such irregularities were committed with a certain sense of self-righteousness by people who felt wronged by the government or left without a choice. The following sections briefly discuss the type of illicit activities that developed in housing as part of the undeclared economy.

Vacant Apartments

One of the first impacts of housing legislation in the eighties was a rise in the number of vacant housing units. The figure was shown by the 1986 population census to be a staggering 1.8 million, yet demand for housing was estimated at about 200,000 units annually. The revelation fell like a bombshell over the public and took the government by surprise. Questions were raised in the Peoples' Assembly, and the Housing Committee requested an explanation from the Central Agency for Public Mobilization and Statistics (CAPMAS). Some raised doubts regarding the accuracy of the figures; others tried to explain away the discrepancy, citing that some people have summer homes and that the figure includes apartments of expatriate Egyptians who will sooner or later return home.

There are other explanations, however. The 1981 Housing Law freed luxury apartments from rent controls and as a result supply exceeded demand in this category. A large number of apartments had no suitable buyers. Did entrepreneurs act irrationally by pricing themselves out of the market? Not entirely. Many owners preferred not to sell but to keep apartments empty for future contingencies, including the housing needs of their offspring. The practice works as a guarantee for the future in a society where housing is in short supply. Other owners prefer to maintain empty apartments for speculative reasons, since prices have been appreciating rapidly. Many entrepreneurs achieve that same objective by leaving an apartment building unfinished, thus keeping it unsuitable for habitation. It is a way of avoiding unfavorable rental laws. In general, since the law allows a very small proportion of units to be put up for sale, while rents are unrewarding apartments remain vacant.

Even public housing became too expensive for the average Egyptian. This was clearly the case in the newly built industrial towns of the Tenth of Ramadaan City, Sixth of October, and al Salaam City. Prospective buyers found that what was offered was inadequate or very expensive. Many of the apartments remained unoccupied, while many workers commuted daily from and to Cairo. In the desert-located al Salaam City, 30 percent of newly built housing units remained vacant.[44] Though there are other reasons why buyers failed to purchase units in those cities, cost has been considered a major factor.

Government regulations have contributed to the phenomenon of vacant apartments in more ways than one. The law stipulated that only 10 percent of the units in an apartment building (raised by law number 136 [1981] to 33 percent)[45] could be offered for sale, and the rest must be rented. To avoid this restriction, entrepreneurs resorted to forming a landowners union composed mainly of relatives and friends, each one of whom would nominally own an apartment unit. The sale then could be made in their names but in the interest of the real owner of the building.

Law number 136 also specified that units designated for rent should not fall below two-thirds of a building's units, while return on rent should not exceed 7 percent of land and building value combined. At the time the law was passed, interest rates were low. But when interest rates went up later to 12 percent and more, no cost adjustments were made in the law. Returns from rental property thus worsened. It became more profitable for one to simply draw interest on deposits in the bank (at about 14 percent) than invest in housing. Had it not been for their ability to evade the law, few entrepreneurs would have ventured into the housing business.

Because of unfavorable official regulations, owners of private housing units assiduously shunned rentals and instead put some of their residential units for sale. To free themselves from unfavorable legal constraints on sales, owners resorted to subterfuge. One approach was to sell the units to cooperatives, since the law exempts cooperatives. Sometimes, the owner remained a partner, real or figurative, with the buyer. Another method was for owners to designate on paper a number of units as high-quality housing, which was not subject to the 7 percent profit rate. It could always be arranged with inspectors to approve the infraction for a small price.

Another reason for the prevalence of vacant housing units was the reluctance of owners to sell by installments; this is because the law worked against them in such instances. The law stipulated that buyers defaulting on payments lost their property claims to the unit, though they could continue to hold onto it as rented property. Purchase by means of installments then became a contrived way to rent, which entrepreneurs originally went to a lot of trouble to avoid. Since the advantages to clients of tenancy are strong—relatively fixed rent rates, lifelong tenure—the law has in effect encouraged customers to default on their mortgages.

Government legislation in housing not only produced counterproductive results but also had a corruptive effect on public conduct. Because of impractical legal provisions, rent contracts became informal and arranged by the parties, according not to the law but to the market rate on which agreement could be reached. Owners could also avoid the strictures of the law by exaggerating building costs when reporting to the government. The largest and most commonly practiced infringement of the law, however, was key-money (*khulu rigl*). It was a required sum, paid in advance of assuming residency in an apartment. One study estimates that 53 percent of new tenants in the period 1976–81 paid key-money, on average £E1,387.[46]

Another way to circumvent the law is for the landowner to cite to the prospective tenant a figure that, though untrue, would set the rent at market rate or close to it. Sometimes this happened before buildings were finished, a situation that gave owners an excuse, in case of official investigation, to claim that uncertainty had been a factor in their estimate. Prospective tenants had ninety days to appeal to the rents committee set up by the government, after which they lost their opportunity to readjust the rent. They could still resort to the courts, a long and costly process. Despite the possibility of circumventing the law, the number of nonluxury units put up for rent on the market remained negligible.

This is not, as we have already seen, the first time in which public conduct turned crooked because the law ran counter to reasonable expectations in economic transactions. A law that forces businesspeople to operate at a loss will also force them either out of the market or underground. In effect, the housing policy led to a situation where customers wanted rentals that were not available, and owners wanted buyers who were in short supply. The result was a sluggish housing market and an increase in the number of vacant units.

Illicit Housing Construction

Housing specialists in Egypt refer to the phenomenon whereby low-income housing is constructed and made available to customers entirely outside official policy parameters as binaa' 'ashwaa'i. [47] One does not have to go outside Cairo to see illegally built housing; Faysal Street, a main thoroughfare leading to the Pyramids, is full of them.

Illicit housing construction has been quite extensive; it is estimated to comprise three-fourths of all housing built from 1970 to 1985.[48] Nearly three thousand hectares of agricultural land around Cairo were built up illegally to provide occupancy to over 1.5 million inhabitants in greater Cairo.[49] Growth in real estate on the periphery of Cairo has been very dramatic, reaching, in 1984, 8 percent compared to 2.5 percent only in the city center.[50] In the provinces, the legal sector in real estate did not cover more than half the housing development.[51] Some specialists have claimed that 40,000 feddans (1 feddan equals 1.038 acres) of agricultural land are converted to real estate annually.[52] Although illegal, housing built on agricultural land has met the needs of low-income people; however, it also deprives Egypt of a considerable part of its scarce agricultural land.[53] One area of over a million inhabitants, northeast of Cairo, was even erected on land that had been reclaimed for agricultural purposes.[54]

By the late seventies, as demand for housing increased and a certain liquidity became present among lower- and middle-class Egyptians, individual entrepreneurs emerged to meet the demand. Some owned agricultural lands located on the periphery of urban centers, where building residences or business establishments was prohibited by law. Entrepreneurs, however, ignored the legal prohibition. Some broke the law by failing to obtain a building license from the authorities in order to save money and time.

The new entrepreneurs who stepped in to exploit this opportunity often did not have liquid capital of their own. Many were small peasant landowners or small entrepreneurs who acquired capital by working abroad. They also included small real estate companies who speculated in land purchases.[55] An entrepreneur would usually purchase a few acres of agricultural land and then divide it up into small plots for sale. Some chose to undertake the construction of housing units themselves on the designated land.

The process worked in this way.[56] Those owning pieces of agricultural land would convert them to housing projects. A very small parcel of land, say, 0.1 feddan, is of practically no value for agricultural investment but could make a lucrative housing project. In cases where the land exceeded what was needed to erect one apartment building, owners would sell part of their land for a good price, then with the acquired funds build an apartment for themselves and their families. The business side of the venture would appear when the owner offered to build an apartment on an additional floor for a customer if the latter would advance a reasonable sum for construction. The advance payment would be deducted from future rent payments. With advance capital, good for some ten years or more of rent, the owner would proceed to add a new apartment, and then another and another.

In some cases, an owner would sell a share of a parcel of land to raise capital with which to erect an entire apartment building on what remained.[57] Either way, poor peasants could change their mode of life from that of a producer to a landlord in real estate. Often, those who became small entrepreneurs followed diverse pursuits and on the whole improved their standard of living.[58] The main questions, though, pertain to the environment and the loss of land in a country where agricultural land is extremely limited. With many of these structures huddled together and lacking proper sanitary conditions, an already serious pollution problem in the capital was made worse.

The transactions described here are extralegal. Starting in 1966, the law prohibited the conversion of agricultural land into housing projects. Nevertheless, violators of this and other housing codes for the most part went unpunished. They connected their housing projects to public utilities such as water and electricity sometimes at their own expense, but more often through the goodwill of local governmental agencies, despite the illegal aspect of the enterprise.[59] In almost all cases, the government consented to the de facto situation and legalized the enterprise.[60] Local authorities not only provided services but also gave licenses to shops and businesses that had been built illicitly.[61] Practices such as these are fairly widespread in other LDCs struggling with poverty and rapid urban growth—for example, in Latin America.[62]

Illicit housing units managed to avoid the disadvantages of rent controls because, being illegal, they went officially unrecognized. These owners enjoyed considerable freedom in setting their rental rates and, in many cases, abused it.[63] In 1987 the Minister of Local Government acknowledged the widespread incidence of illegal housing. He admitted that many people were in violation of the law, building without licenses, paying no taxes, and not subject to rent laws. Apart from continuing to turn a blind eye, the government's alternatives were to dismantle them or to bring the perpetrators to court, both impractical considering the large number of violators, the huge investments in the structures, and the inability of the government to find housing for the would-be evicted residents. The situation, the minister complained, had run out of control.[64]

Governors of provinces facing severe housing shortages tended to accept de rigueur the illegal situation of new houses. The governor of Damietta Province, where severe housing shortages existed, stated clearly that the national government should legalize the underground sector by including the new areas within the urban housing zones. Short of that, the governor continued, alternative houses and shops should be established to take their place. The latter option, he added, is extremely difficult because we have a long waiting list in this province for new houses and we give priority to extreme cases.[65] The Minister of Local Government seems to concur. "In the end," he says, "we are obligated to license them [the illegally built houses]."[66] Thus, there is a general recognition that while this type of housing violated official regulations, it did serve a public need and respond to the logic of the market.

Urban encroachment on agricultural lands has taken another sinister turn with the practice of skimming the topsoil (tagrif) for brick making. Until the late eighties, tagrif was a very serious problem. The flow of silt that the Nile brought down to enrich the land of Egypt almost totally stopped after the completion of the High Aswan Dam in 1965. Builders, thus deprived of their regular supply of raw material for making mud bricks, began using the topsoil of agricultural fields. The seventies and early eighties witnessed an alarming increase in this practice.[67]

The law prohibiting removal of topsoil for brick making reflects the tendency of government to attempt to solve real problems by passing laws and decrees. Those decrees did not answer the public's need for material with which to build bricks. The question of alternatives to mud bricks was not seriously addressed by the government until the eighties. Eventually, however, the choice was made to have bricks made out of clay, of which Egypt had an abundant supply. Clay bricks are considerably more expensive, though, and the practice of skimming topsoil continued unabated until 1985, when the government clamped down firmly on red brick factories. The problem remains, though, on a small scale. To this day one still finds tall chimneys of brick factories ejecting black smoke in the Delta and al Fayyum.

The skimming of topsoil was related to illicit housing practices in that, once the topsoil was removed, owners could make additional profit by using the land for housing projects. The combined profits from tagrif and construction proved to be a strong incentive for development of illegal housing on agricultural land. The tacit official consent suggests that the government was losing control—no longer leading its citizens, but rather, following them. On the other hand, the illegal housing tendency shows a growing public disrespect for government and lack of faith in its ability to solve urgent needs.[68]

Subsidies of building materials for special groups contributed to black market activities. Housing companies of the public sector, local government, brick making industry, private sector companies, and, last of all, merchants were entitled to quotas of subsidized building materials such as cement. For instance, in 1988 a subsidized ton of cement was worth £E53, while in the free market it could fetch anywhere from £E90 to £E120. As a result, the black market in cement developed. The participants included former high-ranking officials who secured quotas for themselves after setting up in business and whose entire business consisted of selling their subsidized shares on the black market. Bona fide contractors and public sector companies also found it more lucrative to trade in black market commodities than to engage in building activities.

Housing policies have also contributed to capital flight and to building dilapidation. Disincentives in urban real estate led harassed entrepreneurs to seek safe havens for their money abroad. Moreover, since owners of rented property had no incentive to spend on maintenance, buildings became dirty and shabby, with elevators that rarely worked. Maintenance in government-owned buildings was generally considered a low priority, and one would have to say that it was nonexistent in most cases.

Insofar as the needs of citizens were concerned, the illicit ventures in housing were functional. They helped meet the housing needs of large numbers of people who otherwise would not have found adequate living quarters. On the other hand, illicit housing activities were disorganized, often unsafe, in violation of basic zoning requirements, destructive of agricultural land and the environment, lacking hygienic and civic services, and ugly. Crowding was typical in city quarters that were built illicitly.

Unlike what de Soto reported from Peru,[69] illicit activities in housing in Egypt were neither collective nor organized. There were no takeovers, except of small areas of government lands by individuals often receiving disguised cooperation from government officials. In the majority of cases, the actors were single household clients and single sellers. Sometimes more than two individuals would be involved, for example, in an extended family of two generations, or groups of friends and neighbors. There was never any coordination of the illicit activity in advance with the neighborhood or local government. Once established, neighborhoods that were built illicitly often sought to secure services such as water and electricity from local government.

Functional as the product of illegal housing turned out to be, it is not a path that has much to recommend it for the future of Egypt or any other developing country. Those individuals who committed the illicit acts, and the government that provided the incentive or the excuse, have both performed poorly. The government failed to provide what was needed and succeeded in obstructing those who could provide, and the needy failed to confront the authorities in an organized and collective effort to introduce reforms. Instead, people resorted to individual acts of subterfuge, with all acting for themselves. This "save myself" attitude reflects a sense of abdication of one's right to affect policy and change what is not right in the system. Thus, it would be inappropriate to endorse, as Hernando de Soto seems to do in *The Other Path*, choices citizens make under duress—in this case, illicit housing as an adequate alternative to sound policy. Wherever illicit conduct becomes the common culture, something serious is plaguing the community and reflecting a condition of disorder in government and society alike.

CONCLUSION

Official housing policy from the time of the Revolution,[70] and even before, has had serious and adverse effects on the national economy and on attitudes of citizens. When the government put limits on the freedom of entrepreneurs, then reduced and finally froze rents, it acted in the name of social justice for low-income people. Rents were not adjusted to inflation but remained frozen for decades, reducing returns on property to practically nothing. Owners receiving meager returns on their property allowed it to deteriorate, thus reducing the number of housing units fit for habitation. Since the law also gave tenants occupancy rights for life to them and their posterity, it practically bestowed property rights on tenants while depriving the actual owners of their full property rights. Thus, the government's position left a great deal of uncertainty about property rights and business returns. In effect, incentives for growth were stifled, and the situation led everyone to understand that wisdom is not to be found in public agencies. What seemed to be an official effort to create conditions of relative equality served neither the supplier nor the customer.

Housing policies such as the ones outlined here breed an uncivic attitude by creating conditions that make it possible and even fair to flout official rules.

This attitude reflects an emerging culture based on the principle that it is right to violate or circumvent the law. A society in which such convictions are common is no longer a civic society and therefore cannot serve as a model for development.

Housing policy reflected the emphasis on central control and transfer of resources in accordance with national objectives. Decision makers showed little sensitivity toward the shifting of burdens as a result of their machinations. The government had the power to make the laws but not necessarily the skill to win public cooperation. The practice of forcing untenable conditions on people for some abstract or generalized goal was proved, as would be expected, self-defeating and obstructive. Overregulation and ineffectiveness prompted one student of housing in Egypt to raise the question of whether the "government errs by its excesses or by its faulty interventionism . . . by being present everywhere, [the government] is impotent everywhere and has lost credibility."[71]

Official housing policy has been criticized from different political and ideological perspectives. One jurist considers government housing policy unrealistic, maintaining that it overlooks inflation and the general cost of capital. This same jurist has also maintained that the policy is unconstitutional. The Egyptian constitution guarantees the right to private property, which includes the right to use and exploit the object owned. This is not true in the case in housing, she argues, since landlords do not enjoy the right to use their property freely. Hence, property rights are nominal, or at best limited. An owner of an apartment has only the right of title but not of free usage. Consequently, owners who leave their apartments vacant are expressing a point of view, she adds. By holding only to ownership title and refraining from using the property, proprietors assert the only right left to them, while denying others any rights.[72] Curiously, these feelings are shared by many high government officials, including former ministers, who find it easier to speak their minds when they are no longer in office.

A diametrically opposite view is advanced by Milad Hanna, a leftist intellectual who is an expert on housing in Egypt and a former member of the Peoples' Assembly. He considers the vacant apartments phenomenon as speculative, immoral, and a deviation from proper conduct.[73] On the other hand, Hanna has criticized the frozen rent policies and the very low returns officially set on real estate property.[74]

Imaginative solutions to real problems such as this one are often more effective than the passing of punitive and restrictive measures. In the eighties, some public sector banks such as the Real Estate Egyptian Bank (al Bank al 'Iqaari al Misri) devised a plan that, in effect, circumvented the limited capital among potential buyers and the fears landlords have of discrimination against them. The plan aims at enabling prospective housing candidates to buy their own apartments. An individual opens a savings account at the bank, beginning with a down payment, then makes monthly deposits for five years. After the completion of the five-year period, the bank enables the depositor to buy an apartment of his of her own choosing, or one chosen by the bank itself. From this point the financing works like a mortgage. With large savings in the bank, the possibility of default by the buyer is reduced and the seller would no longer be wary that the unit might be converted to rental property.

Another successful endeavor was cooperative housing in which the government supported private initiative with concrete measures, without taking over the responsibility for decision making or instituting crippling regulations. Despite criticism of the cooperative sector in housing and the many irregularities committed, it remains the sector responsible for more positive results than any other.

Chapter Nine

The Cultural Dimensions of Economic Policy

CULTURE AND DEVELOPMENT

In the course of a study of economic development policies, cultural factors appear with compelling relevancy. This chapter will therefore be devoted first to showing how certain economic policies reflect cultural norms, and second to discussing how economic policy itself can generate new patterns of cultural behavior. Both tendencies have already been suggested or implied in previous chapters.

Cultural norms do not constitute unsurmountable barriers to change, nor are they fully responsible for policy or outcomes thereof. They play a role whose weight in shaping policy should be determined empirically. Moreover, culture is not being evoked here to attribute in any shape or form underdevelopment or backwardness to Egyptian society. That is not the issue. The issue is that certain culturally conditioned patterns of behavior contribute toward forward movement of the development process while others affect it adversely.

Cultural explanation of economic behavior is far more difficult and less precise than facile statistical generalizations. What follows, though, falls short of cultural explanation. It simply suggests that cultural factors have proven to be relevant to the story of economic policy told in this book.

Economic principles are the subject of science; how people react to them is a question of culture. How people perceive price fluctuations may be different from the way economists see it. To illustrate, a Cairene's typical reaction to an increase in the price of fruits or eggs is to attribute the event to greed on the part of traders. Others may respond by searching first for an economic factor, such as scarcity or transport problems. The first response is moralistic; the second is analytical.

The law of supply and demand may be compelling economically but not culturally. Those who saw in it the preservation of class differences and also found that it discriminated against those who lived below and beyond the market economy tried to use coercive government authority to modify or obstruct its effects. In Egypt, a free market in housing and education was perceived as discriminatory by the July Revolution. The regime thus enacted laws to blunt the effects of supply and demand, but the results of its efforts fell far short of the desired objective. By opting for an integrative rather than a market approach, the leaders of the Revolution followed the dictates of their personal values. The integrative economic development model was in effect predicated on a cultural principle, that of the regime's ideology.

One can detect in cultural interpretations a historical dimension, a time-honored practice, described by Clifford Geertz as "an historically transmitted"[1] pattern, which therefore is associated with traditions. However, those traditions have a direct impact on the present and the future. Again, as stated by Geertz, they are "a system of inherited conceptions expressed in symbolic forms by means of which men communicate, perpetuate, and develop their knowledge about and attitudes toward life."[2]

There is something gripping about the ability to attribute an event to its precedents, yet it is not very assuring, for such attribution is not always very clear or easy to establish. In one instance that I have grappled with in Egyptian economic behavior—that of commitment to self-sufficiency—I have attributed the phenomenon to inherited conceptions only by analogy, and that connection remains tenuous, though fascinating. Another central cultural theme I have been concerned with in this study—illicit behavior as a righteous path—has recently become a general pattern; it challenges tradition and established normative rules. Here, policy created new cultural patterns in society. Geertz, in another context of his analysis, does not insist exclusively on an inherited character of symbolic patterns.[3]

Policy as a Cultural Statement

Viewed in terms of systems of symbolic meanings, economic policies constitute cultural statements, even when they reflect material needs or rational calculations. They are made to send a message, or to signal a position, concerning where policymakers stand in the ideological and class spectra and in what direction they want people to go.

With the economic rational model in mind, it would be very difficult to explain why policymakers such as those we have been concerned with here do not take the right steps when they know full well what the right economic course is. Most cases of irrational economic behavior are due to the ascendancy of other considerations in the minds of policymakers, such as sending special messages.

This is quite a familiar theme in the study of political economy and has been succinctly expressed by Robert Bates, among others.[4] Articulating the political aspects of economic policy, Bates draws the bottom line on what is common to most scholars. Economic policy, he writes, may be "designed to secure advantages for particular interests, to appease powerful political forces, and to enhance the capacity of political regimes to remain in power."[5] In the course of discussing Egyptian economic policies, this book has touched on all three conditions. In addition, I have added here the need to make policy consistent with the demands of an integrative development approach and with the symbolic meanings given to economic objects.

The regime's perspective on development, for instance, did not equate economic development solely with higher production, but rather with sufficiency and justice for all (*kifayah wa 'adl*). Use of the terms sufficiency and justice indicate that economic policy was viewed officially through a cultural perspective. The objective of policy was not boundless growth but enough production to provide a decent living for everyone. This is certainly different from a capitalist perspective, which is the maximization of profits. The welfare of the peasants, therefore, was not seen by policymakers in terms of prices of crops per se but the success of policies that would bring benefits to the nation and every group in it, including peasants.

The matter of whether price and crop controls had one and only one meaning is thus far from being settled. For policymakers, price and crop controls policy was officially justified in terms of its functionality to the national development plan as a whole. It was not seen as exploitation or extractive in nature. This is at least one interpretation that cannot be dismissed offhand, and it underlines the point that attribution of political motivation to policy is not easy to determine with certainty.

Though the cultural orientation of the new leaders is understandable, the policy instruments they devised were obviously counterproductive. This was apparent to Egyptian economists and, by the seventies, to ordinary citizens as well. The regime, on the other hand, continued basically to adhere to its policies because it had not changed its values and because its survival depended on it. The values of the regime were also widely shared by the public, which created something like cultural complicity, overlooking disturbing signals.

Cultural Complicity

Cultural complicity is a reticent social accord that takes the form of general acquiescence in a certain idea or pattern of behavior as if it were a given. It is problematic in that it often contravenes an explicit principle, also professed to and accepted by the same community. Cultural complicity conceals an inconsistency in moral or intellectual positions—in effect, blind spots in a community, a cultural instinct that may be characterized as collective delusion. It is readily accessible and acceptable to the dominant elements of a community that manages to keep discussion of the issue suppressed.

The acceptance of black slavery and the disenfranchisement of women in the newly independent American republic, which was based on equality and liberty, are examples of cultural complicity. It was, of course, realized by some that slavery or discrimination against women was contrary to the Bill of Rights, but most preferred not to make an issue of it.

Collective delusions are a serious social phenomenon, particularly because they work. Once they lose their effectiveness, though, they become worthless relics—discarded, forgotten, passed by unnoticed. When and how these delusions are abandoned remains difficult to establish; there is no rule of thumb by which such an event can be predicted.

ECONOMIC SELF-SUFFICIENCY

The concept and the practice of self-sufficiency show how cultural complicity worked in Egypt. The self-sufficiency concept was developed under Nasser to justify import-substitution policies. It was taken up again seriously by President Mubarak in the eighties. What does it mean when a president declares repeatedly in public that self-sufficiency is the principle that guides him in making national economic policies? To judge from statements made and policy pursued, Mubarak meant, first, that Egypt will export only what is in excess of domestic market needs, and, second, that Egypt will produce everything needed wherever possible and thereby avoid paying hard currency for imports. Thus, Mubarak's message was that Egyptian security resides in Egyptian economic independence.

An Egyptian president is surrounded by experts in economics, and the country itself has a large number of competent economists on whose advice he could draw, yet the self-sufficiency policy that Mubarak resuscitated does not make economic sense. I did not come across any voices protesting or criticizing the policy until recently. On the contrary, knowledgeable ministers made professions at every occasion of their adherence to the self-sufficiency objective and gave exact figures showing how much of its objectives they had realized in their departments. They competed with one another in demonstrating the progress of their ministries toward self-sufficiency. But surely, the president's advisors knew well enough that self-sufficiency was an untenable and self-defeating objective. How could it have enjoyed such ready acceptance in official circles and the nation as a whole? Mubarak is not a tyrant, and therefore one cannot argue that compliance was a matter of coercion.

Self-sufficiency is a concept that enjoys a special charm in the contemporary Egyptian psyche and culture and therefore has widespread acceptance. It has the effect of comforting the feelings of Egyptians who live in a world they perceive as hostile. If it does not bring an assurance of a better tomorrow, the concept at least assures them that their leaders are trying to protect and shield them from an unfriendly world environment. The infitaah, modest as it was, brought in foreign faces that reminded Egyptians of recent history, when the national economy was in foreign and minority hands. Literature of the time is full of scathing criticism of foreigners and Egyptian dependency under the infitaah. San'allah Ibrahim's novella *al Lajnah* is a prime example. It reflects deep suspicions and the fear of having Egypt mixed up in the world economy. Nationalistic and socialist measures were especially popular among ordinary Egyptians, who had always felt that foreigners and foreign residents dominated their economy.[6]

This distrust of the world environment is perhaps currently the most prevalent in matters of food provisions. The slogan "he who owns not the source of his food is not free" (*mann la yamluk ghidha'ahu la yamluk huriyatahu*) is a post–Camp David slogan. It was raised by no less a figure than President Mubarak himself, who steadfastly held to the peace treaty with Israel and pursued the same policy of close relations with the United States. He also held firmly to an economic policy of self-sufficiency during the first ten years of his regime.

Self-sufficiency also speaks to the idea of equality, where all Egyptians are called upon to share the products of Egypt, good or bad. Mubarak's main slogan, "made in Egypt," suggests reassurance against the infitaah world, where ex-patriots, speculators, smugglers, merchants, black marketeers, beneficiaries, and "compradors" enjoyed a European lifestyle while the rest remained condemned to a hard and rough existence. There is nothing the ordinary Egyptian dislikes more than other Egyptians flaunting their wealth.

It would be difficult to see how such an archaic and self-defeating economic idea as self-sufficiency could achieve widespread currency without understanding the phenomenon of reticent cultural accord, or complicity. Self-sufficiency is an idea in harmony with the general culture, consistent with most peoples' predilections and soothing to most peoples' fears. It is part of the common psyche—unspoken, though felt through and through. When structural adjustment was forced upon the Mubarak regime in 1990 by the advanced industrial nations, the concept of self-sufficiency was not openly contradicted, fought out in public, or refuted. It slowly faded away, not through confrontation but neglect. The idea of self-sufficiency cannot be defeated in Egypt, it has to be circumvented and neglected.

Cultural tendencies such as belief in self-sufficiency are something Egyptians share with other formerly colonized countries in Latin America, Africa, and Asia. It is curious to note, however, that Egypt and Argentina, for instance, responded to an aggressive world environment by shielding themselves off through such economic stratagems as import substitution, whereas Asian countries such as Japan, South Korea, and Singapore set out to economically conquer the world that had placed limits on them. One could put this tendency aside as partly rhetorical had it not been generating pressure on decision makers to act toward achieving food self-sufficiency. One should not be surprised, therefore, to hear in Egypt higher officials, journalists, and intellectuals speak, of all things, self-sufficiency in wheat, an objective neither tenable nor economically advantageous.

The powerful deputy prime minister, Minister of Agriculture, and Secretary General of the ruling National Democratic Party, Dr. Yusuf Waali, announced on 16 July 1987 at the celebration of Arab Bread Day that a policy had been set in place to achieve 70 percent self-sufficiency in wheat in the coming two years. Such a move is inexplicable in terms of rational calculation. Not only is it unattainable, but it is generally accepted that Egypt's comparative advantage does not lie in wheat cultivation. The minister and other policymakers know those facts well enough. However, Waali's statement and policy have a cultural meaning accessible and readily acceptable to Egyptians. It is sometimes more important to sound as if you are on the right side than to actually be sound.

Instances of official efforts to seek self-sufficiency abound and have been discussed elsewhere in this book, so a few examples here from recent years will suffice. The Ministry of Industry declared in October 1987 that it would seek self-sufficiency in the production of processed sugar, oil, detergents, and animal feed.[7] However, it is generally known that self-sufficiency in sugar, animal feed, and wheat is out of the question. Another example is from the Ministry of Electricity, which sells its products at highly subsidized rates. The Minister announced in July 1987 his intention to develop electrical industries to produce equipment and electronic products locally to achieve self-sufficiency and thus save hard currency through the reduction of imports.[8]

The warning by the chief executive of the Export Development Bank, Dr. Hazem al Beblawi, that the development of exports should not be thought of as a stratagem to generate hard currency but "as a requirement of catching up with the times" (dukhul al 'asr) has not caught the attention of the public nor become part of even the learned discourse among Egyptians. Beblawi believes that in Egypt, at the level of both officials and common citizens, there are values and traditions that discourage or contradict development of the requirements of joining the modern world. He mentions in particular things that affect exports, such as credibility, lack of concern for quality, punctuality, and an ingrained public suspicion of those who deal with commissions or who facilitate services. Egyptians value above all peasants and government officials, he adds. These are two careers of traditional integrity.[9] Beblawi's comments confirm the analogy made in this analysis with the values and behavioral patterns of the pre-capitalist period of subsistence farming in Egypt.[10]

One symptom of the inwardly drawn tendencies found among Egyptians is revealed in an aspect of the outcry against the Islamic Investment Funds (STAs).

In order to discredit those financial institutions, officials and journalists charged that they had invested large sums of money abroad and that they made various business deals overseas. While there were legitimate economic grounds for concern over some financial practices of certain funds, one is nevertheless struck by the vehemence of the opposition to internationalization of Egyptian business enterprises. In one rare encounter with an STA leader in an industrial fair, President Mubarak's first and only question was whether the fund held capital abroad. When told that the fund's capital was actually deposited in Egypt, the President seemed fully satisfied and asked no other questions.

The funds, it may be observed, were actually the product of a burgeoning trend toward the internationalization of Egypt's economy. They were started by people who earned capital abroad, then sustained by small investors who also earned income abroad and were trying to get the best returns for their money, regardless of national boundaries. The facts, though, did not make a difference, for they did not correspond to the discourse of meaning, which lay on a level separate from reality. They did not fit in with the *idée propre* that the outside world is hostile and not much good for Egypt.

Intellectuals (including economists) in their own turn attacked the practice of investing abroad, stating that it should not be done while there was unemployment at home. The fact that many people in Egypt were receiving revenue from those overseas investments was not seriously considered by critics or government leaders, and neither was the fact that Egypt's domestic capacity to absorb capital was not very great.

The Subsistence Farming Syndrome

The principle of self-sufficiency bears marked resemblance to pre-industrial and pre-capitalist economic attitudes and behavior. It is associated with economic security, which is currently the source of much of the satisfaction Egyptians derive from employment in the public sector. Though pay is low, lifelong tenure and fringe benefits are considered by employees as more important.

The drive for self-sufficiency in a modern economy such as Egypt's may be considered a resurgence of a primordial desire. It is throwback to the past, a swelling out of a deep and persistent subconscious force. The fact that the majority of Egyptian elites, in the broadest sense of the term, are of rural background may contribute to the prevalence of this resurgence.[11]

Egypt's economic policies bear a striking resemblance to household subsistence farming practices of the pre-capitalist period. Both tend to reduce the pace of exchange in the domestic market and with the outside world. Both determine the volume and quality of production relative to domestic needs. The infitaah policy, which reopened the route for the import of some consumer goods, did not lead to a resurgence of exports, primarily because of the decline of production capabilities, the continuing official restrictions on market activities, and the persistence of the idea that satisfying the domestic market should come first.

If one considers a subject such as the production of ceramics, which is politically innocuous and not strategic industrially, one gains a sense of the depth of the tendency for inward-looking self-satisfaction. In the mid-eighties, the Ministry of Industry did not want to increase production of ceramics nor allow imports because it believed that local production actually met the demand of the domestic market. When the ministry learned that shortages in supply did exist, it agreed to increase production, but only to the point of meeting local demands.

This reluctance to accept change reflects misgivings and misunderstanding about the outside world. Such misgivings center on the consequences of having to deal with an outside world that is stronger, as well as expensive, unstable, and unreliable. It also reflects discomfort both with the mechanics of exchange in the world economy and with the unknown.

Egypt's economic policies, though culturally meaningful, cannot be considered progressive, but rather, retroactive. Such ideas as faith in modern science and technology, prominent in the charter drawn up by Nasser in 1962, conceal a deep-seated inward orientation, inconsistent with the principle of specialization in production. Though these observations are only analogies, they leave one wondering about the invisible links between past and present, and between habits of thought and behavioral patterns.

A subsistence farmer whose sources of wealth are fixed and limited resorts to saving and hoarding rather than generating new wealth. One observes a similar behavior pattern in the government's policy regarding foreign exchange, where it tried to conserve rather than to generate more of a scarce resource. Rather than give incentives to Egyptians who actually generated hard currency, the government established restrictions and instituted artificially low rates for foreign exchange.

CLIENTELISM

The Nasser strategy of development showed a conscious effort to free rural Egypt from the clientelism pattern of conduct in favor of establishing peasants as autonomous producers functioning within institutions over which they have some leverage by means of membership and participation.[12] The agricultural cooperatives and worker participation in the management of industrial enterprises are outstanding efforts to break away from reverence to traditional authority and inequalities. The Nasserite tragedy, though, lies in the reversal of the order it sought to install and the evolution of dependency by working citizens on the government's goodwill and handouts. The triumph of clientelism in a new form and on a national scale remains the major distress signal of reform politics in Egypt.

The attitude of the Egyptian government toward citizens is analogous to that of the landlord-tenant farmer relationship of the pre-Revolutionary era. It involves authority, some benevolence, and extraction. Whether extraction is to serve the landlord or the national purpose made no difference in effect to individual citizens.

The Nasser-Sadat model of clientelism is reminiscent of an earlier era where the employer and lord sat in judgment of the value of an individual's work. By valuing them below standards and below the cost of living, they put workers and peasants in a state of indebtedness and through compensatory support made them dependent for their livelihood. The rule applied to most active Egyptians, who were paid below-standard wages and therefore had to be supported by subsidies from the lord of the time, the national government.

The client's advantage is more evident in modern clientelism than in traditional peasant society, for while in peasant society the lord could literally "throw the rogue out" of home and field, the present-day lord is under an obligation not to do so. The collective character into which the client has been absorbed or integrated limits the retaliatory options open to the employer, whether government or private. Thus, to produce conformity employers must use conventional and nonconventional means that do not include cutting off the client from favor.

The widespread controls introduced by Nasser vitiated much of his endeavor to create an autonomous citizenry through institutionalization. Not until the mid-eighties did the government partially retreat from this position by relaxing widespread controls, though not to the point of reversing the new clientelism.

As Egypt plodded along under the strain of finding ways to make itself economically independent of the outside world, the country also suffered from fear of political isolation. This political tendency represents the opposite of economic insularity. Egyptians feel a strong need to consort with other nations politically in order not to be weakened by having to face the world alone. Politically, Egyptians suffer from claustrophobia, as one Egyptian told me. One could clearly notice the two incongruent tendencies during the Nasser period, when Egypt was closed economically and open to Arab allies politically. While Nasser pursued an economic policy of import substitution, which discriminated against Arab countries, politically his discourse was versed in strong Arab nationalist terms. He mounted a tireless drive to surround himself with

Arab allies, going as far as creating one political union with Syria and another with Yemen, plus assuming a leadership role in the Third World bloc of non-aligned nations.

CULTURAL FACTORS AND THE SUBSIDIES

Subsidies are a form of compensation in kind rather than cash. In that respect, they constitute a traditional form of compensation prevalent in pre-capitalistic cultures. Payment of officials and officers were made partly in kind as late as the second half of the nineteenth century. In societies practicing subsistence agriculture, taxes are normally collected in kind, to a greater or lesser degree.

Subsidies for consumer goods in some societies are limited and considered only as temporary stopgap measures. In Egypt, they are co-extensive with the earning and nonearning sectors of the population. That is why they are considered in this study to be a parallel wage system, not only a support system for the poor.

Support for the subsidy system cuts across the ideological spectrum, left and right. The supposedly more progressive political left has tended to be more supportive of subsidies. Indeed, the subsidy system has become a part of their ideology. I have never encountered any statement to the effect that subsidies are actually an outdated system of labor reward coming from any of the various leftist groups. When Ali Lutfi, a former university professor of economics, became a prime minister in 1985, he proposed replacing subsidies for consumer goods with cash compensation. The suggestion received little support and much criticism and was allowed to die an ignominious death.

The support for subsidization policies by the Egyptian left can sometimes reach extreme limits. One such instance concerned the subsidy for high-quality flour. Since much refined flour goes for making sweets, it was argued by some leftist writers that since the poor eat sweets too, subsidization was the right policy. The solution according to that author was for the government to impose a tax on producers of sweets and then spend the returns on the poor.[13] Needless to say, that author's confidence in the competence of the government to collect taxes, let alone distribute benefits fairly, is incongruent with Egyptian realities. Here again we see that policy proposals have a cultural rather than purely objective meaning.

The leftist political party of Egypt, *al Tagamu*ʿ, issued a booklet in 1985 on reform and subsidies entitled *Subsidies of the Rich and Subsidies of the Poor*.[14] It recommends discontinuation of the subsidy for high-quality flour but supports continuation of the bread subsidy across the board on the grounds that in practice it would be difficult to "distinguish between the deserving and the undeserving of the subsidy."[15] For the sake of achieving equity, they recommended that the government heavily tax those who are financially capable to compensate the Treasury for the bread subsidies the rich receive.

If the government is able to identify the rich in order to tax them, why could it not identify them for exclusion from the subsidy benefits? The issue, though, is not economics, or for that matter the ability of the government to implement fair practices, but the fact that subsidies have become a symbol of caring for the needy, true or not. Attacks on any aspect of the subsidy system would be interpreted as a direct or disguised attack on welfare. Again, no one wants to be caught on the wrong side of the fence, and ideological positions are more important than results.

Political parties take a very cautious stand on the subject for obvious political reasons. They avoid the issue by voicing moderate views or no views at all. The Neo-Wafd Party, which is more explicit than any about its opposition to subsidies, is often ambiguous and sometimes speaks with more than one voice on the issue.

Intellectuals, on the other hand, have not informed public opinion or generated a constituency in support of reform on this matter. With the exception of a few, they tended to be lukewarm or outright opposed to reform of subsidies. There are many reasons for this attitude, partly ideological and cultural and partly selfish. Egyptian intellectuals, a mainly propertyless group employed by the government, feel underpaid and resent any reduction in benefits. The same is true of the large bureaucracy and the urban middle class, all of whom benefit disproportionately from subsidies. With little confidence in government leadership, they are not sure who will benefit from a change in the welfare system and thus are unprepared to exchange an evil they know for good alternatives they do not know. Cynicism among some has led to acceptance of a bad situation in which everyone is hurt, as opposed to switching to a system they see as susceptible to manipulation by the rich.[16]

THE LEGALISTIC SYNDROME

Legalism is a cultural syndrome that reflects government's proclivity to resort to formal solutions. Bring to the attention of ordinary Egyptians or members of the elite a problem affecting society or a part thereof and their immediate reaction would be quite predictable: a law should be passed to solve that problem or a government agency should be created to deal with it. The responsibility for solving a public problem, no matter how small, is always relegated to the government. This is matched by very limited local initiative in community and public affairs, with the exception of Islamic organizations. Among Islamists, there is the conviction that religion provides an alternative to the government in providing and regulating social affairs; this conviction gives them an autonomy lacking in the rest of Egyptian society.

The classical pattern of the Mamluke building, a structure some six hundred years old, illustrates modern urban attitudes. The structure is raised in the middle of a yard surrounded by very high solid walls shielding it from the streets. Beauty and cleanliness are reserved for the interior, the private realm. Outside its walls, the street remains untidy, almost a dump. In Zamalek, a fashionable quarter of Cairo today, plush apartment buildings abound. The sidewalks in front of building entrances, however, are often quite untidy. The outdoors is the business of the government, not individual citizens or groups.

Moralizing is another cultural tendency that leads to an emphasis on legal controls and the use of punitive sanctions in order to solve economic problems. This is particularly acute in the case of prices. Though there are very good reasons why prices go up in Egypt and elsewhere in the world, the dominant explanation in the public mind, encouraged unfortunately by the government and the press, is that the corruption and greed of tradespeople are responsible. Sometimes this takes a pathetic turn by placing the blame on poor retail merchants and barrow boys, who are hounded by the police. On a few occasions, the wholesale trader is held responsible. These cultural attitudes prevailed under Nasser and have not abated to this day.

In his last year in office, Sadat instructed provincial governors that "a great part of the increase in prices of food products such as eggs and vegetables is due to exploitation (*istighlaal*) by middlemen and that it is necessary to put an end to that." Therefore, he instructed governors to have their public sector food security companies market these commodities and thereby eliminate those in the middle.[17] Such a suggestion would be understandable only if it came from an outsider who did not know about the performance of Egypt's public sector companies, not to mention the consequences of official price controls, which leave farmers and traders a negligible margin of profit.

One cultural bias existing in Egypt is reflected in the attitudes, held especially by intellectuals, toward services. The provision of services in economic life is downgraded and distrusted as generally exploitative and not in the national interest, especially when compared with production. That is why traders, even the smallest among them, are so widely vilified. A theme that is repeated so frequently both orally and in writing is that production is the only worthwhile, or at least the foremost, economic activity. Services are often viewed as superfluous, even parasitic (*a'maal tufayliyah*).

The business community in Egypt is frequently taken to task for being involved so heavily in nonproductive activities. The fact that production could be superfluous as well never seems to be mentioned, though leftover stocks (*al makhzun al sila'i*) are an endemic problem of the government's industrial firms. Though businesspeople do not choose their activities after consultation with intellectuals, the prevalent intellectual atmosphere creates discord and ambiguity about real solutions. Policymakers who are repeatedly exposed to such ideas may become conditioned to them and to the intellectual mood of their time.

While waiting for real solutions, the easiest thing for those in power to do is to pass new laws. Egypt, according to some observers and legislators, is a prolific producer of laws and statutes. It ranks among the top nations in the world in that respect.[18] Many of these laws are inconsistent with one another, and these inconsistencies are compounded, as they filter down to the implementation level, by executive orders in separate ministries. One such law regulating imports (number 1036, September 1986) is a case in point. The customs officials issued four hundred explanatory memoranda (*manshur tafsiri*) for this one law. Such practices call for increasing governmental supervision and bureaucratic routine, all of which weigh heavily on businesspeople, especially producers who have to continuously seek official approvals from a multitude of government agencies. The practice gives government detailed supervision rights over the business community, without any obligation or provision to provide real control or guidance.

The tendency toward excessive formal regulations as a means of control is ingrained in the culture of distrust. Distrust by individuals of each other and ipso facto by the government of its employees can be seen on every level of the bureaucracy. In order to prevent public officials from abusing their powers or using them to divert benefits to themselves, their families, and their friends, rules are introduced to create a web of formal checks on their activities. Changing a burned out electric bulb in an office requires the signatures of eight or more other officials from various government departments.[19] In effect, offices may go for a long time without a working light bulb, a typewriter ribbon, or paper.

Excessive legislation continues to function as, on the one hand, a panacea offered in the struggle against corruption, and on the other, a means to achieve development objectives that have been elusive. The legalistic way to avoid corruption, however, is demoralizing and obstructive to national development. It may even encourage a greater degree of corruption and the emergence of businesspeople who operate in the middle—cutting deals with officials in gray and black economic spheres where spoils are shared. Such operators abound in Egypt.

The perceived need for control is perhaps what is behind the great reluctance of Egypt to privatize. The feeling that private business is out of control and may defraud the nation if left to its own exploitative means and selfish pursuits is strong in the popular mind and among the elite. The fear that liberalization and privatization would lead to chaos and injustice is reflected in the attitude of writers toward the infitaah. Since most literary writers in Egypt are journalists, their perspectives tend to be dominated by the sensationalism attendant with journalism. Writers like Nagib Mahfouz, in *Al Hub Fawqa Hadabat al Haram,* and Gamal al Ghaytaani, in *Khutat al Ghaytaani,* show just such a preoccupation with what they perceive as loss of control and corruption under infitaah.

Widespread poverty coupled with heightened awareness of public affairs among the masses support anti-business biases. Not only is privilege much resented in the culture, but also the feeling that government controls are necessary to curb its occurrence. It is that same culture of mass poverty that puts a premium on basic needs rather than on political or economic freedoms. Cultural pressures, in effect, combine with the natural desires of political leaders for more control with which to sustain an authoritarian and centralized system of government. The preservation of the public sector, which remains intact to this day, is a meaningful cultural statement, not an economic response to reality.

Another phenomenon is the high level of tolerance Egyptians have for wrongdoers. For instance, government officials who fail to do their job or fail even to show up for work are protected by their colleagues, even those whose workload is affected by such delinquent behavior. It is an attitude that is hard to understand. Lack of commitment and faith in what they are doing may be one explanation. Another could be self-defense: by covering for another they reserve their right to be protected when found delinquent. Or, it could come from a historical, deep-rooted attitude of hostility to authority, an attitude that makes a protective shield necessary for general survival—in other words, today is your turn, tomorrow will be mine.

The tolerance of indolence is manifested not only by ordinary administrators but by their superiors. In particular, officials are spared public exposure and sanction by their superiors. Observers often describe this system as devoid of both punishments and rewards. One sometimes wonders whether Egyptian employees would even respond to rewards or whether they have become habitually indifferent. It is a basic expectation in Egyptian society that a reward is something one wins for being in place, on the right side, or as a favor. The head of the Central Agency for Administrative Affairs made a pertinent remark when he stated that the laws cite thirteen different punishments for nonperformance and for deception, but these punishments are not implemented.[20] Curiously enough, he continued by suggesting that new rules for rewards and punishments be put on the books.

Protection of the culprit was also manifested in other life situations on the mass level. Buyers charged higher prices than the officially set price would neither report the seller to the police nor respond to police inquiries. If pressed they would deny paying more than the official price. On one occasion, a particularly tough Minister of the Interior trying to clamp down on gouging became quite frustrated by the prevailing public attitude and admitted defeat.[21]

CREATING AN UNCIVIC CULTURE

We have dealt thus far with cultural coordinates of economic policy. There is, however, another aspect to the interplay between culture and economics. Economic policies may create new cultural patterns with far-reaching social and political consequences.

In Egypt, economic policies have encouraged uncivic attitudes and behavior regarding the law—including disrespect, evasion, or outright violation. They have, moreover, contributed to citizens' lack of faith in public institutions and officials, disincentives to work, nonachievement, disinterest in the public good, and cynicism. Leaders in government are aware of these tendencies. In an interview in 1990, the head of the Central Agency for Administrative Affairs, Dr. Husayn Ramzi Kazim, shared his thoughts about morale among government officials:

> Hundreds of laws may be issued but none could really be implemented, since the conscience (*damir*) of the government official is non-existent. A segment of employees in government agencies and in the public sector have lost the sense of belonging (*al intima'*) and of responsibility. Such employees live in a constant struggle between truth and falsehood, virtue and vice. [It is a vacillation] between commitment to duty, honesty and loyalty, on the one hand, and carelessness, licentiousness (*tasayub*), and indifference, on the other.[22]

This description may be applicable to a very large segment of Egyptian society, since most employed persons outside agriculture are government employees. Their compensation barely keeps up with the cost of living and they find it necessary to moonlight to make ends meet. Many become disoriented by their status as redundant workers and are overcome by a sense of lack of worth. Since they are not rewarded for merit or punished for shortcomings, they rarely show concern about their work or worry about failure.

Ordinary citizens who have seen the basic needs services that heralded the oncoming of the July Revolution deteriorate have lost faith in the government's ability to deliver on its promises. They had to seek alternatives, quite often in shady practices. For instance, for education they have resorted to private lessons; for housing, to evading the law; for consumer goods, to the black market; and for health services, to private practitioners.

Ordinary Egyptians accept what has been guaranteed them almost for free and seek private ways to make up for shortages. No longer able or interested in reforming the system, they seek to beat it. The fact that there are ways to compensate for what is missing diverts their attention from political activism. "Every law has an exception" is a popular saying.[23] Besides, the regime is too powerful and formidable to take on. Instead of resorting to collective action, all seek private solutions of their own. It may well be that the Revolution raised the level of political consciousness, but it also seriously weakened social and political solidarities, so much so that when political parties were allowed to function again, they could attract only very small followings. Thus, while the government reaps the rewards of political docility, society loses the opportunity for reforms.

Among the religious, however, such lack of seriousness toward the law is infuriating; they see it as indicative of the irresponsibility of government leaders. Leaders in Islam, it ought to be remembered, carry a more somber duty than in secular government, for the law with which they are entrusted is holy. In the case of Egypt, most laws were not holy, nor were the leaders in charge pious. It should not be surprising then to see that those who remained in the grip of a religious consciousness took to violent means to set things right.

The case of the STAs illustrates the way in which strict control policies stimulate deviancy, individual ingenuity, and an attitude of disrespect for the law. The strict and unrewarding rates of foreign exchange imposed by the government stimulated the black market. The STAs started out in the black market and thus were indirectly created by policies that were unfair, impractical, and full of legal loopholes. They found room in the shady sphere of the undeclared economy, and many of them developed crooked means to achieve economic success. They were reared in the uncivic culture, where the real opportunity lay. The situation made them wealthy but also vulnerable. While the government was lax regarding small entrepreneurs in the undeclared economy, it was not indifferent to large ones. The political culture of the time had little tolerance for large-scale entrepreneurial activities, and the STAs became politically visible competitors who had to be suppressed. What the government as an entrepreneur lost in peaceful competition it tried to recover by the use of force.

The culture of strict legal controls is associated with an atitude of righteousness on the part of citizens who violate the law, a feeling of being morally justified in their uncivic attitudes and behavior. For when law or policy strike citizens as unfair—such as when they are not paid adequately or when they are offered less than the going rate for their crops or commodities—they feel cheated by those who were supposed to uphold justice and maintain the law. Feeling cheated by the judge, they consider it their right to outwit the cop. Those who change hard-earned foreign currency in the black market are not only thought of as smart but as doing the only fair thing given the alternative—that is, changing at the government bank at below the market rate. The law, in effect, loses its moral edge.

The phenomenon we encounter here cannot be classified under the rubric of corruption; this is something else. It is induced by policy and thus is more widespread than what usually stems from corruption. It occurs among ordinary citizens and government officials alike. People know that some of their operations in the undeclared economy may be illegal but they do not consider them immoral.

In response to unfair demands placed on them, people have tried to circumvent, evade, or violate the law. Such widespread deviant economic behavior has been treated in this book as a distinct set of economic activities under the label "undeclared economy." Examples of activities that fall under the undeclared economy include paying for private lessons, dealing in foreign exchange in an unauthorized way, using flour and bread for chicken feed, and illicit housing. The term *undeclared economy* suggests clandestine, perhaps illegal, behavior, but not overt deviancy. A veil separates them from the world of open and legal transactions. The undeclared economy is not exactly the same thing as the black market.

The undeclared economy consists mostly of covert transactions made necessary by legalistic prohibitions or the failure of institutions to deliver.[24] They are not immoral activities, and usually they are the most rational. Activities under the undeclared economy are perfectly normal transactions that are only covert because the government prohibited them or, through its policies, drove people to commit them.

In contrast, the black economy, or black market, refers to economic activities that violate the law and ethical norms at the same time; these include drug trafficking, smuggling, tax evasion, embezzlement, bribes, theft, and appropriating public funds. This is not a phenomenon we are concerned with here,[25] though sometimes it is difficult to draw a sharp line between the undeclared and the black economy.[26]

The presence of an undeclared economy means that something is fundamentally wrong with economic policy. It also points to the transformation in Egypt's political culture: the resort to individualistic and illegal solutions, weakening of political solidarities, and the belief in one's right to break the law. Moreover, it raises the premium on official resort to police action to run the economy.

The leaders of the July Revolution set in place national and morally high objectives for themselves and future generations. That their very earnestness should defeat their purpose is of course one of the tragic aspects of the enterprise.

Chapter Ten

The Illusive Path to Development

The economic policies discussed in this book have led to the kind of problems that typically arise when governments expand disproportionately at the expense of private activities in the marketplace. They also underline the distortions and unfathomable complexities of substituting an administrative structure for the free market.

Governments and markets are interdependent institutions.[1] We often see in them contrasts and contradictions. Government works according to peremptory administrative methods, while markets function by means of discretionary choice and adjustment. The one seeks to control and fashion reality, while the other respects its diversity and seeks to make use of it.

Despite those clear differences governments and markets reflect philosophies and legal precepts that overlap and contrast at one and the same time. Concepts such as justice, order, choice, wealth, scarcity, access, security, rights, and obligations are at the base of both institutions. That is why markets are regulated and governments are responsive to public concerns.

In a national effort to redefine the philosophy behind the two institutions, leaders of the July Revolution by and large substituted government for the market. Centralized agencies acting within the context of a national plan took the place of private actors. Subordinating the market almost totally to central authority blocked those channels that make government responsive to the public. It also disturbed the complementary equation between market and government by determining wages, prices, and the production of commodities in accordance with a national design and using authoritarian means.

The merger of markets and central authority represents a radical development strategy that applies peremptory administrative measures where discretionary choice is the norm, thus blurring the specialized function of each. Under those conditions, balance and maintenance takes the place of growth and profit. Moreover, the merger disturbs the delicate balance between rights and obligations. Where individual actors claim rights by law and convention, their claims are voided by official claims, making government the source of all laws and decisions. At best, individual rights become an official gift; at worst, an obligation.

As this study has shown, the market proved to be inimical to the control and management necessary under the integrative economic development model. Rising difficulties led to a parallel, illicit system of economic exchange that provided some relief from strict controls but also complicated management of the economy. Thus, the need for reform did not take long to arise; in fact, it developed less than two decades after the integrative model was introduced.

STRUCTURAL ADJUSTMENT AND REFORM

As the integrative development program unfolded, the patron state found itself increasingly caught up in a game of self-entrapment. When the Revolutionary fervor of radical policymaking collided with the insurmountable difficulties of economic development, the patrons of the project started to idle in place and muddle through. Leaders became increasingly bothered by their inability to provide and awed by the magnitude of the task of reshaping the massive edifice they had created. Decision makers started to realize how hard it was to move forward and how costly and painful to stay in place. A compromise solution was reached in the vain hope of capturing the future without losing the past.

The reform process, which initially started in the mid-seventies, consisted mainly of efforts to gradually disaggregate the two institutions—government and market—allowing the latter greater freedom. Though reforms provided some relief, it was nevertheless clear that full recovery could not be achieved piecemeal and without abandoning the integrative development model altogether.

The indifferent results of Egypt's reforms and their slow pace endured until 1990 and beyond, for many reasons. Structural reform is often considered difficult to implement due to political and economic considerations. In the first place, post-Nasser leaders were not intellectually or ideologically prepared to perform a surgical operation. Nasser's successors did not have the education or vision of, for instance, Turkey's Turgut Ozal; they were not equipped to lead Egypt into a new economic future. Second, the political constituency, those with a vested interest in reform, such as the business class, remained weak and dependent on government favors. Private businesspeople who had survived the Nasser onslaught basked in the protected market of the patron state. New entrants, mainly small entrepreneurs, were not strong enough and tended to exploit the weaknesses of the system rather than face up to them.

Because of their background and ideological predilections, most intellectuals remained adamantly opposed to a free-market economy and continued to associate the predominant role of government with social justice and nationalism. Organized labor was in alliance with the ruling party and rather secure in that collaborative relationship. The bureaucracy had much to fear from reform in terms of loss of benefits and loss of jobs. In short, the dependency aspect of society in the patron state continued to be a predominant feature during the reform period and slowed the process down.

It would be deceptive, however, to believe, as did Sadat and Mubarak, that irritants could be mended or removed without affecting the entire edifice. Prices cannot be freed and subsidies removed without at the same time allowing collective labor to bargain freely and business firms to run autonomously. Exports cannot be freed without abandoning self-sufficiency objectives and removing restrictions on exchange rates. Private business enterprises cannot be allowed full freedom without undermining most public sector firms and government allocations of production shares and product mixes. These changes constitute a big order and require tremendous effort and will to undertake. It can be done, though. Such reforms have been relatively successful in Mexico, Argentina, Chile, Tunisia, and Turkey, among other countries.

Finding one's way out of the patron state trap can be enhanced by changes in the political regime, plus international pressures and assistance. Economic collapse also contributes to change. This latter phenomenon could be termed a *Malthusian syndrome*, a situation where reform is not undertaken until the disaster point is reached.

Structural adjustment does not occur without agony and social destabilization, that is clear enough. Still, the economic cost of reform tends to be exaggerated by policymakers and writers.[2] Continuing the drain is more costly than the remedy. The economy will not suffer if subsidies to the rich and to inefficient firms are eliminated, nor if the production of unwanted and high-cost goods at public expense is stopped. Economies that suffered from counterproductive and financially deleterious policies such as the ones described in this book have no better remedy than turning around, and turning around has been successful in many LDCs.

In Egypt the transformation to a rentier economy in the early seventies, when the crisis had reached its peak, reduced the need for radical change. The rentier economy helped Sadat stay the course, for he did not have the will, the knowledge, or the conviction to abandon Nasser's legacy. His effort to reduce minor subsidies in 1976/77, which led to popular outburst and immediate recision of the measures, is often taken as an example of the near political impossibility of reform. This is not, however, the case. Sadat's subsidy reform was so inappropriate that it was bound to fail, even without mass disturbances. He started with the marginal subsidies, which were the subsidies most equitably distributed and basic for low-income people. Heavyweight subsidies such as energy were not touched. Raising the price of bread, cooking oil, or tea could not remedy the ills of the Egyptian economy.

Sadat's infitaah initiative was not a major economic turnaround but a ruse intended to maintain the flow of rents into Egypt. As the source of these rents, the West and the region's oil-rich countries were mollified by Sadat's shift into a pro-Western and anti-Soviet stance. Economic liberalization was added to serve as a palliative and a signal of Sadat's seriousness and goodwill.

Sadat never envisaged a radical redefinition of economic strategy, let alone abandonment of the integrative economic development model.[3] Symbols, Sadat understood well enough, were quite effective political tools. With a symbolic stance, Egypt could henceforth count on being bailed out by its new political allies, and indeed it was bailed out repeatedly during the seventies, eighties, and during the Kuwait crisis in 1991.

Since neither Sadat nor Mubarak felt the force of a constituency for economic change, they devoted their careers to crisis management rather than to a new project or a new start. It was the deceleration in the flow of rents and persistent pressure from international economic agencies that eventually convinced Mubarak between 1987 and 1991 to move ahead with serious reforms. Even then, his moves remained cautious and calculated.

Yet, as Egypt prepares itself to become a free-market system, little intellectual discourse has taken place to prepare the country for the expected shock of a new order. The debate remains at the stale level of ongoing argument about the injustices of the free market. The critical issue of how much interdependence between the government and the market is desirable and how it should be fashioned remains practically unexplored. Broached even less is the question of why and under what conditions political leaders intervene in the interest of the market.

It may be useful here to recall that the integrative economic development approach was adopted by the July Revolution to break away from the imperfections of the free market. Now, after more than thirty years of the new order, we have seen that imperfections and distortions characterize the managed approach as well, and perhaps to a greater extent. Among these, we have identified inefficiency, huge deficits, low productivity, shortages, noncompetitive products, low investment rates, slow to negative growth, debt, general poverty, and an uncivic culture. Advocates of privatization may be well advised to keep abreast of the experiences of Egypt and other countries where serious shortcomings characterized *both* orders, a fact underlining the importance of interdependence.[4]

Under national conditions of scarcity, glaring inequalities, and underdevelopment, the free market functions poorly as a self-regulating mechanism. This is not made any easier by the fact that we live in a world economy whose main actors are governments and multinational corporations. It would require selective government involvement to prevent monopolistic tendencies and clandestine suppression of competition. Selective government involvement would also be needed to support and promote small and underendowed entrepreneurs for defined periods of time.

The growing challenges of the global marketplace and modern technology mean that government would have to continue even more strenuously to mediate in the international economic arena on behalf of its entrepreneurs and traders. Government activism is needed in the international market and on behalf of autonomous private entrepreneurs, whose cooperation with the national government and international agencies is indispensable.

DEVELOPMENT THESES RECONSIDERED

The Egyptian experience in which the market became a function of government constituted a radical approach to economic development. It has had its bright moments but also a long period of economic stagnation and general decline.

The literature on development offers an array of explanations for the developmental experience of countries such as Egypt. In this book, the indifferent results of an ambitious economic development strategy had to be explained without the benefit of those theories for the following reasons.

First, LDCs are often criticized for stressing heavy industry in their development strategy, a choice that is cumbersome and inconsistent with the comparative advantage or economic endowments of developing countries. The regime that followed the July Revolution, however, emphasized traditional and consumer goods industries rather than heavy or intermediate industries.

Second, urban bias has often been a source of serious distortions and lopsided development. *Urban bias* refers to a condition in which the rural population and agriculture have to pay for maintaining the living standards of urban residents and for the cost of industrialization. As the chapters on agriculture and industry have shown, the terms of trade between urban and rural societies have been relatively balanced under the patron state, and official exactions have affected urban and rural interests alike. The common practice of extracting from the countryside to finance industrialization has been vitiated by the availability of other sources of finance, such as foreign loans and aid, expatriate remittances, foreign investments, and general rent sources.

In fact, the Egyptian case highlights the new trend regarding terms of trade between rural and urban areas and the ability of governments to resort to alternative sources of funding. The contention that resources were diverted from the countryside to urban centers has been shown to be an incomplete picture, one which fails to be consistent with the whole policy perspective. In Egypt, farmers were not treated differently from any other producers. Those resource transfers made were in line with a functional integrative strategy, the purpose of which was to move society in the direction of the grand design envisaged by the leaders of the Revolution, Nasser in particular.

Third, the soft state thesis maintains that governments of developing countries are too tender to make the hard economic decisions. Paradoxically, the idea of an all-powerful government enjoying hegemony over the economy has been alternately described in the literature as both despotic and soft.

The idea of a soft state was introduced in Gunnar Myrdal's *Asian Drama*, which highlights the observation that political regimes in developing countries in Southeast Asia "are reluctant to place obligations on people."[5] For instance, one hardly finds policies of forced savings or compulsory measures to reduce mass consumption. Moreover, income-tax collection remains very inadequate. John Waterbury has seen in Egypt a comparable situation.[6]

A number of observations are in order here because the soft state notion shifts the emphasis from where the real development problem lies to what could be an illusory terrain. In the first place, accumulation from domestic sources does not by itself raise sufficient capital for rapid growth, given the widespread poverty in most Third World countries. Whether the means used are coercive or not is therefore irrelevant. Still, relative to their small national income, the ratio of national savings is quite respectable in many developing countries. As for mass consumption in LDCs, it is limited to food and basic essentials, hardly an area for cutbacks.

The Nasser regime was, moreover, firm and coercive rather than reluctant to impose obligations. Egypt's progressive income-tax laws have one of the steepest rates in the world. Moreover, the regime forcefully transferred material resources from all sectors. We have seen in this study how harsh and extensive that transfer could be.

For governments to be more forceful is not enough. When put in the hands of unqualified managers, investment capital obtained through extraction or other means will not result in growth. Nor would it foster growth under faulty development strategy.

THE EXTRACTIVE REGIME THESIS

Excessive taxation in various forms has been viewed in the literature as extractive. During most of my research on this subject, which spanned a period of almost ten years (1981–90), I considered the extraction phenomenon as an example of the inevitable consequence of unchecked power of an authoritarian regime. In short, I accepted the phenomenon of excessive taxation of one sort or another as an extractive policy not much different from the practice exercised by those landlords and crop merchants overthrown by the Free Officers. The July Revolution, moreover, extended the practice of excessive exactions to cover other groups.

The possibility of extraction by the government was vividly drawn to my attention in 1966, when I was studying the impact of national reforms on a village in the Delta. A weary, dust-laden young agronomist on his way home after sunset complained that he worked longer hours than he was paid for by the government and added, "that is the meaning of exploitation. I am being exploited by a socialist system." Though I never forgot that statement, I was not then ready to deal with it, especially at a time when the benefits of Nasser's reform measures were evident all over the village.

Obviously, once the extraction thesis is accepted, the next logical step is to conclude, along with the village agronomist, that the reform regime of the Revolution exploited everyone: peasants, workers, schoolteachers, businesspeople, manufacturers, property owners, and others. In short, the regime fixed the returns on labor and capital at unrewarding rates, far below what those rates could be if left to market forces.

The quandary, however, remained unresolved, since the same extraction-prone government provided extensive welfare services and subsidies in various ways to all the above-mentioned groups and to consumers in general. Subsidies are a form of compensation and, in this case, can be interpreted as a means to make things right for those whose returns on labor or capital had been officially set low. They functioned as a kind of balance, a trade-off.

Why, one may ask, did the regime choose this method? One possible answer is that the choice of subsidies as a form of compensation is a favor to the consumer. Things, however, become complicated when further evidence shows that almost all producers received subsidies, and in disproportionate shares. What is one to think then? Does the regime support producers or consumers? Are subsidies a form of favoritism in which some partisans, classes, or regime supporters are rewarded at the expense of the public or a segment thereof?

Though some groups received more than their fair share of the subsidies, hardly anyone was excluded. Since subsidies were universal, it does not seem that they were introduced to favor a particular partisan. Nor is it easy to say that the consumer was particularly favored over others, for in exchange they received low wages. And though nearly all industrial producers received subsidies, research evidence points to differential subsidization advanced to various public enterprises.[7]

The existence of differential rewards to various government-owned enterprises and the fact that the public sector itself was not exempt from "official extraction" suggests that claiming that the government extracted from the private sector to subsidize its own enterprises does not adequately explain the situation. Such a claim has of course been made, if not explicitly, at least implicitly in the urban and industrial bias arguments.[8]

When it is realized that the same government-owned enterprises that enjoyed subsidies also suffered from official extraction, the policy panorama gets more perplexing. Official extraction has been manifested in such policies as price controls, product mix, crop controls, inputs, outputs, and outlets. But those were exactly the same restrictive practices inflicted on such private actors as peasant producers and businesspeople. In whose interest was the extraction then made? To be meaningful, extraction must be made in the interest of some segmentary body—an individual, clan, class, band of warriors, armed gang, grasping officials, adventurer governments, or somebody else.

Some authors have maintained that was exactly what had happened in Egypt after the Revolution. Authors with a leftist outlook tended to claim that even though Nasser and his successors steadfastly upheld the public sector, they had in reality put it in the service of the bourgeoisie.[9] Others have argued that the loot found its way to the pockets of politicos and bureaucrats in collusion with businesspeople.[10] None have offered convincing evidence to make their claims credible. The truth of the matter is that every group that received benefits through the new order also suffered an official exaction of one sort or another.

In cases such as Egypt, in which the public sector is subjected to price controls just as the private sector, one needs an explanation that goes beyond attribution of bias against the private sector in a socialist economy. There is no doubt that the private sector was at a disadvantage, but that observation does not explain the behavior of the regime vis-à-vis the public sector, which suffered similar handicaps. It needs to be explained why policymakers set prices at a rate detrimental to their own firms, and why governments appropriated some of these firms' profits. When the same government-owned firms are subjected to extraction and subsidization at the same time, one cannot continue to remain content, claiming favoritism to the public sector, nor can one make the opposite claim that this sector had been exploited by the government.

When the private sector, on the other hand, is reduced to a fraction of its former size and subjected to heavy government regulation, then it makes no sense to say that the regime is in the service of the private sector and puts the surplus at its disposal. Moreover, the infitaah did not restore nationalized private enterprises to their original owners or significantly limit heavy government regulations and restrictions.

When urban as well a rural actors are the subject of extraction, then we need to go beyond the classical explanation of policy in terms of an urban bias. Whether there was a total balance or not between official exactions and benefits distributed is immaterial. The beneficent attitude of the government is clearly shown by their support, even if it fell short. Some sort of balance was the aim of government policy.

When sums spent by the government on military involvements and foreign policy adventures constituted a relatively small portion of the national budget[11] and official investments and welfare spending a disproportionately large portion, then the needs of the government thesis ceases to be a convincing argument in support of the extraction theory.

One should feel compelled at this point, as I did, to drop the extraction hypothesis as an explanation for the Egyptian government's policy. But what explanation remains?

THE GLOBAL EQUILIBRIUM THESIS

An alternative hypothesis that seems to put the pieces together is that the policies officially set across the board are measures of equilibrization, a balancing act operating in a relatively closed political and economic system. The regime had a national project of a developmental nature that rested on a strategy whereby government functioned as a patron agency in charge of business and welfare at one and the same time. This grand project for society and the economy devised by the leaders of the Revolution had to be kept artificially in balance, since the design itself was not inherently self-sustaining. As leaders of the regime put the entire economy under their managerial control, they had to weigh all parts in relation to one another and to the ultimate national objective they had already defined. It was necessary that the component parts of the grand design work in unison and not be allowed to affect each other adversely in a serious way. Such constraints required a managed approach.

The phrase "a relatively closed political and economic system" is used here to mean an arrangement in which an autonomous authority controls most of the economic and political resources in society and makes the critical decisions regarding investments and distribution. Very limited consultation, if any, is conducted with the affected parties, and minimal intervention occurs from other actors, domestic or exogenous. The Nasser regime had achieved that point of control by 1962. The situation remained largely unchanged under Nasser's successors.

Not only was the regime successful in controlling the domestic economy, but it wrested control of foreign trade and foreign investments from the hands of private agents, national and foreign. While it could not exactly control the impact of world economic forces on Egypt, it could and did determine the kind of responses made toward the world order. To reduce the preponderant effect of the world economy on the national development project and uphold the ability of national leaders to make autonomous decisions, it sought to reduce international economic interactions to a minimum and rely on a state of relative self-sufficiency.

The Egyptian development approach may then be described as an integrative model with balance as its focal point. Functional equilibrium, the balancing act, required that each part in the national economy perform as expected and make its contribution to other components. If, under the integrative model, increasing production under conditions of scarcity is an objective, then the planner seeks to reduce production cost by cutting wages or setting the prices of inputs below their market rate by means of an administrative decision. If urban rents are not balanced with workers' salaries, rents are brought down by decree to make them within the reach of wage earners.

Under a system of functional equilibrium, the object of a business enterprise is neither profit nor growth. Its value is determined by its functionality in the system. An enterprise has to meet the needs of other enterprises in the system; contribute to economic self-sufficiency; and generate value added, part of which means employment and social services. Individual enterprises and the economy as a whole are considered to be performing satisfactorily if they fulfill those functions. But since functionality can be sustained only by intervention of the patron, the system proved to be both authoritarian and artificially maintained.

As mentioned, business enterprises were considered functional when they contributed to each other's needs, whether in inputs or outputs. This included transfers of resources from financially successful enterprises to less fortunate ones. Under national self-sufficiency conditions, not all enterprises were economically viable or had comparative advantage. Thus, while ideally every part was expected to perform as planned, in practice that objective fell far short of expectation. Inconsistent performance and deficits by various firms were endemic. Some public enterprises with disposable income saw policymakers divert their surplus to help balance the sheets of less viable government-owned enterprises. Liquidation of a chronically losing enterprise made no sense where functional equilibrium was required by an integrative development model.

Resource transfers were made from such industries as pharmaceutical, energy, petroleum, metals, and engineering to other enterprises. Whether directly or indirectly, they subsidized those which received large sums, such as textile, chemical, and food industries. For example, direct governmental assistance to textile industries in 1985/86 came to £E101 million, £E17 million more than the profits made by public sector textile industries, not taking into account direct and indirect subsidies. Similarly, aid to chemical industries came to about £E121 million, which exceeded returns from chemical firms by £E24 million. In contrast, engineering industries received only £E21 million, though the sum was raised in 1986/87 to £E72 million, exceeding profits by more than £E14 million. Metals, petroleum, and energy received no cash assistance at all in the mid-eighties. Also the allocation of assistance discriminated in favor of some industries at the expense of others.

Transfers from some industries to others were also reflected in tax rates. As we have already shown, food industries of the public sector paid the least amount in taxes, 10.87 percent of the surplus in 1985/86 and 14.42 percent in 1986/87. This compares with 42.89 and 52.09 percent for the pharmaceutical industry during two different periods in the eighties. The industries hit hardest by taxes were, in descending order, pharmaceutical, energy, petroleum, metals, and engineering. The argument regarding the adverse effects of direct government cash claims on industry is applicable to some industries but not all. Some are beneficiaries while others turn out to be providers.

The wisdom of such procedures may be called to question, but the procedure itself was not motivated by a desire to extract or to punish but rather to make the national project work according to plan. It represents, in short, an integrative approach in which value transfers are made in accordance with the requirements of the national design rather than basic economic principles. Instead of economic development, however, the model has produced, as has been seen in this volume, low growth and scarcity to the detriment of the national project and the interests of the various groups in society.

The most detrimental aspect of the value transfers has been the policy known euphemistically as social returns in government public enterprises.[12] Broadly understood, *social returns* refers to those benefits accruing to individuals from the purchase of products of industrial and other firms at low prices. In addition to other functions, a firm's performance is measured by its contribution to consumers' savings from buying products at low prices. Also taken into account are the benefits of employment, whether that employment is redundant or not. The difference between the price government industrial firms could charge in the marketplace and the low official sale price of its commodities was officially considered a free credit extended by government industrial firms to the public as a social welfare measure. Thus, policymakers and defenders of the public sector have argued that the returns of government-owned firms are higher than their book values show and that they are profitable when viewed in social terms.[13]

On the face of it, the social returns argument seems to have merit. It has enjoyed the support of many Egyptian economists and public figures who take pride in the social contribution industry has made toward easing the economic conditions of citizens. In fact, the social returns policy constitutes not welfare but a distorted wage system. Discount rates on consumer goods are no substitute for a sound and rewarding wage system. All those subsidies and special discounts were nothing but a partial correction to a distorted price and wage controls system. Such policy, in addition, put the employing firm in financial difficulties, impairing its normal growth. It was, moreover, a primitive labor compensation system, one that relied on exchange in kind in conjunction with monetary compensation. Compensation in kind may also have contributed to the problems of increased and more irrational consumption.

When the welfare load is blamed for weighing heavily on the development project and leading to its failure, we should understand that such claims are not based on proper analysis of economic facts. Egypt's economic problems lay in its economic strategy rather than in what it spent on welfare, which was indeed quite modest though deceptively extensive.

The social returns policy, which has often been characterized as distributive, was in fact a distorted wage system, pernicious and obstructive to the economic development process. Social returns consume investment capital; they are not cut from the value generated by investment. The role of the public sector as an agent of growth was, as a result, stifled. Since the public sector was made the spearhead of the industrialization drive, the stifling of its freedom to pursue productive policies for growth has been the major cause behind Egypt's failure to become one of the newly industrialized nations. The cumulative effects of this nearly thirty-year drain on the national economy accounts for much of the economic stagnation. Needless to say, had it not been for the rent income flowing into Egypt as of the mid-seventies,[14] the Egyptian economy would have collapsed long ago. It nearly reached that point in 1973 and on many other occasions in the eighties.

In a difficult and not adequately understood economic game, policy can only be made consistent by artificial acts of interference. There is no conspiracy theory behind it, nor a particularly hidden and favorite beneficiary, whether individuals or a class. The regime's land distribution scheme was made decisively and with great fanfare during the first decade of the new regime, not secretly behind closed doors. The beneficiaries and the losers were clear for everyone to see. Peasants and industrial workers became beneficiaries, while landlords and businesspeople lost out. But once the new order was set, the integrative development policies of the regime affected almost all groups designated by the regime as part of a coalition of the working forces: peasants, workers, intellectuals, soldiers, and native capitalists, in addition to employees of government-owned enterprises.

It is as futile under the circumstances to claim that low prices given to agricultural produce favor urban and industrial interests as it would be to claim that suppressed industrial wages betray the bourgeois leanings of the regime. The fact of the matter is that policies were made to keep the national project afloat and more or less delivering. That objective affected the fortunes of all parties: urban and rural, business firms and employees, producers and consumers, civilians and bureaucrats, public sector and private. For should the national project collapse, the prestige and future of the regime would follow suit.

Peasants, who were favored and championed by the regime, benefited from land distribution and an assortment of other reform policies but had to submit to consolidation plans, nationalized market of inputs and outputs, and crop and price controls. The policy measures taken to improve agriculture had to be consistent and not detrimental to the rest of the national project. Thus, the favor extended to peasants was not necessarily the ultimate target by itself, nor were peasants the object of extraction when they became strictly regulated. It was simply that their role in the economic equation had been redefined in light of the national economic project.

Similarly, industrial workers who had been given privileges in the workplace had to give up in return their autonomy, collective bargaining, and striking rights.

Policies such as those of prices, rents, wages, profits, and subsidies were part of a grand design intended to propel the economy as an integrated whole into modernity and equity. They failed for the reasons discussed above. They cannot, however, be viewed as specific extraction measures against one actor or the other. It is pointless to look in a piecemeal fashion at one specific act of unbalanced distribution and consider it exploitative. One must see the issue as it fits into the whole design and ask whether that design is a sound and efficacious model of development.

The extraction thesis, however, cannot be dismissed in its entirety. For while it has no place or explanatory powers in the analysis of policymaking, when viewed from the perspective of a private actor, excessive transfers have no other name but extraction. While a holistic approach here may enhance our understanding of the patron state phenomenon, to the affected producer or wage earner, price fixing and wage controls are a tax, an extraction to be avoided by any means. Unlike the design masters, the affected actors' judgment is not based on a view of the complete picture, in which all transfers are balanced, but on how they themselves are faring. Hence, the flourishing of the uncivic culture since the early sixties.

It is important, therefore, to see the extraction thesis in its proper perspective. It is a perception, but as a perception it affects the attitudes and behavior of the actors who hold it; thus it constitutes an important social and political fact. It is one thing, however, to examine the impact of policy on attitudes and behavior and quite another to adopt, as analysts, the subject's perception of policy as an explanation of reality. To understand the Egyptian paradox, indeed the paradox of development, it is necessary to see the issue from both perspectives—the global approach of integrative economic development, on the one hand, and the affected actors, on the other.

Maintaining functional equilibrium within a relatively closed system is an extremely vulnerable undertaking for any national leader, not only in Egypt but in countries with more resources as well. The integrative economic development system has a very high propensity to self-destruct and to generate an uncivic culture, if its travails are prolonged. In Egypt the crisis of poor performance was prolonged; but due to the incidence of favorable exogenous factors coupled by minor adjustments during the seventies and eighties, it did not take the form of a violent breakdown.

The tendency of the managed system to self-destruct is greater than that of other models. An obvious risk is the likelihood for severe shortages—first in capital, which leaves projects incomplete, and second in foreign exchange, which leaves enterprises without the necessary intermediate goods and machinery. Projects begun remain inactive, and ipso facto firms operate below capacity.

A second major risk of the managed system results from manipulation of domestic resources. Transfers from one sector to another or from one firm to another prevent capable productive forces from using their potential for growth, re-investment, and renovation. "Good money thrown after bad" is the expression that best characterizes this process.

Self-destructive practices are not limited to unproductive and wasteful management of capital but also to loss of control over the extensive organizations that implement the design and take their orders from above. The government had no sufficient resources to make the various actors in its service conform to the spirit or letter of commands or to instill initiative. Political appointments in positions of responsibility engender political not economic accountability. Moreover, impractical and intractable decisions descend from above (the president or cabinet members) and leave little for executives to salvage.

Under the integrative development model, the sector or the economy at large became the center of attention rather than the individual enterprise. Such a shift in priorities resulted in a downward pressure on productive forces, a sort of production depressant. The weakening of the individual firm in the interest of the national project had, as is to be expected, an adverse effect on the national economy.

The Vicious Circle of Intervention

Unwilling to give up its national design or make a hard choice in the face of terrible shortages, the regime chipped away at the edges of its programs beginning in the seventies and continuing into the late eighties. To deal with the scarcity of funds, it cut back on the tendency to determine prices artificially and drew closer to market determinants of exchange. But it stubbornly refused to eliminate wasteful enterprises or programs, tending rather to spend less and less. It artificially shifted the burden to national banks by allowing deficit-ridden firms to cover their annual deficits by loans. In the production area, it increased its stringent measures to lower investment and contain wages. As these efforts proved, the greater the exigencies and range of government intervention and hegemony, the greater the slide away from actual control. Compliance with the regime's express objectives progressively diminished, and a new and uncivic culture emerged.

The founders of the patron state began in the late fifties with an assumption opposite from what actually occurred. Their understanding was that the greater the range of the regime's control over the nation's economic resources, the greater the political power of its leaders. In reality, more extensive governmental powers proved eventually to be a political and economic liability, not an asset.

EQUALITY, PRIVILEGE, AND SOCIAL CONSCIOUSNESS

Nasser and his successors established a social system of relative equality and adhered to it throughout. The system was intended to remove the excesses of inequality by taking on the very wealthy and providing basic needs for the poor. Equal opportunity became the law of the land, especially in social welfare services such as free education and health care. The question here is whether equal opportunity resulted in equal benefits and whether such benefits compensated for the controls imposed on society in the name of social justice and national development.

This study has shown that contrary to express policy statements, under a regime striving for equal access to benefits, status holders and skilled individuals actually enjoyed a greater share of what the government offered than other groups in society. Prevailing social advantage rather than express government policy is responsible for this relative distortion in distribution. Thus, when a policy such as free education for all is put into effect, those who enjoy status, wealth, and skills are able to use or manipulate the system to their advantage and receive a disproportionate share of the available educational resources. Though the policy might have been originally made expressly to open the doors to the disadvantaged, their share remained not fully utilized. Egypt is not alone in that respect;[15] an egalitarian system of education in France ended up with similar results.[16]

In education, for instance, the privileged can afford the opportunity costs of sending their children to school, while the poor cannot afford to forgo the earnings of their children's labor for the duration of the school term. The privileged may also enjoy access to other resources that give their offspring better chances, such as ability to pay for private lessons. Education is not the only area with such distortions; in all the policies examined in this book, it has been found that equal opportunity does not automatically translate into equal shares.

The advantaged, however, do not constitute a closed circle, nor do they have a committee that presides over the management of their interests. The fact of the matter is that a regime of equality is porous, and the skilled actors surface on top, despite formal rules giving others equal opportunity. At any rate, the socially advantaged are not to be found in one place or one career type but are a category dispersed among government officials and better-off citizens in various walks of life.

The privileged do not necessarily achieve their bigger share by conspiracy, solidarity, or collective action as socialist thought would have us believe but by individually using and manipulating the system. Some tacit group agreement undoubtedly exists; the point, however, is that under the patron state, advantage could be achieved by a large number of people on an individual basis without resort to collective action.

By prohibiting collective action for social improvement, national leaders fostered individual and private solutions to common problems. Individual solutions increase the opportunities for the privileged and contribute to the attitude of political disengagement and cynicism. The culture generated by the Revolution has been the antithesis of what it had set out to achieve—nationalism and public sharing in one uplifting enterprise. Instead, we have seen individualism, familism, cronyism, and cynicism prevail. Most politically damaging has been the decline in collective action to mend social problems and the prevalence of an individualistic attitude of everyone for himself. So long as obtaining social advantage was a matter of maneuvering on the edges of an entrenched and insurmountable system, collective action was deemed nonproductive by most Egyptians. Spontaneous mass eruptions did occur from time to time, but were not organized into sustained operations.

The preceding account should not imply that the regime of equality did not benefit the traditionally underprivileged; the point is rather that they were unable to fully or equally exploit opportunities. Upward mobility in Egypt has been clearly in evidence, however, and an impressive number of low-income people have found their way into the ranks of the privileged.

The individualistic approach to social problems and the public cynicism have politically served the regime well. The resulting tendencies—greater shares for the advantaged and upward mobility for many of the poor—have produced relative social stability. The privileged were pacified by their enjoyment of the larger share of the public good, while aspirants to privilege were accommodated by access to the means of social mobility. The conjunction of these two tendencies reduced the incidence of social discord and dissension and contributed to the survival of the class coalition organized by the nationalist-oriented patron state system. This may be the main reason why the patron state system survived for so long in Egypt under conditions of slow economic growth.

THE UNCIVIC CULTURE

One particularly disturbing phenomenon resulting from the integrative development approach was the cultivation of illicit behavior by citizens and officials alike—particularly cynicism and disrespect for the law. Economic development rests on a moral commitment as much as on clear vision and sound economic policies. The idealism and promise of the Egyptian Revolution in its earlier phases faded within a relatively short period of time. Instead, national leaders became resigned to routine crisis management and citizens to cynicism and frustration. In effect, the regime failed to convince most Egyptians that the policy hardships it had inflicted on them were morally justifiable and developmentally functional.

Government policies are supposed to be more or less rational, politically and economically, but they may also reflect cultural patterns of behavior set in place over a number of generations. Not only may public policy reflect cultural norms but it may in turn generate new cultural patterns of behavior. The Revolutionary regime set out to inspire and instill idealism and public spiritedness but inadvertently produced a culture of evasion and undercover behavior. In the last few decades, we have witnessed the creation of a mass culture in Egypt that has been termed in this book *uncivic* and that can be attributed to distortions in official economic policies.

The predominant feature of the uncivic culture is the common readiness of citizens to see violation of the law as a matter of right and as a sign of clever social aptitude.[17] In many areas, especially economic ones, breaking the law is not considered by ordinary Egyptians as antisocial behavior.

The uncivic culture is not synonymous with forms of corruption, such as embezzlement and bribery, for corruption is recognized as immoral and reprehensible, whereas uncivic behavior is considered a justifiable response to unfair or impossible official impositions. The practice is a feature of common everyday life among the mass population, including officials of the government themselves. Perhaps the most damaging aspect of the uncivic culture is the generation of a tendency for each individual or family to go it alone. It has become a matter of beating the system at its game, not reforming it. Group spirit and group action have fallen victim to the spirit of cynicism that pervades today's culture in Egypt.

The uncivic culture thus is associated with widespread cynicism regarding public affairs, frustration over lack of progress, and lack of incentive to contribute to the common good. Cynicism is indicative of the ambiguity of moral imperatives in society and may generate extremism among some as a revulsion against loss of public moral standards. Some of those capable of such moral revulsion are also gifted with religious talent and zeal, such as are some Islamic revivalist groups, who have become opponents of and the only credible alternative to the Revolutionary regime.

It is not unusual for an observer of regimes in developing countries to take the uncivic culture phenomenon lightly as yet another statistical instance of corruption, grasping officialdom, and elite disrespect for their own commitments. Such an attitude, however, does not provide an answer. An accurate explanation must go beyond facile complaints of grasping officialdom, especially because the level of explicit corruption in Egypt, no matter how much focus has been placed on it, is in fact comparatively low when judged against standards in other developing countries. Officials of the government, high and low, continue to live with means that can be described as modest to poor. The uncivic culture phenomenon is directly related to the type of development policy pursued by a regime. Understanding it brings one to the heart of the development process affecting more than two-thirds of the world population.

Underdevelopment

We shall extrapolate from the preceding observations a view of underdevelopment based on the scarcity of entrepreneurship. The new perspective offers the hope that development can be achieved without having to make a choice between growth and equity.

The Marxian concept of surplus value is basic to the explanation of both the distribution and production processes. Surplus value is equivalent to the value generated by a worker in excess of the subsistence requirements for him and his families. This idea is analogous to tenancy conditions and wage labor in less-developed agricultural economies. Workers retain of the value they generate only what is necessary for keeping body and soul together, the rest is taken away by the landlord. What is taken by the "inactive" landlord is called the surplus value of labor and goes to the benefit of the employer, not the worker.

The simplicity of the landlord-peasant model is deceptive. Marx's concepts of *subsistence* and *surplus value* are subjective and therefore not precise enough to serve as benchmarks for determining the value of work or as bases for a coherent economic theory.

The subsistence concept is always defined from someone's point of view. A family with only a roof over its head and enough food not to starve could be said to be living at subsistence level. But food and shelter may be so deficient as to make the life expectancy of its members ten years shorter than that of better-situated families. If subsistence, on the other hand, is defined in terms of the minimum required calories and protein intake that are recommended by medical wisdom, then should other basic needs such as education, housing, medical services, and leisure be included? And by how much? Where does one draw the line? Who defines subsistence, the donor or the beneficiary? It is clear that subsistence can be upgraded or downgraded continuously without changing the term itself. Similarly, if it is not possible to determine what constitutes an economic surplus, then the concept cannot serve as a basis for a theory of exploitation and poverty, in other words, of underdevelopment.

Another Marxian concept pertinent to the subject of underdevelopment is determining the value of work, especially when the calculation involves machines. The question is, what level of technology should be used when machine work is compared to human labor? Human labor and its output cannot be separated from some level of technology. Using a flint tool to plant corn would give an output per hour of labor quite different from that when a wooden or metal plow is used. Should the output of a tractor be compared to that of a man using a hand pick, a wooden plough, or a metal plough? One may have to define the technological level arbitrarily in order to make it useful for comparison, yet to do so in order to discover the value of work is more archaic than the gold standard in finance.

Marx, according to some of his interpreters, recognized the differential in labor skills and productivity.[18] Workers with highly developed skills contribute more to production than others with lesser or no skills. In that case, a differential reward system, in which the more skilled produce more and should be rewarded more, must be accepted. Hence, inequality and social classes under communism are admissible. For Lenin to say later on that such inequality is temporary and would disappear under the last stage of socialism is quite arbitrary.

Economic value, it follows, is not created by the quantity of labor alone, as Marx and Lenin asserted, but by the quality of labor and by the ideas guiding and organizing it. Hence, the importance of entrepreneurship. A successful idea of a business opportunity is worth many times more than the amount of labor spent on production of a commodity. The skilled find a better price for their labor because the returns they generate are greater. Service thus has an economic value all its own—a reality that is underplayed, almost ignored, in favor of production by Marxism and by an alarming number of intellectuals in the Third World.

If it is admitted that economic value is generated by the quality of labor and by the ideas guiding and organizing an enterprise, then the source of underdevelopment can also be identified as a lack of entrepreneurial skills and adequate quality work. Long hours put in by unskilled workers may prove more costly than the going market rate for the product. Under those circumstances, the cost to produce is greater than the returns, the solution for which is to desist from production or to substitute machines for human labor.

Low economic standards prevail when (1) labor returns are low; (2) the labor cost of a commodity relative to production cost is too high; (3) the skills necessary for production are too crude or totally lacking; or (4) the quality of products precludes their competitiveness in the market.

The illusion that in a controlled market economy, competitiveness (in price, cost, and quality) does not matter obscures the underdeveloped nature of the process. A commodity in a controlled market economy is inexpensive because it is artificially priced, not because of lower production cost or high returns of labor. In a market economy, a product that is too costly and inferior would be ejected and its producer marginalized. Poverty then is a function of the engagement of skills that are irrelevant to the market; it is a prevalence of dispensable labor. It is indicative of the economic marginality of the labor force.

Economic marginality of work occurs when the cost of employment is greater than the value of its returns. This point stands on its head the Marxist argument that poverty occurs under conditions where the value of returns is greater than labor cost. Admittedly, the deprivation of workers from a proper share of the surplus leads to their impoverishment, but so does low productivity. Given freedom of action, an employer will not use an extra unit of labor that does not give an extra unit of profit. Disregard for this basic rule, under whatever pretext, is at the heart of the economic crisis of many centrally managed economies. A great deal of the poverty and misery in LDCs is due to low labor productivity, scarce employment opportunities, and the absence of competent entrepreneurship.

In short, when dealing with LDCs the issue is how to avoid generating a deficit, not how to distribute a surplus, which is rarely there. Since LDCs have a high ratio of unskilled to skilled workers, their production of goods and services is meager, a fact manifested in a generally low GNP and a low standard of living.

But how then, one may wonder, have some developing countries—such as South Korea and Taiwan—succeeded in becoming industrialized and wealthy nations despite a large proportion of unskilled to skilled labor? In the sixties, South Korea was at the same economic level as Egypt and Peru, but in the eighties South Korea left them both far behind. Since only the briefest possible treatment of NICs could be included here, suffice it to say that the private sector was encouraged in those countries, even during the import-substitution phase.[19] Government involvement in NICs took the form of providing outstanding incentives and support, aside from its direct role as an entrepreneur and manager, which was not exclusive as in the case of the integrative development model. Guided and supported by the government, the private sector became the major agent of growth in conjunction with a large public sector. Here is where the issue of entrepreneurship in its basic meaning comes in as an answer to our query.

The starting point is that production of economic value is a social rather than an individual act. The importance of individual skill pales in comparison to the social aspect of an economic action—the organization of skills, decision-making and managerial. The key issue becomes one of entrepreneurship, for what is needed are ideas and the ability to organize and coordinate elements of an enterprise. Economic marginality of labor is a social condition more than an individual one, and therefore underdevelopment is a function of the level of entrepreneurial skills even in an economically nonobstructive environment.

An entrepreneur is a prime mover, an agent with a valuable idea and the managerial skills necessary for its implementation. Skill means the use of the labor of others effectively. Unskilled labor under expert entrepreneurial management can be put to better use than under less capable management and get transformed effectively. Likewise, skilled labor in the absence of entrepreneurship and effective management will be wasted and perform below capacity. The argument here is that the whole is greater than the sum of its parts, for taken alone a unit of labor may be unproductive even if skilled, but taken as part of a well-conceived enterprise its relevance becomes magnified. That is why we can dare to think that equality will be enhanced with economic growth, for growth inspired by skillful entrepreneurship will improve the capacity of labor to be productive. Moreover, a more skilled and productive labor force has greater political weight and is in a better position to claim its share of national wealth. We know statistically that the more economically advanced a country, the more equitable the distribution.

In light of the preceding argument, it would be more appropriate when discussing underdevelopment to refer to entrepreneurial scarcity than to labor marginality. Entrepreneurs are the ones who put together elements of production and services effectively. They are the agents of growth, and where there are few such agents, underdevelopment and its correlates prevail. Thus, ideas and managerial skills should be assigned greater weight in the generation of material values in an economy than sheer quantities of labor.

The problem with the integrative economic approach has been the setting up of a single entrepreneur as a central intelligence to guide and manage the totality of the national economy and social welfare. A more inimical formula to entrepreneurial success one can hardly find.

Development is not a function of the ingenuity of one or very few entrepreneurs but of a culture that is permissive and supportive of creative energies. The prevalence of small business entrepreneurs should not be viewed negatively as a prerequisite that condemns LDCs to remain at a low level of growth and technology, for enterprise is by nature dynamic, and what is small can become large. In the absence of capital accumulation, low purchasing power, adequate infrastructure, and advanced skills, small enterprises are the most appropriate undertakings for the initial stages of growth in most developing countries.[20] Not backyard steel furnaces, as might be imagined by some; no steel furnaces at all is the point. Continued use of public funds on quixotic adventures in fancy industrial complexes is not an affordable proposition.

One of the paradoxes of development is that government's competence as entrepreneur is extremely poor, yet institutionally governments are an essential part of the development environment. Though their supportive role is essential, governments should not set priorities or assume managerial functions.

Entrepreneurship does not exist in a vacuum; its most significant environment is the state system. Governments are called on to play a more active role than just a protector of a free economic environment. One of the main reasons is that entrepreneurs are not necessarily self-regulating or autonomous agents acting in the general interest. The self-seeking principle and private interest of entrepreneurs is an essential aspect of the process that cannot be taken away without incurring great risks. Moreover, government services are an essential substitute for lagging market mechanisms in LDCs and sometimes in advanced industrial countries. Educational services and other external economies provided to a large extent by public authorities are cases in point.

In addition to the fact that the market is not self-regulating, the self-centered perspective of entrepreneurs makes the role of the government a necessary complement; for a government, in principle, looks after the general interest. Entrepreneurs in a free, especially developing, market manifest serious shortcomings that, through government action, can be avoided.

First, entrepreneurs are subject to inertia, satisfaction with the regular course taken, and inability (in a significant number of cases) to adjust to change. We may be reminded here of tendencies among entrepreneurs to wallow in protectionism. Shock treatment may be necessary and may come from government action, regional market changes, new technology, or new blood in the entrepreneurial class.

Second, entrepreneurs are prey to habits of self-indulgence. The nouveau riche especially may easily slip into lives of conspicuous consumption, luxurious living, and waste.

Third, entrepreneurs have tended to exhibit predatory inclinations, which is manifest through monopolization of the market and of business enterprises. When the free market economy fails to uphold competitiveness, antitrust legislation may prove necessary.

Fourth, access to capital is not entirely free or equal in the market, especially in LDCs. In some very poor LDCs, farmers may not even have enough credit to buy seeds and other inputs on their own and so may fail to cultivate the land without outside assistance. Again, the government, or some community action, may be a valuable mediator or provider in this case, but not necessarily the only one.

Finally, the exchange of labor as a commodity in democratic societies has shown that the price of labor is influenced by factors other than supply and demand. Unionization and collective bargaining are only an illustration of the mediation of the market mechanism by social factors.

Whether visibly or not, government is a partner with business, but government should earn that role and not think of it as one of right and privilege. A government is a prime candidate for that partnership by virtue of its functions and public character, in addition to other factors such as modern technology and the global marketplace, an increasingly important factor in the equation. Governments are becoming more involved in the international market, mediating between the domestic and the global trading arena.

A public authority has potentially the right qualities to balance and cope with entrepreneurial privateness and fragmentation, but not every government is willing to play that role, is able to play it, or plays it effectively. There is no guarantee against incompetence, partnership in corruption, or blinding sectional interests. These potential shortcomings of governments have to be addressed one way or another, for very few success stories can be found where government has not effectively played the double role of arbiter and support provider. In contrast, the government's role as a monopoly entrepreneur has proved to be a sure formula for failure.

NOTES

Chapter 1: Introduction

1. See Evans, "The State as Problem and Solution," 140.

2. Sartori, *The Theory of Democracy Revisited*, 279.

3. Held, "Introduction: Central Perspective," 1.

4. *Webster's New Collegiate Dictionary*, 10th ed.

5. For more on this view, see Harik, "Privatization."

6. Kahler, "Orthodoxy and Its Alternatives."

7. Waterbury, *The Egypt of Nasser and Sadat*, 18.

8. Richards and Waterbury, *A Political Economy*, 215.

9. Ibid.

10. The handmaiden role is more applicable to Saudi Arabia and the Gulf states; see Krimly, *The Political Economy of Rentier States*.

11. Handoussa, "Siyasaat al islaah."

12. Cooper, "State Capitalism." Richards and Waterbury, *A Political Economy*, owe much to Ghunaym, who started to write about state capitalism and the new class in Egypt since 1968: see *Al Namoudhaj al Misri*. For a detailed discussion of the neo-Marxist view of state capitalism, see Jessop, *State Theory*.

13. Waterbury, *The Egypt of Nasser and Sadat*, 19.

14. Richards and Waterbury, *A Political Economy*.

15. Springborg, *Mubarak's Egypt*; Seddon, "Austerity Protests"; Ayubi, *The State and Public Policies*. Richards and Waterbury, *A Political Economy*, reiterates the "state capitalist" thesis with some reservation, as can be understood from the casual remark, "public sector enterprises generally operate at a loss" (216).

16. See Waterbury, *The Egypt of Nasser and Sadat*, 18–20.

17. Ibid., 20.

18. Waterbury maintains that the public sector was competitive "in production, sales and profits" from 1956 to 1961: ibid., 19. I have not found any evidence to support that assertion.

19. Waterbury, *The Egypt of Nasser and Sadat*, 19.

20. See the discussion that follows and chapter 10.

21. Writing in December 1988, Handoussa was still able to make that assertion; see "Siyasaat al islaah," 9.

22. See chapter 2.

23. For the strategic minority concept, see Harik, "The Political Elite as a Strategic Minority."

24. Richards and Waterbury, *A Political Economy;* also Mursi, *Hadha al Infitaah;* and Ghunaym, *al Namoudhaj al Misri.*

25. It should also be added here that Nasser received American and European financial aid.

26. About three-fifth of exports were cotton and yarn.

27. Issawi, *Egypt in Revolution,* 45.

28. For this period, see Hansen and Nashashibi, *Egypt;* Vatikiotis, ed., *Egypt Since the Revolution;* Abdel-Fadil, *The Political Economy of Nasserism.*

29. O'Brien, *The Revolution in Egypt's Economic System.*

30. Nasser stated in 1963 that control of the means of production, not total nationalization, is the object. See English translation in Karpat, ed., *Political and Social Thought,* 293.

31. Handoussa, "The Impact of Liberalization."

32. Hansen and Marzouk, "Planning and Economic Growth"; and Amin, *Qissat Duyun Misr.*

33. Theoretically, the government had drawn up a seven-year plan, but in fact it was just a face-saving device for the regime, not a real plan.

34. Mabro and Radwan, *Industrialization of Egypt;* also Baroudi, "The Performance of the Egyptian Export Economy."

35. Bianchi used the term *fitful* to describe the discontinuous and fragmentary nature of Egyptian policymaking since the Revolution: see Bianchi, *Unruly Corporatism.*

36. According to Nasser during the unity dialogues: see *Mahaadir Muhaadathaat al Wahdah,* 304. With respect to industry alone, see the table listing the share of public sector involvement for each branch of manufacturing in Mabro and Radwan, *Industrialization of Egypt,* 103.

37. For a detailed statement of the open-door policy, see Oweis, ed., *The Political Economy;* Ayubi, *The State and Public Policies;* Springborg, *Mubarak's Egypt;* and Hinnebusch, *Egyptian Politics.* For primary sources on the infitaah, see CAPMAS, *Mawqif al Infitaah al Iqtisaadi.*

38. Handoussa, see "Siyasaat al islaah," 8.

39. After restrictions on exports were mostly lifted in the early nineties, there were still twenty commodities whose export was banned, seventeen subject to quantitative restrictions, and thirty-seven whose export required prior permission.

40. Handoussa, "Reform Policies," 3–4.

41. Ibid., 4 and 5. Springborg maintains that public employment increased four-fold between 1970 and 1986: *Mubarak's Egypt,* 137.

42. 'Idl, "al qitaa' al 'aam," 207.

43. Handoussa, "Reform Policies," 4.

44. Figures given by Naggar, *Nahwa Istratijiyah Qawmiyah,* 71; and *Al Ahraam al Iqtisaadi* (cited hereafter as *al Iqtisaadi*), 10 June 1991.

45. See Springborg, "Egypt," in *Economic and Political Liberalization in the Middle East,* edited by Tim Niblock and Emma Murphy (London: British Academic Press, 1993), 152.

46. Handoussa, "The Impact of Liberalization," 24.

47. See Beblawi and Luciani, eds., *The Rentier State;* also Handoussa, "Reform Policies," 3 and 4.

48. According to Prime Minister Kamal Hasan Ali: see *al Ahraam,* 14 June 1985.

49. According to the Minister of the National Economy: see *al Ahraam,* 14 March 1988. Private entrepreneur spokespeople usually question this figure and consider it biased upward.

Chapter 2: Industrial Policy and Decision Making

1. From the text of the first Five Year Plan, quoted by Issawi, *Egypt in Revolution,* 169.

2. Hansen, *Egypt and Turkey,* 153; CAPMAS, *Al Kitaabal Ihsaa'i al Sanawy,* table 11.3.

3. Issawi, *Egypt in Revolution,* 170.

4. See Mabro and Radwan, *Industrialization of Egypt,* tables 5.2 and 5.3. For the record of the Nasser regime in general, see Hansen and Nashashibi, *Egypt;* and Harik, "Azamat al Tahawwul al Ishtiraaki."

5. Handoussa, "Reform Policies."

6. Muhieddin, "taqiym istraatijiyat al tasniy`," 189.

7. For a more elaborate statement on this subject, see Bianchi's study, *Unruly Corporatism;* and al Sayyid, *Al Mujtama'wa al Siyaasah;* also Amani Qindil in various papers and contributions to the weekly publication *al Iqtisaadi.*

8. For the economic history of this period, see Issawi, *Egypt in Revolution;* and Mabro, *The Egyptian Economy.*

9. al 'Idl, "al qitaa' al 'aam."

10. Regarding the political aspects of a populist regime in Egypt, see Hinnebusch, *Egyptian Politics.*

11. Sullivan, "The Political Economy of Reform."

12. Bianchi, *Unruly Corporatism;* and al-Sayyid, *al Mujtama'wa al Siyaasah;* also Posusney, "Labor as an Obstacle to Privatization."

13. For the situation under President Sadat, see Qindil, *Sin'al Siyaasaat al 'Ammah.*

14. These agencies were transformed into holding companies in 1991. See the rest of this chapter for details.

15. Law number 60, 1971; and law number 11, 1975.

16. al 'Idl, "al qitaa' al 'aam," 209–11.

17. See Waalil's article in *Al Iqtisaadi,* 3 January 1983. The editor of the journal confirmed to this writer that the article was sent by the minister unsolicited.

18. See discussion by the Minister of Industry in *al Ahraam,* 12 June 1987.

19. *Rose el Yousef,* 23 June 1986.

20. Government of Egypt (GOE), al Majaalis al Qawmiyah al Mutakhassisah (MQM), *al Qitaa' al 'Aam,* 130–36; also GOE, MQM, *al Shu'un al Iqtisaadiyah,* 46.

21. Ahmed, *Public Finance in Egypt,* 71.

22. This was reorganized in 1991 and made into holding companies.

23. General organizations that undertook actual business or industrial activities remained intact as general managers of actual enterprises such as railways or electricity.

24. GOE, MQM, *al Qitaaʿ al ʿAam*, 130–36.

25. This belief has been frequently expressed by government officials and at times by business leaders. For documentary purposes, we may mention GOE, MQM, *al Qitaaʿ al ʿAam*, and other publications of al Majaalis al Qawmiyah. See in particular *al Dawrah*, 14; and Handoussa, "The Impact of Liberalization"; also Handoussa, "maʾaal al qitaʿ al ʿaam," 451–56.

26. According to a former Minister of National Economy, ʿAbd al Munʿim al Qaysuni, in the article "Qadiyat al Daʿm fi Misr," *Ahraam*, 6 September 1977.

27. Dr. Hamed el Sayeh, interview by author.

28. Text of statement given to author by Dr. el Sayeh, December 1979.

29. Rivlin, *Dynamics*, 80.

30. Ibid.

31. Ibid.

32. Hansen and Nashashibi, *Egypt*, 92.

33. Qaysuni, "qadiyat al daʿm fi misr," *Al Ahraam*, 6 September 1977.

34. See chapter 3 regarding this issue.

35. Press conference given by the Minister of Industry and quoted in *al Ahaaly*, 10 February 1988.

36. Ibid.

Chapter 3: Industry

1. Handoussa, "The Impact of Liberalization," 8; Handoussa, "maʾal al qitaʿ alʿaam," 457.

2. Handoussa, "Public Sector Employment," 21.

3. Ibid., 22.

4. Ahmed, *Public Finance in Egypt*, 66.

5. For the positive economic returns from traditional industries and negative returns from metals industries and engineering during that period, see the study results reached jointly by the World Bank and the Ministry of Industry and reported by Hatim, *al Iqtisaad al Misri*, 267; and Handoussa, "Public Sector Employment," 33.

6. Ahmed, *Public Finance in Egypt*, 65.

7. These include 0.5 percent for sports, 5 percent for reserves, 5 percent for bonds, and 5 percent for inflation reserves.

8. Handoussa, "maʾal al qitaʿalʿaam," 456.

9. Handoussa, "The Impact of Liberalization," 3; and GOE, MQM, *al Qitaʿ alʿAam*.

10. In principle, the measure that devalued the pound should have added to the production cost of public sector enterprises that previously had been entitled to a special foreign-exchange rate. In practice, though, the change was nominal to most GIE transactions, because government banks charged a high commission for foreign exchange provided to GIEs, making their rate equal or more costly than the black-market rate.

11. See chapter 6, on foreign exchange.

12. Handoussa, "maʾal al qitaʿ alʿaam," 456.

13. Ibid., 456–57.

14. *Al Ahraam,* 16 December 1988.

15. Ibid.

16. Net profit made by state industrial firms in 1987 was reported by the government think tank, al Majaalis al Qawmiyah of Majlis al Shura, to be 2.5 percent. GOE, MQM, *al Shu'un,* 42. The IMF and the World Bank usually put the figure at 1 to 2 percent. However, it is not clear what these figures include or exclude in a distorted economic system.

17. One Egyptian pound (£E) was equal to 45 cents in the free market (here, the black market) in the early seventies and about 30 cents in the late eighties.

18. Rivlin, *Dynamics,* 91.

19. Qaysuni, *al Ahraam,* 1 July 1977.

20. Ibid., 5 September 1977.

21. Ibid., 7 September 1977.

22. See chapter 4, on agriculture.

23. Handoussa, "ma'al al qita' al 'aam," 456.

24. See budget report in Qaysuni, *Al Ahraam,* 3 September 1988.

25. Reported in *al Iqtisaadi,* 12 December 1988.

26. For details, see Ahmed, *Public Finance in Egypt,* chapters 4 and 5.

27. *Al Ahraam,* 9 July 1988.

28. Ibid.

29. Ibid.

30. Figures for the years 1984/85 to 1986/87 were obtained from GOE, Ministry of Finance, *Al hisaabaat al khitaamiyah,* which covers all state industrial enterprises in the following industries: textiles, chemicals, foods, minerals, engineering, mining, petroleum, energy, and pharmaceuticals.

31. The record of the Ministry of Finance shows that net returns (al faa'id) of state industrial firms in 1985/86, after accounting for losses but before paying taxes, came to £E799,771,000. Taxes paid then came to £E216,051,000.

32. *Al Ahraam,* 20 August 1988.

33. The Minister of Industry, Muhammad 'Abd-al-Wahhab, who gave this figure added that the asset value of the GIEs was 77 billion pounds, which makes the debt value larger than 50 percent of the assets. Considering that the asset value figure is debatable, the seriousness of the GIEs' situation can no longer be in doubt.

34. GOE, MQM, *al Shu'un,* 42.

35. Based on figures obtained from the Ministry of Finance, *al hisaabaat al khitaamiyah.*

36. This compares with thirty-one firms in the previous year.

37. *Akhir Saa'ah,* 9 March 1988.

38. Ibid.

39. *Ahraam,* 16 December 1988.

40. See *al Iqtisaadi,* 21 February 1983.

41. Head of the marketing and export sector, Ministry of Industry, interviews, December 1987 and January 1988.

42. For the Nasser years, see Hansen and Marzouk, "Planning and Economic

Growth," p. 35, table 9. For the seventies, see Ahmed, *Public Finance in Egypt*, chapters 4 and 5.

43. GOE, Ministry of Planning, *Summary of the Second Five Year Plan*. Public sector investment accounts for about 70 percent of total investment in the economy: Ahmed, *Public Finance in Egypt*, 59.

44. World Bank, *World Development Report*, 1986.

45. *Al Ahraam*, 6 November 1988.

46. Ibid.

47. World Bank, *Fertilizer Industry Review*, iii; see also price table, p. 25.

48. Ibid., 26.

49. *al Iqtisaadi*, 17 October 1988, 74.

50. Quoted by Richter, *The Energy Problem*, 12 November 1986, 18; see also World Bank, *Fertilizer Industry Review*, 27, which finds the energy cost to be 5.9 times more than in comparable modern firms elsewhere.

51. World Bank, *Fertilizer Industry Review*, 27.

52. See ibid., 26.

53. See table in ibid., 6.

54. Ibid., 7.

55. Handoussa, "The Impact of Liberalization," 19.

56. Minister of Industry, interview by the weekly publication *Akhir Saa'ah*, 9 March 1988.

57. World Bank, *Fertilizer Industry Review*, 9.

58. Ibid., 27.

59. Ibid., 28.

60. Ibid., 25.

61. Ibid., iv, 17, and 21.

62. Ibid., 4.

63. Minister of Electricity, *al Musawwar* conference; see *al Musawwar*, 9 September 1988.

64. See the Electric Authority statement in *al Iqtisaadi*, 8 August 1988, 73.

65. Data given by the Minister of Electricity at *al Musawwar* conference; see *al Musawwar*, 9 September 1988.

66. Ibid.

67. Ibid.

68. The Electric Authority of Egypt confirms this view with regard to electricity sold to the aluminum firm: *al Iqtisaadi*, 8 August 1988.

69. Minister of Electricity, *al Musawwar* conference, op. cit.; and World Bank, *Fertilizer Industry Review*.

70. Richter, *The Energy Problem*, 17.

71. See *al Iqtisaadi*, 21 July 1986.

72. Richter, *The Energy Problem*, 16.

73. Ibid., 17, n. 1.

74. Minister of Electricity, *al Musawwar*, 9 September 1988; also, see statement by the prime minister's office in *al Iqtisaadi*, 21 July 1986.

75. Figures based on data in statement published in *al Iqtisaadi*, 8 August 1988.

76. Former Minister of the National Economy, Abu-'Ali, in *Al Tanmiyah al Sinaa'iyah*, 58.

77. This figure was 20 percent of world prices, according to a speech by President Mubarak; see text in *al Ahraam*, 25 August 1988.

78. Minister of Health to *Rose al Yousef*, 21 March 1988.

79. Qaysuni, *al-Ahraam*, 1 July 1977.

80. *Rose el Yousef*, 21 March 1988; this statement is attributed to official sources.

81. The Minister of Health prepared a list of 248 medicines whose import he prohibited. He then set up a committee to examine the list, and the committee approved the prohibition of most items.

82. See table 3.1.

83. Government official in charge of sales, interview, 1988.

84. See Riyad, *Sinaa'at al Dawaa'*, 213–16.

85. *Rose el Yousef*, 21 March 1988.

86. See Muhieddin, "taqiym istraatijiyat al tasniy'."

87. GOE, Ministry of Finance, al *hisaabaat al khitaamiyah*.

88. See table 3.1.

89. See Sherif, "Poor Incentives, Poor Performance."

90. *al Ahaaly*, interview, 27 January 1988.

91. See statement by former Minister of the National Economy, Abu-'Ali, "al Siyasaat al Iqtisaadiyah," 58.

92. World Bank, *Agricultural Price Management*, ii, considers Egypt in this category.

93. Harik, "Continuity and Change."

94. Harik, "Azamat al Tahawwul al Ishtiraaki."

95. For a scholarly and detailed statement on Egyptian exports, see Baroudi, "The Performance of the Egyptian Export Economy."

96. Some public sector managers brought success to their firms under rather hard conditions. For the successful ones, see Handoussa, "The Impact of Liberalization."

Chapter 4: Agricultural Policy

1. For a detailed statement on this strategy, see Harik, *The Political Mobilization of Peasants*, and "Continuity and Change."

2. Of this 25 percent, 8 percent went to the High Aswan Dam. See on this subject Hansen and Marzouk, *Development and Economic Policy*, 8; see also a World Bank report with Ikram as a coordinating author, *Egypt: Economic Management*, 73; and Richards, *Egypt's Agricultural Development*, 190.

3. For this view of African agriculture, see Bates, *Markets and States*.

4. See Abdel-Fadil, *Development, Income Distribution, and Social Change*, 120; and Radwan, *The Impact of Agrarian Reform*, 76; also Korayem, "Tawzi' al dakhl" and *The Impact of Economic Adjustment*.

5. For the extent of social services extended to the countryside, see Harik, *The Political Mobilization of Peasants*.

6. Ibid.

7. Regarding this view of the regime's single party, see Harik, "The Single Party as a Subordinate Movement."

8. Harik, *The Political Mobilization of Peasants.*

9. Ibid.

10. It was 8 percent in 1976 and fell to 5.3 percent later. For the eighties figures, see what follows in this chapter.

11. Land distributed to peasants remained legally government-owned, though peasants held it as if it were actually their private property and they could pass it on to progeny with due legal process. In the eighties, many farmers were able to purchase land-reform orchards from the government.

12. World Bank, *Agricultural Price Management,* iv.

13. Nassaar and Mansur, "al Siyasaat al Si`riyah," I:28.

14. Ibid., 31.

15. Ibid., 28.

16. This seems to be the case in tropical Africa, according to Bates's interpretation: see *Markets and States.*

17. See *al Ahraam,* 31 May 1987.

18. For details, see GOE, Ministry of Agriculture, *al Siyasaat al Si'riyah,* vols. 1 and 2.

19. The frustration of one minister—Yusuf Waali, the Minister of Agriculture— with this situation led him to take the action described in chapter 2.

20. World Bank, *Agricultural Price Management,* iii.

21. See in particular the monthly *al Tali'ah* and the weekly *Rose el Yousef.*

22. World Bank, *Agricultural Price Management,* 15–16.

23. In the case of maize, the surplus was not transferred to consumers only but also was spent in the form of subsidies to poultry farmers and to maize growers.

24. World Bank, *Agricultural Price Management,* iii.

25. Ibid., 16.

26. Ibid., iv.

27. Ibid., 16.

28. Ibid.

29. Nassaar and Mansur, "al Siyasaat," 39.

30. See World Bank, *Agricultural Price Management,* v.

31. The low return to farmers from rice, as compared to the government's profit share, was confirmed by then Minister of Agriculture Yusuf Waali: *al Iqtisaadi,* 3 January 1983, 18. The minister gives the same figures: £E19.8 for the farmer's share and £E346.2 for the government.

32. Area planted with garlic rose to 15,000 feddans in 1984, then dropped to 8,000 and 9,000 the following two years: CAPMAS, *Statistical Yearbook, 1952–1986;* see also a discussion by former Minister of Agriculture Mustapha al Gibali: *Ahraam,* 17 September 1987. It will be noticed from the table that the area of crops with highly priced by-products, such as wheat and sugarcane, were not greatly affected by low prices.

33. In 1991 I collected a number of official price lists for vegetables distributed to retail store owners in Cairo.

34. See *Ahraam*, 14 September 1988.

35. GOE, Central Bank, *Annual Report, 1986/87*, table 4, p. 10.

36. World Bank, *Agricultural Price Management*, vi.

37. Adams, "Development and Structural Change," 711–15.

38. Ibid.

39. Ibid.

40. Ibid.

41. This occurred first in a personal interview by this author just before Waali became a minister and later in many public utterances.

42. Mu'tamar al Khubz al 'Arabi (MKA), (1) *Raghif al Khubz*, 62, table 3.

43. Ibid., 61, table 2.

44. Minister of Agriculture, *al Ahraam*, 8 May 1988.

45. The international wheat price saw a rapid escalation during the decade. The price for a ton of wheat rose from $70 in 1972 to $175 in 1981, reflecting the peaking of oil prices and the devaluation of the import exchange rate of the Egyptian pound in 1979.

46. Mustapha, *Tarshid Faaqid al Khubz*, MKA, vol. 6, al Buhuth al Fardiyah, 1.

47. Official statements, *al Ahraam*, 25 July 1987; and *Sabah al Khayr*, 23 July 1987.

48. MKA, *Dirasaat*, 1:60, table 1. According to the Minister of Supplies, consumption and import figures rose in 1988, and that year Egypt consumed 8,892,000 tons of wheat, with 1,916,000 tons (21 percent) locally produced and the rest (79 percent) imported. See declaration in *al Ahraam*, 12 March 1988.

49. Waterbury, *The Egypt of Nasser and Sadat*, 199.

50. Ahmad al Juwayli, then Governor of Damietta (and an acknowledged expert in questions of agriculture and the bread industry), Bread Conference, Cairo, July 1988.

51. For details, see chapter 5.

52. *Rose el Yousef,* editor's interview, 2 June 1986, 20.

53. CAPMAS, *Statistical Yearbook;* also Mustapha al Gibali (former Minister of Agriculture), *Ahraam*, 17 September 1987.

54. Hindi and al Amir, "Nahwa tatwiir al nizaam al taswiqi lil-huboub," in GOE, MOA, *Siyasaat*, II:9. Compulsory deliveries were abolished in 1975 and restored in 1983: ibid., 36.

55. Ibid., 37.

56. Minister of Agriculture, *Ahraam*, 13 July 1988.

57. Minister's statement reported in *al Ahraam*, 17 July 1987.

58. Ibid.

59. Yusuf Waali to *al Ahraam* correspondent, *Ahraam*, 30 July 1988. The minister has a habit of giving varying figures from time to time. The area planted in 1988 was said on another occasion to be 1.373 million feddans and the production 2.722 million tons: *Ahraam*, 5 August 1988.

60. Minister of Agriculture, *Ahraam*, 25 July 1987.

61. *Al Ahraam*, 1 January 1988.

62. See Habashi, "Nahwa tatwiir al nizaam al taswiqi," in GOE, MOA, *Siyasaat*, II:14.

63. Underpricing and many of its causes are discussed in GOE, Ministry of Agriculture, *al Siyasaat al Si'riyah*, vols. 1 and 2.

64. In 1990 I collected a number of official price lists distributed to retail merchants, who generally ignored them.

65. Officially though, mandatory pricing continues. See *al Ahraam*, 2 August 1987.

66. General Secretary of the Poultry Farmers Association, *al Ahraam*, 12 November 1987. The figure seems to be a reasonable estimate. Egypt's need for all animal feed reached 4 million tons annually in the mid-eighties, while in 1986 local production of feed ingredients amounted to 1.5 million tons.

67. 'Isaam Shabanah (head of the General Organization for Poultry and Animal Resources), interview with *al Musawwar*, 26 August 1988. Other estimates by industry observers are a little lower, but not by much.

68. Sharaf et al., "Nahwa tatwiir," in *Siyasaat*, II:11.

69. Ibid., 44.

70. The public sector share of the egg market was actually larger (some industry sources estimate it at 25 percent) when public sector projects such as those run by the various governorate and agrarian reform organizations are included.

71. Statement by 'Isaam shaba-nah, head of the Public Sector Organization for Animal Resources, in *al Musawwar*, 26 August 1988.

72. Sharaf et al., "Nahwa tatwiir," in *Siyasaat*, vol. 2, 36.

73. See interviews in *al Musawwar*, 26 August 1988.

Chapter 5: Subsidization Policies

1. Subsidies in Egypt are higher than in any other Middle Eastern country, including Syria and Tunisia.

2. al Qaysuni, "Qadiyat al Da`m fi Misr," *al-Ahraam*, 6 September 1977.

3. Ibid.

4. Dr. 'Abd al Razzaq Rizqallah, Egyptian expert at the United Nations, in *al-Ahraam*, 20 August 1988. This means that inflation was averaging 35 percent annually.

5. Figure based on data given in GOE, Central Bank of Egypt, *Annual Report, 1986/87*, 14.

6. Central Bank of Egypt, *Annual Report*, 2.

7. GOE, Central Bank, *al Majalla al Iqtisaadiyya*, vol. 26, no. 2, 1986, p. 150.

8. See announcement in *al-Ahraam*, 9 October 1988.

9. World Bank, *Agricultural Price Management*, iv.

10. Ibid., 16.

11. Ibid.

12. *Al-Ahraam*, 25 August 1988.

13. Handoussa, "Reform Policies," 10.

14. Ibid.

15. See Bank Misr, *al Nashra al Iqtisaadiyah*, year 29, number 2, 31–32.

16. According to Kamal Higaab, head of the Water Authority of Greater Cairo, in a declaration to *al-Ahraam*, 5 May 1986.

17. Ibid.

18. Figures given by Kamal Higaab, head of the Water Authority for Greater Cairo, *Akhir Saa'ah*, 16 March 1988.

19. Ibid.

20. Official statement in *al-Ahraam*, 5 May 1986. This situation still existed in 1991, as a statement by the head of Water Authority of Greater Cairo confirms: see Sa'd al Deeb, *al-Ahraam*, 13 November 1991.

21. Statement by head of the Water Authority of Greater Cairo, *al-Ahraam*, 13 November 1991.

22. I have personally seen, in an apartment I briefly occupied, an instance where years of trickling water due to an unfixed faucet had caused the bathtub enamel to wear off, showing the black substance underneath.

23. See *al-Ahraam*, 28 May 1985.

24. See official statements in *al-Ahraam*, 8 and 12 March 1988; *al Sha'b*, 8 March 1988; and other dailies.

25. At times officials give a figure of 30 kilograms.

26. See for instance, statement by the Minister of Industry to *Akhir Sa'ah*, 9 March 1988, which was repeated in debates in the Peoples Assembly and in the upper house, Majlis al Shura.

27. Minister of Supplies, *al-Ahraam*, 2 August 1988. In another interview, the same minister estimated the cost to the state of a kilogram of sugar at 135 piastres, *al-Ahraam*, 3 March 1988.

28. Based on data given by the Minister of Supplies to *al-Ahraam*, 12 March 1988.

29. Minister of Supplies, in statement to the Peoples Assembly, *al-Ahraam*, 4 March 1988. The figure for wheat and flour is a little higher than other official figures.

30. USAID, *Report*, 15 February 1987, 6.

31. The data on the 1970s situation are drawn from the following sources: USAID, *Egypt's Food and Energy Subsidies*, an unpublished study that describes the situation in 1979; GOE, Ministry of Supplies, *Subsidy List Per Item*; and Richter, *The Energy Problem*.

32. Presidential address on the 34th anniversary of the July Revolution: see text in *al Iqtisaadi*, 28 July 1986. The figure given for 1980–81 in CAPMAS, *Statistical Yearbook*, is £E17,149 billion. The exact figure for 1985–86 is £E26,572 billion: GOE, Central Bank of Egypt, *al Majalla al Iqtisaadiyya*, 170.

33. USAID, *Egyptian Food and Energy Subsidies*, 1979.

34. *al Iqtisaadi*, 19 May 1986, 33.

35. USAID, *Egyptian Food and Energy Subsidies*, 1979.

36. This conclusion is confirmed by studies made by the Food Policy Research Institute: see Alderman and von Braun, "Egypt's Food Subsidy Policy."

37. Richter, *The Energy Problem*, 1986.

38. Ibid., 20.

39. Ibid., 9.

40. Figure cited by Minister of Electricity in interview in *al-Musawwar*, 9 September 1988.

41. Exception should be made for 1988, when the price of wheat in the United States went up sharply due to a drought.

42. *Al-Ahraam*, 19 August 1988.

43. Minister of Supplies, *al-Ahraam*, 2 August 1987.

44. The coupons remained despite the reduction in subsidies in the 1990s. See statement to that effect by the Minister of Supplies, *al Ahraam*, 15 May 1992.

45. International Bank of Reconstruction and Development, Development Research Department, discussion papers, no. 289 (Washington, D.C., 1987).

46. *Rose el Yousef*, 2 June 1986.

47. See MKA, *Dirasaat 'ala al Khubz al Masri*, vol. 3.

48. See MKA, *Dirasaat*, vol. 3, 38–39.

49. See MKA, *Dirasaat*, vol. 1.

50. Every sack makes 850 loaves. Officials claim that a sack makes 880 loaves, which would fetch 17,00 piastres.

51. Statements made at the officially sponsored conference on bread, entitled Mu'tamer al Khubz al 'Arabi, held in Cairo, July 16–19, 1988.

52. This writer witnessed three attacks made against bakers by detectives of the MOS within a six-month period in 1987.

53. On the average a bakery used about twenty-five sacks a day, thus giving a baker about £E11.

54. It may be noted here that the price for diesel fuel, which most bakeries used, was raised from £E7.5 to £E28 per ton in 1987.

55. Statements made during the discussions in the Mu'tamer al Khubz al 'Arabi, Cairo, 1988.

56. This continued to be the estimate of the Ministry of Supply in October 1987.

57. *Sabah al Khayr*, 23 July 1987.

58. Their share by 1988 had risen slightly, though no reliable estimate is yet available.

59. See, in confirmation of this, official admission in *MKA Dirasaat*, vol. 1, 45.

60. For a discussion of these problems, see ibid., vol. 3, 43–45.

61. For the number of infractions, see *al-Ahraam*, 1 February 1988.

62. Rose el Yousef, June 2, 1986, the same journalist who interviewed the bakers. The figures here differ, for bakers admit to receiving only twenty-five sacks per day on average.

63. *Al-Ahraam*, 9 July 1987.

64. Mursi, *Taqwim Faa'iliyat Nizaam al Da'm*, estimates between 10 and 20 percent; Mustafa, *Tarshid Faaqid al Khubz*, estimates 13 percent.

65. Also explicitly stated in *MKA, Dirasaat*, vol. 1, 27.

66. *Al-Ahraam*, 20 September 1988.

67. Shlomo, *On the Effects of Subsidies*, p. 1.

Chapter 6: Foreign Exchange Controls

1. Hatim, *Al Iqtisaad al Misri*, 391. In 1975 own-exchange transactions were expanded by means of trade law number 118: ibid., 173.

2. Ikram, *Egypt: Economic Management*, 261.

3. Egyptian apologists among economists and other writers often assert that the financial crisis did not appear until the 1967 war and as a result of it. This is not true. As an example of such writers, see Zaki, *Dirasaat fi Azamat Misr*.

4. Hansen and Nashashibi, *Egypt*, 108.

5. Hatim, *al Iqtisaad al Misri*, 196. Figures showing high liquidity in the Egyptian market have often been cited by the Minister of Tourism, Fu'ad Sultan.

6. The manner in which hard currency was transferred and smuggled out of Egypt has been described by former Minister of Planning Isma'il Sabri 'Abdallah: see statement in *al Ahaaly*, 7 December 1988.

7. See Zaki, *Dirasaat fi Azmat Misr*, 207–11, for the relevance of such policy to Egypt. Zaki considers exchange controls a successful policy, though he gives no substantiation of this claim.

8. Report by a special committee of the Peoples' Assembly, *al Ahraam* 19 June 1987.

9. Hatim, *Al Iqtisaad al Misri*, 161–65.

10. Ibid.

11. See Girgis, *Industrialization and Trade Patterns*, 100–101; also Hatim, *Al Iqtisaad al Misri*, 170–72.

12. See details in Hatim, *Al Iqtisaad al Misri*, 172–73.

13. This law was introduced by Minister of the National Economy 'Abd al Magid 'Abd al Razzaaq. See documentary evidence in *al Iqtisaadi*, 21 July 1986.

14. *Al Iqtisaadi*, 25 July 1983.

15. For a summary of the various rates, see Luciani, "Multiple Puzzle."

16. For the rates in 1986 as reported by a special committee of the Consultative Council (*Maglis al Shawra*), see report in *al Iqtisaadi*, 16 June 1986. The only marked difference is the increase in the incentive rate.

17. See Hatim, *al Iqtisaad al Misri*, 200.

18. See statement by former Minister of the National Economy 'Abd al Razzaaq in *al Iqtisaadi*, 21 July 1986.

19. *Al Iqtisaadi*, 25 July 1983.

20. Interview granted by the minister to *Rose al Yousef*, 1 May 1987.

21. See, for instance, statement to that effect by former minister of the National Economy 'Abd al Razzaaq in *al Iqtisaadi*, 21 July 1986.

22. Al dollar al gumruki was worth 40 piastres until Mustafa al Sa'id raised it to 70 piastres. In 1986 it was raised again to 135, then in 1987 to 189 piastres.

23. For the concept of the rentier state and its application to the Middle East, see Beblawi and Luciani, eds., *The Rentier State*.

24. Nabil Sabbagh of *al Iqtisaadi* finds this to be the realistic estimate among those made by local and international sources. See *al Iqtisaadi*, 17 October 1988.

25. See report by a special committee of the Peoples' Assembly, *al Ahraam*, 19 June 1987.

26. Hatim, *Al Iqtisaad al Misri*, 165.

27. Ministerial decree number 354, 1981.

28. Ministerial decree number 28, 1982.

29. Figures given by Minister of Tourism, Mr. Fu'ad Sultan, *al Ahraam*, 2 December 1988.

30. Statement by the Minister in the Economic Committee of the ruling National Democratic Party: see *al Iqitsaadi*, 28 July 1986.

31. See terms in Hatim, *al Iqtisaad al Misri*, 163.

32. For details, see Girgis, *Industrialization and Trade Patterns*, 88ff.; also Mabro and Radwan, *Industrialization of Egypt*, 226; and Hatim, *al Iqtisaad al Misri*.

33. Finding by Peter O'Brien, quoted in Mabro and Radwan, *Industrialization of Egypt*, 215–16.

34. For the seventies, see Girgis, *Industrialization and Trade Patterns*, 185.

35. Girgis, *Industrialization and Trade Patterns*, 142–44.

36. Mabro and Radwan, *Industrialization of Egypt*, 213; and Ahmed, *Public Finance in Egypt*, 59.

37. See Baroudi, "The Performance of the Egyptian Export Economy."

38. Countertrade deals though were another matter.

39. Decree number 126, *qaraar*, 1983, of the Minister of the National Economy.

40. Decree number 361; see text in *al Ahraam*, 16 August 1988.

41. For an example, see the article by former Minister Fu'ad Mursi, "Madha fa`ala al infitaah."

42. According to the Central Bank report; see summary in *al Ahraam*, 23 July 1988.

43. Khayr-al-Din et al., "al siyaasah al himaa'iyah," 15.

44. Hatim, *al Iqtisaad al Misri*, 303.

45. Import/export law number 118.

46. Abd al Latif al Sharif is an outstanding exception to the rule. Al Sharif started out manufacturing plastics and in the construction business. He is now one of the largest and most successful of Egypt's private entrepreneurs. Like the other STAs, his business was hurt by the June 1988 decrees.

47. For a relatively detailed statement, see Springborg, *Mubarak's Egypt*.

48. For the dynamics of their dealings with high-ranking officials, see ibid.

49. The other shareholders are: Daqahliya governorate, 10 percent; the National Development Bank of Daqahliya, 25 percent; Abd-al-Raouf family, 15 percent; individual shareholders, 12 percent.

50. Among the supporters were the dailies *al Akhbaar*, *al Gumhuriyah*, and occasionally *al Ahraam*. Critics included the weeklies *Rose el Yousef*, *al Musawwar*, *and al Ahraam al Iqtisaadi*.

51. For a detailed statement of the new laws and official clarifying statements made a few weeks later, see, in addition to the daily press, Sharaf-al-Din, *al Dalil al Qaanuni*.

52. See comments made by various specialists and commentators in *al Iqtisaadi*, 13 June 1988, and subsequent issues.

53. See his comments in *al Iqtisaadi*, 13 June 1988.

54. The politically strident attitude of al Rayyaan stands out in this respect. He paid a heavy price for ignoring his politically experienced confidants' advice to avoid standing up to the government and to engage in large projects considered strategic by the government, such as the transport project in Giza.

55. Sharing this view of political meddling by STAs is the leftist political party, *al*

Tagamu, whose newspaper, *al Ahaali*, was the most outspoken critic of the STAs and repeatedly called on the government to regulate them.

56. *Al Ahraam*, 14 August 1987.

57. Ibid.

58. Ibid., 14 August 1987.

59. Ibid., 22 July 1988.

60. Khayr-al-Din et al., "al siyaasah al himaa'iyah," 15.

61. See *al Ahraam* 15 September 1987.

62. *Al Ahraam*, 15 May 1987.

63. Abdel-Fadil, *Ta'ammulaat*, 120.

Chapter 7: Educational Policy

1. For a testimony on this subject by one experienced professor and administrator, see al Minufi, "al ta`lim fi al khitaab al siyasi," 200 and 243–44.

2. It was introduced in 1948 for elementary and in 1951 for secondary education.

3. Mansfield, *Nasser's Egypt*, 121–22.

4. National Planning Institute, *Mustaqbal al Qitaa' al 'aam*, 61.

5. According to experts working with USAID, the inflation of student numbers in elementary schools was about 14 percent in the mid-eighties, while that of preparatory schools reached 100 percent.

6. See al Safty, "malaamih tatawur," 22.

7. World Bank, *World Development Report 1991*, table 29, p. 260.

8. Based on data in Safty, "malaamih tatawur," table 2, p. 28.

9. Based on data in ibid., tables 1 and 2, 25, 28.

10. Legal opinion is divided on this question, but officials introduced fees surreptitiously in 1989 in a new system called the Open University. Special students who enroll in this system pay £E100 per course per semester and are set aside from the regular university students in that they do not have to attend classes and are subject to a different examination.

11. Dr. Hasanein Rabi', Dean of the College of Arts, Cairo University, interview, March 1991.

12. A report in the newspaper *al Sha'b*, 25 August 1987, that the rate was raised to £E20 is not true, according to Cairo University officials.

13. See breakdown in the statement by the Ministry's higher officials in *al Ahraam*, 18 October 1987.

14. Reexaminations were possible once in the first year, twice in the second and in the third, and three times in the fourth: Dr.Hasanein Rabi', Cairo University's then assistant dean of Student Affairs, interview by author, February 1988.

15. Ibid.

16. *Al Musawwar*, 20 November 1989.

17. See Mansfield, *Nasser's Egypt*, 120.

18. In a speech on the tenth anniversary of the Revolution, quoted by al Minufi, "al ta`lim," 155. Official figures should be taken as an approximation only, since contradictory accounts are abundant. See, for instance, an example given in ibid., 174–75.

19. See ibid., 155.

20. In another account, expenditure on university education in 1961 was only £E105 per student: Amir Bokhtor, quoted in Abdel-Fadil, *The Political Economy*, 362.

21. See al Safty, "malaamih tatawur," 115. A very close figure, £E262,328,000, is given by UNESCO for the same year: *UNESCO 1990 Statistical Yearbook*.

22. Figures given by the Ministry of Education in the major document on education reform: GOE, Ministry of Education, *Istraatijiyat Tatwiir al Ta'lim*, July 1987. See also *The Development Strategy of Education of July 1987*, Center for Educational Research, 88–89, also quoted in Amani Qindil, *With Our Own Hands*. The National Planning Institute (NPI) cites the figure of £E1.4 billion for all levels of education three years earlier: NPI, *Mustaqbal al Qitaa' al 'aam*, 60. In a speech on Labor Day in Egypt, President Mubarak cited the figure of £E1.85 billion: al Minufi, "al ta'lim," 190. The Minister of Education, however, stated in the weekly roundtable held with editors of *al Musawwar* on 20 November 1987 that government expenditure on education was "about £E2.5 billion." However, one has to accept the lower figure, which is more consistent with figures for past years and is what most education specialists in Egypt have accepted: see al Safty, *Siyasat al Ta'lim*, 116.

23. For instance, the same Minister of Education, Fat'hi Srour, gave the figure of £E2.5 billion before Maglis al Shawra. Officials often cite the figure 2 billion.

24. Based on figures for 1987 of £E18 billion as government revenue and £E40 billion as GDP.

25. World Bank, *World Development Report 1991*, 66.

26. *UNESCO 1990 Statistical Yearbook*, tables 2.12 and 4.1.

27. See al Safty, "malaamih tatawur," 116. The figure al Safty cites from UNESCO for 1983 is 4.1 percent of GDP and 8.9 percent of the state budget. The World Bank, *World Development Report 1991*, table 11, p. 224, gives the figure of 11.9 percent of all government expenditure. This figure is one of the lowest in the middle-income economies group identified by the World Bank. The NPI gives the figures of 4.7 percent of GDP in 1970 and 5 percent in 1983: *Mustaqbal al Qitaa' al 'aam*, 60.

28. USAID has contributed up to $200 million for educational purposes, mostly for building schools in the provinces.

29. Safty, "malaamih tatawur," 116–17. The expenditure per university student continued to decline in the nineties. According to Labib al Sibaa'i, "al 'aalam al sirri lilimtihaanaat al jaami'iya," *al Ahraam*, 9 May 1991, the figures were £E40 for a medical student, £E25 for an engineering student, and £E18 for an arts student.

30. This is based on the fact that the number of students at all levels in 1987 was a little over 11 million, while the budget was £E1.3 billion: see figures in CAPMAS, *Statistical Yearbook, 1952–1986*; and al Safty, "malaamih tatawur."

31. NPI, *Mustaqbal al Qitaa' al 'Aam*, 60.

32. Education experts working with USAID.

33. *UNESCO 1990 Statistical Yearbook*, table 2.12.

34. See Safty, "malaamih tatawur," 56–63.

35. Ibid., 58.

36. See Qindil, "muqaddima: al ta'lim wa al siyasah," 8. Similar results are reported for 1991 with some improvement in the ratio in business schools (1:192) and a slight

deterioration in law schools (1:161). In education, the ratio is reported to be 1:115. See Labib al Sibaa`i, "al `aalam al sirri lil-imtihaanaat al jaami`iya," *al Ahraam*, 9 May 1991.

37. Safty, "malaamih tatawur," 57.

38. Qindil, "muqaddima," 8.

39. Based on figures given by the Minister of Education (*al Ahraam*, 18 October 1987), there were 14,500 university teachers to 669,000 students. The last figure is from al Safty, "malaamih tatawur," 25.

40. Mahmoud Abdel-Fadil argues strongly that the poorer classes receive less of the state subsidy for education; see his article "Educational Expansion."

41. In a speech made in December 1968, Nasser complained about the decline of educational levels and mentioned the widespread resort to private lessons. See al Minufi, "al ta`lim," 173–74.

42. Mustafa Kaamil Murad, a member of Maglis al Shawra and head of the Liberal Party, in a statement made in Maglis al Shawra; see *al Ahraam*, 6 December 1987.

43. Qindil, *With Our Own Hands*, 96.

44. GOE, Ministry of Education, al Diwan al 'Aam, *al Muwazanah al 'Aamah*, vol. 2.

45. By 1992 these figures had grown to 12.5 million students and 750,000 teachers.

46. Private lessons were the subject of criticism in the last policy document in the Nasser period, The National Program (*Wathiqat Barnaamaj al 'Amal al Qawmy*), July 1971.

47. In a roundtable discussion with the editors of *al Musawwar*, 20 November 1987.

48. See Qindil, "al qitaa` al khaas," 143.

49. Qindil, "Al Qitaa` al Khaas wa al Siyaasah al Ta`limiyyah fi Misr" (paper given at the Conference on the Private Sector and Decision Making in Public Policy, organized by the Centre for Political Research and Studies, Cairo University, al Fayyum, 17–19 November 1988), 36. Published later in a briefer form.

50. Lecture given by the Minister of Education, Fat/hi Srour, at the Gezira Club, Zamalek, Cairo, 31 October 1987, attended by the author. The statement was reported in the daily press.

51. Ibid. Figures were reported by the daily press repeatedly. In a meeting with the teachers' union, Minister Srour mentioned that students often sit on the floor and that the length of a class session is fifteen minutes: *al Ahaaly*, 11 November 1987.

52. Srour lecture, Gezira Club, Zamalek, Cairo, 31 October 1987. The World Bank, *World Development Report, 1991*, table 29, p. 260, gives a teacher-to-student ratio of 27 in primary education in 1988. This figure, undoubtedly obtained from official sources, bears no relation to reality.

53. Srour lecture, Gezira Club, Zamalek, Cairo, 31 October 1987.

54. NPI, *Mustaqbal al Qitaa' al 'Aam*, 62.

55. Statement made by the Minister of Education in a roundtable discussion with editors of *al Musawwar*, 20 November 1987.

56. NPI, *Mustaqbal al Qitaa' al 'Aam*.

57. *Al Ahraam*, 3 November, 1987.

58. Statement by a former Minister of Education, Abd al Salaam Abd al Ghaffaar, *Rose el Yousef,* 23 November 1987.

59. See *al Musawwar,* roundtable discussion, 20 November 1987.

60. Ibid.

61. *al Ahraam,* 20 May 1987.

62. See interview in *Akhir Saa'ah,* 10 June 1987.

63. Ibid.

64. *Akhir Saa'ah,* 10 June 1987.

65. *Hawaa',* 13 June 1987.

66. The teachers union had 450,000 members in 1988.

67. NPI, *Mustaqbal al Qitaa' al 'Aam,* 60. According to the Minister of Education, distribution was as follows: 5.5 percent in elementary levels, 1.7 percent in preparatory, 14.3 percent in secondary, and 14.6 percent in business secondary schools: *al Ahraam,* 16 November 1987

68. Ministry of Education, *Istraatijiyat Tatwiir al Ta'lim,* 124; and the Minister of Education, in *al Ahraam,* 16 November 1987. This is true also for an earlier period; see Abdel-Fadil, *The Political Economy,* 357.

69. See al Minufi, "al ta'lim."

70. Qindil, "al qitaa` al khaas."

71. Ibid.

72. Roundtable discussion with the editors of *al Musawwar,* 20 November 1987.

73. When he later changed his mind with respect to the university, he did not do anything to bring it about.

74. The idea came up originally in the fifties, died down in the sixties, and was resurrected in 1973. See Rabi', "qadiyat al jaami'ah al ahliyah," 376–85.

75. Actually, the principle of a public university charging full tuition has been in effect for a long time at the Egyptian university called The Arab University of Beirut. After 1975, because of the civil war in Lebanon, the Beirut University moved to Alexandria, where its student body became predominantly Egyptian. It has only recently restricted admission to Egyptians. See details in al Safty, "malaamih tatawur," 88–93.

76. Dr. Minufi has recently been promoted to chairperson.

77. Dr. al Safty is referring to the great demand for American University in Cairo graduates, both in the private sector and in the foreign service of the national government.

78. Safty, "malaamih tatawur," 99.

79. Reference to the great demand now for AUC students in the private sector and in the foreign service of the national government.

80. Minufi, "al ta'lim," 213.

81. Ibid., 218 and 237.

82. Reported in *Al Mujtama' al Madani,* published by the Ibn Khaldun Center, Cairo, March 1992, p. 12.

Chapter 8: Housing Policy

1. See Hanna, *al Iskaan,* 44.

2. Ibid.

3. Ibid.

4. See ibid., 46 and 56. Also, Hanna, *Uridu Maskanan*, 116.

5. See Hanna, *al Iskaan*, 49.

6. Large, foreign contracting companies have taken on very large projects, such as hotels and infrastructure, rather than family housing units, which will not be examined in this chapter.

7. See what follows in this chapter.

8. See chapter 4, on agricultural policy.

9. On this point, see Harik, "Privatization: The Issue."

10. See 'Abd-al-Mu'ti, *al Siraa' al Tabaqi*.

11. Undersecretary of the Ministry of Planning, *al Ahraam*, 10 January 1989. The head of the public sector organization for construction, Mohammed Mahmoud, cited the figure £E950 million, but that includes housing companies not under the Ministry of Housing and Construction: *Business Monthly* (September 1987).

12. As one example, see Hanna, *al Iskaan*, 78.

13. *Ahraam*, 17 August 1987.

14. Publication of Bank al Ta'mir wa al Iskaan (Reconstruction and housing bank).

15. See Hansen and Marzouk, "Planning and Economic Growth"; also Harik, "Azamat al Tahawwul al Ishtiraaki."

16. *al Iqtisaadi*, 23 January 1989, 24 and 25.

17. 'Amr Muhieddin maintains that investment in housing showed absolute decline since 1956 and that by 1959 it was 50 percent less than in 1956: see *Income Distribution*, 62.

18. Based on data in ibid.

19. Ibid.

20. Ibid.

21. See *Business Monthly*, Cairo (September 1987), 10.

22. Statement by the Minister of Planning, Kamaal al Ganzouri: see *al-Musawwar*, 3 July 1987.

23. See Hanna, *al Iskaan*, 97.

24. These figures correspond to those reached by Hanna for the year 1983/84: *al Iskaan*, 98.

25. The same ratio was found by Hanna for the year 1983/84: *al Iskaan*, 98. The figure cited by Richards, who states that "roughly three-quarters of all dwellings constructed during the infitaah period were luxury housing," bears no relation to reality: "Ten Years of Infitaah," 329–30.

26. Hanna, *al Iskaan*, 98.

27. Hanna, *al Iskaan*, 98–99.

28. Cairo, bulletin of *Bank al-Ta'mir wa al-Iskaan* (Construction and housing bank).

29. See Hanna, *al Iskaan*, 97.

30. Bank al Ta'mir wa al Iskaan.

31. Al-Bank al-'Iqaari al-Misri (Egyptian real estate bank).

32. According to al Majaalis al Qawmiyah (National Committees of the Consulta-

tive Assembly), public sector investment in 1981 reached £E1,100 million, while that of the private sector was £E400 million (£E200 by *al-qitaa ͨ al-istithmaari,* i.e., newly formed investment companies, and £E200 million by *al-khaas al mubaashar).*

33. Ghunaym, *al Namoudhaj al Misri,* 352.

34. Bank al Taͨmir wa al Iskaan, using data from GOE, Ministry of Planning, *al Khuttah al Khamsiyah,* vol. 1, pp. 112 and 127. The total number of units officially reported built during the entire period of the first Mubarak Plan was 812,000 units. The figure, however, does not include units built illicitly by private entrepreneurs and individual families.

35. Report of Al-Majaalis al Qawmiya, published in *al Iqtisaadi,* 21 February 1983.

36. Ibid.

37. Statement made by Mohammed Mahmoud, President of Public Sector Organization for Construction, *Business Monthly* (September 1987), 18.

38. Hanna, *al Iskaan,* 57.

39. See Kadi, "L'articulation," 173; of the 1,400 housing co-ops, only 50 function according to cooperative rules, the rest are in the speculation business.

40. Ibid.

41. Based on figures given by Bank al Taͨmir.

42. See *al Ahraam,* 12 June 1987.

43. Housing Committee Report in the Peoples' Assembly: see *al Ahraam,* 21 May 1987.

44. Hanna, *al Ahraam,* 26 January 1988.

45. Law number 47, 1977.

46. A study report submitted to USAID, quoted in Abdel-Fadil and Diab, "Abʾaad wa Mukawimaat al Iqtisaad," 31.

47. This account is based on numerous interviews I conducted with housing specialists, entrepreneurs, and individuals who built their own illicit houses during the periods 1987–89 and 1990–91.

48. Drosso, "La politique de l'habitat au Caire," 28; Hanna gives the figure of 80 percent, *al Iskaan,* 58. Figure first appeared in a report to USAID entitled *Informal Housing in Egypt* and presented in 1981. For a different point of view, see Abdel-Fadil and Diab, "Abʾaad wa Mukawimaat," 33, which puts the figure at 40 percent of the formal housing sector.

49. Kadi, "L'urbanisation."

50. Ibid.

51. Drosso, "La politique de l'habitat," 29.

52. Ibid., 32.

53. Interview with Dr. Galila el Kadi, 1988.

54. Kadi, "L'articulation," 1.

55. Ibid., mimeo, 10–11; and Drosso, "La politique de l'habitat au Caire."

56. Dr. Galila el Kadi, interview by author, Cairo, October 1988.

57. Kadi, "L'articulation," 10; and "L'urbanisation," 102.

58. Kadi, "L'articulation."

59. Kadi interview. See also her article "L'articulation"; and Drosso, "La politique de l'habitat," 29.

60. Kadi, "L'articulation."

61. See *al Ahraam*, 30 August 1987.

62. See de Soto, *The Other Path;* and Collier, *Squatters Settlements.*

63. *Al Ahraam*, 30 August 1987.

64. Ibid.

65. Ibid.

66. Ibid.

67. See Kadi, "L'articulation," 173–74.

68. For the government's loss of credibility and lack of effectiveness, see Drosso, "La politique de l'habitat," 30–31; and Kadi, "L'articulation," 2.

69. De Soto, *The Other Path.*

70. For an assessment of this period, see Kadi, "La division sociale," 48–49.

71. Drosso, "La politique de l'habitat," 30.

72. *Al Ahraam*, 2 July 1987.

73. Milad Hanna, lecture at Centre de documentation et d'etudes economiques, juridiques et sociales, Cairo, June 1987. Dr. Hanna has expressed his views widely in the press and at conferences, as well as in his two books on housing.

74. See Hanna, *Uridu Maskanan* and *al Iskaan.*

Chapter 9: The Cultural Dimensions of Economic Policy

1. Geertz, *The Interpretation of Cultures,* 89.

2. Ibid.

3. Ibid., 249–52.

4. See Bates, *Markets and States;* and *Beyond the Miracle of the Market.*

5. Bates, *Markets and States,* 5–6.

6. This attitude is reflected in popular sayings such as "diyar Misr khairha li ghairha" (the bounty of Egypt is always siphoned off by aliens).

7. *Al Ahraam*, 22 October 1987.

8. *Al-Ahraam*, 6 July 1987.

9. Dr. Beblawi, interview by author, 1987.

10. See what follows in this chapter.

11. As used here, *Egyptian elites* incorporates all modern educated persons, including those with a secondary education: see Shils, "Political Development in the New States." Note that Binder, *In A Moment of Enthusiasm*, attributes a preponderant influence to rural elites in the national affairs of Egypt.

12. See Harik, *The Political Mobilization of Peasants.*

13. Amin, *Mihnat al Iqtisaad,* 118.

14. Sa'd-al-Din et al., *Da'm al Aghniyaa' wa Da'm al Fuqaraa'.*

15. Ibid., 76–77.

16. See the case of resistance to educational change discussed in chapter 7.

17. *Ahraam*, 29 January, 1981; see the merchants' point of view in *al Iqtisaadi*, 19 January 1981.

18. In fairness, it may be said that Egypt ranks behind some Latin American countries such as Peru: see de Soto, *The Other Path.*

19. Regarding the electric bulb case, see al-Maraaghi, *Al Mudiir al Masri,* 101–3.

For excessive bureaucratic practices in general, see in particular Ayubi, *Bureaucracy and Politics.*

20. Interview in *al Ahraam*, 5 January 1990.

21. See *Ahraam*, 20 June 1986.

22. Interview with Sa'dani, *Ahraam*, 5 January 1990.

23. *Kul qaanun wa lahu mizraab.*

24. This is very close to the way Abdel-Fadil uses the term covert economy (*al iqtisaad al khafi*): see Abdel-Fadil and Diab, "ab'aad wa mukawimaat."

25. Other authors have discussed corruption of this kind in Egypt: see Waterbury, *The Egypt of Nasser and Sadat;* Husayn, *Al Iqtisaad al Misri,* vols. 1 and 2; Ayubi, *The State and Public Policies;* and Hinnebusch, *Egyptian Politics;* among others.

26. See study by Abdel-Fadil, *Informal Sector Employment.*

Chapter 10: The Illusive Path to Development

1. For more on this point in relation to LDCs, see Callaghy, "Toward State Capability."

2. A notable exception is Nelson, "Poverty, Equity."

3. For the continuity of the Sadat and the Nasser regime from a different angle, see Bianchi, *Unruly Corporatism,* chapter 1.

4. For the joint role of government and free enterprise, see Harik, "Privatization."

5. Myrdal, *Asian Drama,* 66 and passim.

6. Waterbury maintains that since the emergence of Nasser in the early fifties, Egypt has been a soft state: Waterbury, "The 'Soft State.'"

7. See chapters 2 and 3, on industrialization; also Sherif and Soos, "Egypt Liberalization Experience."

8. See, Lipton, *Why Poor People Stay Poor;* and Bradshaw, "Urbanization and Underdevelopment," 52 and 224–39.

9. Scholars who have shared that view include Richards and Waterbury, *A Political Economy;* Ghunaym, *Al Namoudhaj al Misri;* Mursi, *Hadha al Infitaah;* and the leftist monthly journal *al Tali'ah,* which singled out middle-class farmers as the beneficiaries of the Revolution.

10. See Waterbury, *The Egypt of Nasser and Sadat,* particularly chapter 8; Ayubi, *Bureaucracy and Politics* and *The State and Public Policies;* Hinnebusch, *Egyptian Politics;* and Baker, *Sadat and After.*

11. Despite several armed conflicts since 1956 in which Egypt was involved, the economic cost of war has not been a decisive cause of economic stress: see Harik, "Azamat al Tahawwul Al Ishtiraaki."

12. The term used is *al 'aa'id al ijtimaa'i* or *al as'aar al ijtimaa'iyah.*

13. Amin, *Mihnat al Iqtisaad,* 119; also Handoussa, "Time for Reform."

14. See Beblawi and Luciani, eds., *The Rentier State.*

15. For comparative view of other Middle Eastern countries, see al-Amin, *al Laatajaanus al Ijtimaa'i.*

16. See Boudon, *L'Inégalité des chances.*

17. The term *uncivic culture,* as used here, should not be viewed as the antithesis of

the civic culture concept propagated by Gabriel Almond and his associates. See Almond and Verba, *The Civic Culture*. Almond's civic culture is concerned with the attitudinal attributes associated with liberal democracy. Here we are concerned with attitudes that may be considered deviations from the normally accepted moral standards of behavior in any political order endowed with general legitimacy.

18. See Howard and King, *The Political Economy of Marx*, 130.

19. For a balanced account of the NICs, see Haggard, *Pathways from the Periphery*.

20. This explains why economists like John W. Mellor stress agriculturally based growth as a prime mover for development in LDCs: see Mellor, *The New Economics of Growth*.

WORKS CITED

'Abd-al-Mu'ti, 'Abd al Baasit. *al Siraa'al Tabaqi fi al Qariyah al Misriyah* [Class struggle in the Egyptian village]. Cairo, 1977.

Abdel-Fadil, Mahmoud. *Development, Income Distribution, and Social Change in Rural Egypt, 1952–1970: A Study in the Political Economy of Agrarian Transition.* Cambridge: Cambridge University Press, 1975.

———. *Informal Sector Employment in Egypt.* Vol. 1. Geneva: International Labor Office, 1980.

———. *The Political Economy of Nasserism.* Cambridge: Cambridge University Press, 1980.

———. *Ta'ammulaat fi al Mas'alah al Iqtisaadiyah al Misriyah* [Observations regarding the economic question in Egypt]. Cairo: Dar al Mustaqbal al 'Arabi, 1983.

Abdel-Fadil, Mahmoud, and Jihaan Diab. "Ab'aad wa mukawimaat al iqtisaad al khafi" [Dimensions and elements of the covert economy]. *Majallat Misr al Mu'aasirah* 76, no. 400 (April 1985).

———. "Educational Expansion and Income Distribution." In *The Political Economy of Income Distribution in Egypt,* edited by Gouda Abdel-Khalek and Robert Tignor. New York: Holmes and Meier, 1982.

Abu-'Ali, Sultan. "al Siyasaat al iqtisaadiyah" [The economic policy]. In *Al Tanmiyah al Sinaa'iyah fi Misr.* Al Ahraam: Kitaab al Ahraam al Iqtisaasdi, 7. Cairo, 1988.

Adams, Richard H., Jr. "Development and Structural Change in Rural Egypt, 1952 to 1982." *World Development* 13, no. 6 (1985).

Ahmed, Sadiq. *Public Finance in Egypt: Its Structure and Trends.* Staff Working Papers, no. 639. Washington, D.C.: World Bank, 1984.

Alderman, Harold, and Joachim von Braun. "Egypt's Food Subsidy Policy: Lessons and Options." *Food Policy* (August 1986).

Almond, Gabriel A. "The Return to the State." *American Political Science Review* 82, no. 2 (June 1988).

Almond, Gabriel A., and Sydney Verba. *The Civic Culture: Political Attitudes and Democracy in Five Nations.* Princeton: Princeton University Press, 1963.

Amin, Adnan al. *al Laa-tajaanus al Ijtimaa'i* [Social discordance]. Beirut: Sharikat al Matbu'aat, 1993.

Amin, Galal. *Mihnat al Iqtisaad wa al Thaqaafah fi Misr* [The tragedy of the economy and culture in Egypt]. Cairo: al Markaz al 'Arabi lil-Bahth wa al Nashr, 1982.

———. *Qissat Duyun Misr al Khaarijiyah* [The story of Egypt's external debt]. Cairo: Dar ʿAli Mukhtaar, 1987.

Ayubi, Nazih. *Bureaucracy and Politics in Contemporary Egypt.* London: Ithaca Press, 1980.

———. *The State and Public Policies in Egypt Since Sadat.* London: Ithaca Press, 1991.

Baker, Raymond. *Sadat and After: Struggle for Egypt's Soul.* Cambridge, Mass.: Harvard University Press, 1990.

Bank Misr. *Al Nashra al Iqtisaadiyah* [Economic bulletin], year 28, no. 1, 1984; year 29, no. 2, 1985. Cairo, 1985.

Baroudi, Sami. "The Performance of the Egyptian Export Economy in the Open-Door Period: Explaining the Deterioration in Agricultural Exports, 1974–1991." Ph.D. Diss., Indiana University, 1992.

Bates, Robert H. *Beyond the Miracle of the Market: The Political Economy of Agrarian Development in Kenya.* Cambridge: Cambridge University Press, 1989.

———. *Markets and States in Tropical Africa: The Political Basis of Agricultural Policies.* Berkeley: University of California Press, 1981.

Beblawi, Hazem, and Jiacomo Luciani, eds. *The Rentier State.* New York: Croom Helm, 1987.

Bianchi, Robert. *Unruly Corporatism: Associational Life in Twentieth-Century Egypt.* Oxford: Oxford University Press, 1989.

Binder, Leonard. *In a Moment of Enthusiasm: Political Power and the Second Stratum in Egypt.* Chicago: University of Chicago Press, 1978.

Boudon, Raymond. *L'Inégalité des chances, la mobilité sociale dans les sociétés industrielles* [Inequality of opportunity: social mobility in industrial societies]. Paris: Collin, 1973.

Bradshaw, York. "Urbanization and Underdevelopment: A Global Study of Modernization, Urban Bias, and Economic Dependency." *American Sociological Review* 52, no.2 (April 1987).

Callaghy, Thomas M. "Toward State Capability and Embedded Liberalism in the Third World: Lessons for Adjustment." In *Fragile Coalitions: The Politics of Economic Adjustment,* edited by Joan M. Nelson. Washington, D.C.: Overseas Development Council, 1989.

Central Agency for Public Mobilization and Statistics (CAPMAS). *Al Kitaab al Ihsaʾi al Sanawi, 1952–86.* Cairo, 1987.

———. *Mawqif al Infitaah al Iqtisaadi fi Jumhuriyat Misr al ʿArabiya hatta 12/31/ 1983* [The situation of the economic open-door policies in the Arab Republic of Egypt until 12/31/1983]. Cairo, 1985.

———. *Statistical Yearbook, 1952–1986.* Cairo, 1987.

Collier, David. *Squatters Settlements and the Incorporation of Migrants into Urban Life: The Case of Lima.* Cambridge, Mass.: Massachusetts Institute of Technology, Center for International Studies, 1976.

Cooper, Mark N. "State Capitalism, Class Structure, and Social Transformation in the Third World: The Case of Egypt." *International Journal of Middle East Studies* 15, no. 4 (November 1983).

Davis, Eric. *Challenging Colonialism: Bank Misr and Egyptian Industrialization, 1920–1941*. Princeton: Princeton University Press, 1983.

de Soto, Hernando. *The Other Path: The Invisible Revolution in the Third World*. New York: Harper and Row, 1989.

Drosso, Ferial. "La politique de l'habitat au Caire entre 1952 et 1981" [Housing policies in Cairo between 1952 and 1981]. *Monde Arabe: Maghreb Machrek* (Paris) 110 (1985).

Evans, Peter. "The State as Problem and Solution: Predation, Embedded Autonomy, and Structural Change." In *The Politics of Economic Adjustment*, edited by Stephan Haggard and Robert Kaufman. Princeton: Princeton University Press, 1992.

Evans, Peter, Dietrich Rueschemeyer, and Theda Skocpol, eds. *Bringing the State Back In*. Cambridge: Cambridge University Press, 1985.

Geertz, Clifford. *The Interpretation of Cultures: Selected Essays*. New York: Basic Books, 1973.

Ghunaym, ʿAdil. *Al Namoudhaj al Misri li-Raʾsmaaliyat al Dawlah al Taabiʿah* [The Egyptian model of dependent state capitalism]. Cairo: Dar al Mustaqbal, 1986.

Girgis, Maurice. *Industrialization and Trade Patterns in Egypt*. Thbingen: Mohr, 1977.

Government of Egypt (GOE), Central Bank of Egypt. *al Majalla al Iqtisaadiyya* [Economic journal] 26, no. 2 (Cairo, 1986).

——, Central Bank of Egypt. *Annual Report 1986/1987*. [Cairo]: CBE Printing Press, [1987].

GOE, MQM. *al Qitaaʿ al ʿAam* [The public sector]. Cairo, 1981.

GOE, MQM. *al Shuʾun al Iqtisaadiyah* [Economic affairs]. dawrah 14, (1987/88).

GOE, Ministry of Agriculture and Land Reclamation and United Nations Food and Agricultural Organization (*MOA*, Siyasaat). *al Siyasaat al Siʿriyah wa al Taswiyqiyah fi Jumhuriyat Misr al ʿArabiyah* [Pricing and marketing policies in the Arab Republic of Egypt]. Edited by Fahmi Bishay, Saʿd Nassaar, and Zuhayr ʿAbdallah. 2 vols. Cairo, 1987.

GOE, Ministry of Education, al Diwan al ʿAam. *al Muwazanah al ʿAamah, 1986–1987* [The general budget]. Vol. 2.

GOE, Ministry of Education. *Istraatijiyat Tatwiir al Taʿlim* [The strategy of change in education]. Cairo: Al Markaz al Qawmy lil-Buhuth al Tarbawiyah, July 1987.

GOE, Ministry of Finance, Department of Current Account for Public Sector Companies. *Al hisaabaat al khitaamiyah lil-muwaazanaat al jaariyah wa la raʾsmaaliyah li-sharikaat al qitaaʿ al ʿaam, 1984/85 and 1986/87* [The final account of the public sector budget]. Unpublished document.

GOE, Ministry of Planning. *Summary of the Second Five Year Plan (1987/88–1991/92)*. Cairo, July 1987.

GOE, Ministry of Supplies. *Subsidy List Per Item* (published in Arabic). Cairo, Ministries of Supplies Publications, 1986.

Habashi, Nabil. "Nahwa tatwiir al nizaam al taswiqi li-mahaasiil al khudar" [Toward a new system of marketing vegetable.] In GOE, MOA, *al siyasaat al Siʿriyah*, vol. 2.

Haggard, Stephan. *Pathways from the Periphery: The Politics of Growth in Newly Industrializing Countries*. Ithaca: Cornell University Press, 1990.

Halim, Fawzi, and al-Atrubi, Muhammad Subhi. "Al Siyasaat al Siʿriyah wa Istihlaak al Ghidha" [Pricing policies and food consumption]. In GOE, MOA, *al siyasaat al Si'riyah,* vol. 2.

Handoussa, Heba. "The Impact of Liberalization on the Performance of Egypt's Public Sector Industry." Paper presented at the second B.A.P.E.G. conference, "Public Enterprise in Mixed Economy LDCs," sponsored by Boston University and the Harvard Institute for International Development, April 1980.

———. "ma'aal al qita' al 'aam" [The future of Egypt's public sector]. In *al Infitaah: al Judhur wa al Hisaad wa al Mustaqbal* [The open-door policy: The roots, the harvest, and the future], edited by Gouda 'Abd al Khaaliq.

———. Mulakhas al bahth 'an siyasaat al islaah fi gitaa' al sina'ah al misriyah [Summary of the study on reform policy in the Egyptian industrial sector]. Paper presented to a conference on Investment Strategy. Cairo, Minister of Labor and ILO, December 1988.

———. Public Sector Employment and Productivity in the Egyptian Economy. Report prepared for the ILO Comprehensive Employment Strategy Mission, September 1980.

———. "Reform Policies for Egypt's Manufacturing Sector." In *Employment and Structural Adjustment: Egypt in the 1990s,* edited by Handoussa and Gillian Potter. Geneva: ILO, 1991.

———. " Mulakh as al bahth 'an Kiyasaat al islaah fi qitaa' al sinaa'ah al misriyah" [The reform policy in the Egyptian industrial sector]. Paper presented at a conference on the strategy of employment in Egypt, sponsored by the ILO and the Egyptian Ministry of Labor, Cairo, December 1988.

———. "Time for Reform: Egypt's Public Sector Industry." In *Studies in Egyptian Political Economy,* edited by Herbert M. Thompson. Cairo Papers in Social Science, vol. 2. American University in Cairo, 1979.

Hanna, Milad. *al Iskaan wa al Masyada: al Mushkila wa al Hal* [Housing and the trap: the problem and the solution]. Cairo: Dar al Mustqabal al 'Arabi, 1988.

———. *Uridu Maskanan: Mushkilah laha Hal* [I want a residence: a problem that has a solution]. Cairo: Maktabat Rose el Yusef, 1978.

Hansen, Bent. *The Political Economy of Poverty, Equity, and Growth: Egypt and Turkey.* New York: Oxford University Press, 1991.

Hansen, Bent, and Girgis A. Marzouk. *Development and Economic Policy in the UAR (Egypt).* Amsterdam: North-Holland Publishing, 1965.

———. "Planning and Economic Growth in the UAR (Egypt), 1960–65." In *Egypt Since the Revolution,* edited by P. J. Vatikiotis. New York: Praeger, 1968.

Hansen, Bent, and Karim Nashashibi. *Egypt.* New York: National Bureau of Economic Research, 1975.

Harik, Iliya. "Azamat al Tahawwul al Ishtiraaki fi Misr" [The crisis of socialist transformation in Egypt]. *Majallat al 'Ulum al Ijtimaa'iyah,* Jaami'at al Kuwayt, 15 (Spring 1987).

———. "Continuity and Change in Local Development Policies in Egypt: From Nasser to Sadat." *International Journal of Middle East Studies* 16 (March 1984).

———. "The Political Elite as a Strategic Minority." In *Leadership and Development in Arab Society,* edited by Fuad Khuri. American University of Beirut, 1981.

————. *The Political Mobilization of Peasants: A Study of an Egyptian Community*. Bloomington: Indiana University Press, 1974.

————. "Privatization: The Issue, the Prospects, and the Fears." In *Privatization and Liberalization in the Middle East*, edited by Iliya Harik and Denis J. Sullivan. Bloomington: Indiana University Press, 1992.

————. "The Single Party as a Subordinate Movement: The Case of Egypt." *World Politics* (October 1973).

————. "Subsidization Policies in Egypt: Neither Economic Growth nor Distribution." *International Journal of Middle East Studies* 24, no. 3 (August 1992).

Harik, Iliya, and Denis J. Sullivan, eds. *Privatization and Liberalization in the Middle East*. Bloomington: Indiana University Press, 1992.

Hatim, Sami ʿAfifi. *Al Iqtisaad al Misri bayn al Waaqiʿ wa al Tumuh* [The Egyptian economy: ambition and reality]. Cairo: Al Dar al Masriyah al Lubnaaniyah, 1988.

Held, David. "Introduction: Central Perspective on the Modern State." In *States and Societies*, edited by David Held et al. New York: New York University Press, 1983.

Hindi, Muhammad Kaamil, and Muhammad Rajaaʾ al-Amir. "Nahwa tatwiir al nizaam al taswiigi lil-houboub" [Toward development of the marketing system for grain]. In GOE, *al Siyasaat al Siʿriyah*, vol. 2.

Hinnebusch, Raymond, Jr. *Egyptian Politics Under Sadat*. Cambridge: Cambridge University Press, 1985.

Hopwood, Derek. *Egypt: Politics and Society, 1945–1984*. London: Allen and Unwin, 1985.

Howard, M.C., and J.E. King. *The Political Economy of Marx*. London: Longman, 1988.

Husayn, ʿAdil. *Al Iqtisaad al Misri min al Istiqlaal ila al Tabaʿiyah* [The Egyptian economy: from independence to dependency]. 2 vols. Cairo: Dar al Mustaqbal al ʿArabi, 1982.

ʾIdl, Muhammad Rida al. "al qitaaʿ al ʿaam wa haykal al sinaaʿah al misriyah" [The public sector and the structure of Egyptian industry]. In *al Iqtisaad al Misri fi ʾIqd al Thamaaninaat* [The Egyptian economy in the eighties], edited by Muhammad Zaki Shafiʾi. Al Jamʾiyah al Misriyah lil-Iqtisaad al Siyaasi, Cairo: Daar al Mustaqbal al ʾArabi, 1988.

Ikram, Khalid. *Egypt: Economic Management in a Period of Transition: The Report of a World Bank Mission*. Baltimore: Johns Hopkins University Press, 1980.

al-ʿIsawi, Ibrahim. *al-Daʿm*. Cairo: Dar al-Mawqif al-ʿArabi, 1987.

Issawi, Charles. *Egypt at Mid-Century*. London: Oxford University Press, 1954.

————. *Egypt in Revolution: An Economic Analysis*. Oxford: Oxford University Press, 1963.

Jessop, Bob. *State Theory: Putting the Capitalist State in its Place*. Pennsylvania State University Press, 1990.

Kadi, Galila el. "L'articulation des deux circuits de gestion foncière au Caire." *Peuples Mediterraneens: Egypte Recompositions*, nos. 41–42 (October 1987–March 1988).

————. "La cite des morts, un abri pour les sans-abri [The city of the dead, a refuge for those without refuge]. *Monde Arabe: Maghreb Machrek* (Paris), no. 127 (1990).

————. "La division sociale de l'espace au Caire: segregation et contradictions" [Social divisions by geographical zones in Cairo: segregation and contradictions]. *Monde Arabe: Maghreb Machrek* 110 (1985).

————. "L'urbanisation spontanée au Caire" [Unorganized urbanization in Cairo]. *Urbanisme* 204 (1984).

Kahler, Miles. "Orthodoxy and Its Alternatives: Explaining Approaches to Stabilization and Adjustment." In *Economic Crisis and Policy Choice: The Politics of Adjustment in the Third World*, edited by Joan Nelson. Princeton, N.J.: Princeton University Press, 1990.

Karpat, Kemal H., ed. *Political and Social Thought in the Contemporary Middle East.* New York: Praeger, 1968.

Khayr-al-Din, Hanaa', et al. "al siyaasah al himaa'iyah wa ta'thiruha ʿala tashjiʿ intaaj al qitaaʿ al khaas al sinaaʿi fi misr" [The protectionist policy and its impact on the industrial private sector]. Paper presented to the Conference on Public Policy and the Private Sector, organized by the Center for Political Research and Studies, Cairo University, 19 November 1988.

Korayem, Karima. *The Impact of Economic Adjustment Policies on the Vulnerable Families & Children in Egypt.* A report prepared for the United Nations Children's Fund, Egypt, 1987.

————. "Tawziʿ al dakhl bayn al hadar wa al rif, 1952–1975" [Income distribution in the urban and rural areas]. Paper presented to the Third Annual Conference of Egyptian Economists, Cairo, 1978.

Krimly, Khalid. *The Political Economy of Rentier States: A Case Study of Saudi Arabia in the Oil Era, 1950–1990,* Ph.D. diss., George Washington University, 1993.

Lipton, Michael. *Why Poor People Stay Poor: A Study of Urban Bias in World Development.* Cambridge, Mass.: Harvard University Press, 1977.

Luciani, Giacomo. "Multiple Puzzle: Egypt's Exchange Rate Regime Controversy." *Journal of Arab Affairs* 5, no. 2 (Fall 1986).

Mabro, Robert. *The Egyptian Economy, 1952–1972.* Oxford: Clarendon Press, 1974.

Mabro, Robert, and Samir Radwan. *Industrialization of Egypt 1939–1973: Policy and Performance.* Oxford: Clarendon Press, 1976.

Mahaadir Muhaadathaat al Wahdah bayn Misr-Suriyah-al ʿIraq, 1963 [The minutes of the unity talks between Egypt, Syria, and Iraq]. Vol. 1. Beirut: Dar al Masirah, 1978.

Mansfield, Peter. *Nasser's Egypt.* London: Penguin Books, 1965.

Maraaghi, Mahmoud al. *Al Mudiir al Masri fi Libaasen ʿAsri* [The Egyptian executive in a modern attire]. Cairo: al Qaahira lil-Thaqaafah al ʿArabiyah, 1975.

Mellor, John W. *The New Economics of Growth: A Strategy for India and the Developing Countries.* Ithaca: Cornell University Press, 1976.

Minufi, Kamaal al. "al taʿlim fi al khitaab al siyasi al misri" [Education in the political literature of Egypt]. In *Siyasat al Taʿlim al Jaamiʿi fi Misr* [University education policy in Egypt], edited by Amani Qindil. Cairo: Cairo University, Markaz al Buhuth wa al Dirasaat al Siyaasiyah, 1991.

Mitchel, Timothy. *Colonising Egypt*. Cambridge: Cambridge University Press, 1988.

Moore, Clement Henry. *Images of Development: Egyptian Engineers in Search of Industry*. Cambridge, Mass.: MIT Press, 1980.

———. "Money and Power: The Dilemma of the Egyptian Infitah." *Middle East Journal* 40, no. 4 (1986).

Muhieddin, ʿAmr. *Income Distribution and Basic Needs in Urban Egypt*. American University in Cairo, Cairo Papers in Social Sciences, vol. 15, no. 3 (1982).

———. "taqyim istraatijiyat al tasniyʿ fi Misr (1939–1973): al siyaasah wa al idaaʾ" [Evaluation of industrialization strategy in Egypt]. In *Istraatijiyat al Tanmiyah fi Misr* [Development strategy in Egypt]. Cairo: al Hayʾah al ʿAmmah lil-Kitaab, 1978.

Mursi, Fuʾad. *Hadha al Infitaah al Iqtisaadi* [That economic opening]. Beirut, Dar al Wahdah, 1980.

———. "Madha faʿala al infitaah al iqtisaadi bil-qitaaʿ al ʿaam" [What has the opendoor policy done to the public sector?]. *al Manaar* (September 1986).

Mursi, Sawsan. *Taqwim Faaʿiliyat Nizaam al Daʿm wa Atharuhu ʿala Suluk al Mustahlik al Misri* [The efficacy of the subsidy system and its effects on the behavior of consumers in Egypt]. Jamiʿat al Azhar, Kuliyat al Tijaara, 1986.

Mustafa, Muhammad Samir. *Tarshid Faaqid al Khubz ʿala al Maʿida* [Rationalizing bread waste on the dining table]. Cairo: Maʿhad al Takhtit al Qawmi, 1988.

Muʾtamar al Khubz al ʿArabi (MKA [Arab Conference on Bread]). Driasaat ʿala al Khubz al Misri [Studies on Egyptian bread]. 3 vols. Cairo: Acadimiyat al Bahth al ʿIlmi, wa Hayʾat al Qitaʿ al ʿAam, July 1988.

Myrdal, Gunnar. *Asian Drama: An Inquiry into the Poverty of Nations*. New York: Pantheon Books, 1968.

Naggar, Saʿid al. *Nahwa Istratijiyah Qawmiyah lil-Islaah al Iqtisaadi* [Toward a national strategy of economic reform]. Cairo: Dar al Shuruq, 1991.

Nassaar, Saʿd and Mahmoud Mansur. "al Siyasaat al Siʿriyah wa al Intaaj al Ziraaʿi" [Pricing policies of agricultural produce]. In *al Siyasaat al Siʿriyah wa al Taswiyqiyah*, vol. 1, edited by Fahmi Bishay, Saʿd Nassaar, and Zuhayr ʿAbdallah. Cairo, 1987.

National Planning Institute (NPI). *Mustaqbal al Qitaaʿ al ʿAam* [The future of the public sector]. Cairo, 1988.

Nelson, Joan. "Poverty, Equity, and the Politics of Adjustment." In *The Politics of Economic Adjustment*, edited by Stephan Haggard and Robert Kaufman. Princeton: Princeton University Press, 1992.

Niblock, Tim, and Emma Murphy, eds. *Economic and Political Liberalization in the Middle East*. London: British Academic Press, 1993.

Nordlinger, Eric A., et al. "The Return to the State: Critiques." In *The American Political Science Review* 82, no. 2 (June 1988).

O'Brien, Patrick K. *The Revolution in Egypt's Economic System: From Private Enterprise to Socialism, 1952–1965*. Oxford University Press, 1966.

Oweis, Ibrahim, ed. *The Political Economy of Contemporary Egypt*. Washington, D.C.: Georgetown University, CCAS, 1990.

Posusney, Marsha. "Labor as an Obstacle to Privatization: The Case of Egypt." In *Privatization and Liberalization in the Middle East*, edited by Iliya Harik and Denis J. Sullivan. Bloomington: Indiana University Press, 1992.

Qaysuni, 'Abd al Mun'im al. "Qadiyat al Da'm fi Misr" [The subsidy issue in Egypt]. *Al Ahraam* (1 July 1977; 5–7 September 1977).

Qindil, Amani. "muqaddima: al ta'lim wa al siyasah wa al tanmiyah" [Introduction: education, policy, and development]. In *Siyasat al Ta 'lim al Jaami 'i fi Misr* [University education policy in Egypt], edited by Amani Qindil. Cairo: Cairo University, Markaz al Buhuth wa al Dirasaat al Siyaasiyah, 1991.

———. "al qitaa' al khaas wa al siyasah al ta'limiyah fi Misr" [The public sector and educational policy in Egypt]. In *Al Qitaa' al Khaas wa al Siyaasaat al 'aamah fi Misr.* Cairo: University of Cairo Center for Research and Political Studies, 1989.

———. *Sin' al Siyaasaat al 'Ammah fi Misr* [The making of public policy in Egypt]. Ph.D. Diss., College of Economics and Political Science, Cairo University, 1985.

———. *With Our Own Hands.* Ottawa: IDRC, 1986.

Quandt, William B. *Egypt: A Strong Sense of National Identity.* Washington, D.C.: Brookings, 1989.

Rabi', 'Amr Hashim. "qadiyat al jaami''ah al ahliyah fi siyasat al ta'lim al jaami'i" [The issue of the private university in higher education policy]. In *Siyasat al Ta 'lim al Jaami 'i fi Misr* [University education policy in Egypt], edited by Amani Qindil. Cairo: Cairo University, Markaz al Buhuth wa al Dirasaat al Siyaasiyah, 1991.

Radwan, Samir. *The Impact of Agrarian Reform on Rural Egypt (1952–1975).* Geneva: The International Labor Organization, 1977.

Richards, Alan. *Egypt's Agricultural Development, 1800–1980: Technical and Social Change.* Boulder, Col.: Westview Press, 1982.

———. "Ten Years of Infitaah: Class, Rent, and Policy Stasis in Egypt." *The Journal of Development Studies* 20, no. 4 (July 1984).

Richards, Alan, and John Waterbury. *A Political Economy of the Middle East: State, Class and Economic Development.* Boulder, Col.: Westview Press, 1990.

Richter, Charles. *The Energy Problem.* USAID, Staff Working Paper, 12 November 1986.

Rivlin, Paul. *The Dynamics of Economic Policy Making in Egypt.* New York: Praeger, 1985.

Riyad, Wagdi. *Sinaa 'at al Dawaa'* [The medicine industry]. Cairo: Kitaab al-Ahraam al-Iqtisaadi, August 1988.

Sa'd-al-Din, Ibrahim, et al. *Da 'm al Aghniyaa' wa Da 'm al Fuqaraa'* [Subsidies of the rich and of the poor]. Cairo: Kitaab al Ahaali, 1985.

Safty, Madiha al. "malaamih tatawur siyasat al ta'lim al 'Aali" [Evolution of higher education policy]. In *Siyasat al Ta 'lim al Jaami 'i fi Misr* [University education policy in Egypt], edited by Amani Qindil. Cairo: Cairo University, Markaz al Buhuth wa al Dirasaat al Siyaasiyah, 1991.

Sartori, Giovanni. *The Theory of Democracy Revisited.* Chatham, N.J.: Chatham House Publishers, 1987.

Sayyid, Mustafa Kamel al. *Al Mujtama' wa al Siyaasah fi Misr: Dawr Jama 'aat al Masaalih fi al Nidhaam al Siyaasi al Misri, 1952–1981* [Society and politics in Egypt: the role of interest groups in the Egyptian political system]. Cairo: al Mustaqbal al 'Arabi, 1983.

———. *Privatization: The Egyptian Debate.* Cairo Papers in Social Science, vol. 13. Cairo: American University in Cairo, 1990.

Seddon, David. "Austerity Protests in Response to Economic Liberalization in the Middle East." In *Economic and Political Liberalization in the Middle East,* edited by Tim Niblock and Emma Murphy. London: British Academic Press, 1993.

Sharaf-al-Din, Ahmad. *al Dalil al Qaanuni li-Tawzif al Amwaal* [The legal guide to money investment companies]. Cairo: Kitaab al Ahraam al Iqtisaadi, no. 9, 1988.

Sharaf, Muhammad Fahim et al. "Nahwa tatwiir al nizaam al taswiqi lil-haywanaat" [Toward development of the marketing system of livestock]. In GOE, MOA, *al Siyasaat al Si'riyah,* vol. 2.

Sherif, Khaled. "Poor Incentives, Poor Performance." Cairo: *Business Monthly* 4, no. 5 (May 1988).

Sherif, Khaled, and Gina Soos. "Egypt Liberalization Experience and Its Impact on State-Owned Enterprises." In *Privatization and Liberalization in the Middle East,* edited by Iliya Harik and Denis J. Sullivan. Bloomington: Indiana University Press, 1992.

Shils, Edward. "Political Development in the New States." *Comparative Studies in Society and History* 2 (1960).

Shlomo, Yitzhaki. *On the Effect of Subsidies to Basic Commodities on Inequality in Egypt.* International Bank for Reconstruction and Development, Discussion Papers, no. 289. Washington, D.C., 1981.

Springborg, Robert. *Mubarak's Egypt: Fragmentation of the Political Order.* Boulder, Col.: Westview Press, 1989.

Sullivan, Denis. "The Political Economy of Reform in Egypt." *International Journal of Middle East Studies* 22, no. 3 (August 1990).

Tignor, Robert. *State, Private Enterprise, and Economic Change in Egypt, 1918–1952.* Princeton: Princeton University Press, 1984.

UNESCO 1990 Statistical Yearbook.

USAID. *Report.* Washington, D.C., 15 February 1987. Unpublished document.

USAID. *Egypt's Food and Energy Subsidies in 1979.* Washington, D.C., 1979. Unpublished document.

Vatikiotis, P.J. *The Modern History of Egypt.* New York: Praeger, 1969.

———, ed. *Egypt Since the Revolution.* New York: Praeger, 1968.

Waterbury, John. *The Egypt of Nasser and Sadat: The Political Economy of Two Regimes.* Princeton: Princeton University Press, 1983.

———. "The 'Soft State' and the Open Door: Egypt's Experience with Economic Liberalization, 1974–1984." *Comparative Politics* 18, no. 1 (October 1985).

World Bank. *World Development Report.* Washington D.C., 1986.

———. *World Development Report, 1991.* New York: Oxford University Press, 1991.

———. *Agricultural Price Management in Egypt.* Staff Working Paper, no. 388. Washington, D.C., April 1980.

World Bank, EMENA Technical Department. *Fertilizer Industry Review.* Confidential Report, no. 6969 EGT. January 1988.

Zaki, Ramzi. *Dirasaat fi Azamat Misr al Iqtisaadiyah* [Studies in the Egyptian economic policies]. Cairo: Madbouli, 1983.

Index